S0-BFB-244

BOOK PUBLISHING

A BASIC INTRODUCTION

BOOK PUBLISHING

A BASIC INTRODUCTION

NEW EXPANDED EDITION

JOHN P. DESSAUER

CONTINUUM • NEW YORK

1989

The Continuum Publishing Company
370 Lexington Avenue
New York, NY 10017

Copyright © 1974, 1981 by Xerox Corporation
New Material Copyright © 1989 by The Continuum Publishing Company

All rights reserved. No part of this book may be reproduced,
stored in a retrieval system, or transmitted, in any form or by
any means, electronic, mechanical, photocopying, recording, or
otherwise, without the written permission of
The Continuum Publishing Company.

Printed in the United States of America

Library of Congress Cataloging-in-Publication Data

Dessauer, John P.
   Book publishing : a basic introduction / John P. Dessauer. — New
expanded ed.
     p.   cm.
   Bibliography: p.
   Includes index.
   ISBN 0-8264-0446-4
   1. Publishers and publishing.   2. Book industries and trade.
I. Title.
Z278.D47   1989
338.4′30705—dc20   89-7302
                                                              CIP

A.M.D.G.

To the many book people,
living and dead,
who have taught me
by their wisdom and example

Contents

Publisher's Foreword

During all of my thirty years in American publishing there have been ongoing debates and concerns over the conflicting identity of book publishing, over the threatened culture of literacy in our country, and over the role and responsibility of the publishing people who are serving the wider community of the book. However, in an industry characterized by conflicting paradigms, good publishers consistently have opted for quality over quantity, culture over commerce, mission over money. And because publishing commitments have always been personal as well as professional, and publishing decisions either intensely private or insistently public, most publishers have succeeded or survived conscientiously, courageously, and creatively.

New technologies and business strategies, conglomerate owners, and new capital all have transformed much of publishing into a more obviously result-oriented industry for increasingly global commercial markets. But the book publishing community has never utterly abdicated its commitment to a holistic understanding of the human person. It seems quite certain that there is something about the printed word, with its anchorage in the heritage of the past and its demand for conceptual thinking, and about the printed page as catalyst of the creative imagination, which is keeping book publishing true to its better self.

Today most knowledgeable publishing executives continue to express great optimism over the future of book publishing and the humanistic values of our culture of literacy, which will endure beyond our time of work and hope. But the conflict between publishing as a medium of literature, scholarship, education, or entertainment, and as a business enterprise managed as a private or public risk-taking venture guided by the principles of profit and loss and short term return-on-investment, is still very much alive both inside and outside our publishing industry.

For nearly fifty years, Sir Stanley Unwin's half-true dictum, "publishing has rewards greater than money," which he made in *The Truth About Publishing,* remained the unchallenged final word on the subject—until 1974, when the first edition of John P. Dessauer's *Book Publishing* established a completely new standard of open and comprehensive discussion of all the facts and truths of both the publishing business and of the business of publishing. Everyone in publishing now knows that books, and by extension the dissemination of ideas, knowledge, and wisdom are also a very real form of money, investment, product, merchandise. To publish not only means "to make public," but also to risk capital and above all to have the courage of your entrepreneurial conviction. Indeed, "a book is not published until it is sold," and publishers must "publish or perish."

Let us also agree that the truth about publishing becomes much more concrete when we say, "Publishing has *responsibilities* greater than money." To be a publisher today requires the full knowledge and affirmation of our complex and less and less serendipitous or accidental profession. When we say that you cannot be in publishing without being a *publisher,* we emphasize the wholeness of the publishing job. As every staff member represents a functional extension of the publisher's role, everyone in publishing is indeed a publisher—and *Book Publishing* continues as the basic introduction for all of us in the book community.

John Dessauer completed this new edition of *Book Publishing* as he officially concluded his forty-five-year career as bookseller and publisher, writer and editor, book industry analyst and independent consultant, and friend of all book people. As one of our industry's foremost professionals, he not only made numerous cutting-edge contributions to the publishing world, but also achieved his always challenging goals with a gentle determination that was uniquely his own.

Since 1943, John Dessauer managed bookstores and book clubs, directed university presses, and worked with national educational and professional organizers before establishing his own publishing consulting firm in 1972. He has also directed the Center for Book Research, edited its *Book Research Quarterly,* and prepared the annual statistical *Book Industry Trends.* For twenty years he has been a contributing editor to *Publishers Weekly*, issued by R. R. Bowker, which in 1974 also published the first edition of this book.

I am confident that this revised and updated third edition of *Book Publishing* will bring further credit and gratitude to John Dessauer, and I fervently hope that it will inform and inspire all publishing people, writers, booksellers, librarians, and educators, as well as those countless general readers who are curious about the wondrous world of book publishing.

Werner Mark Linz

Author's Preface

When this book was first published in 1974, the audience I had in mind were the staffs and prospective employees of the more than 2,000 book publishers then active in the U.S. This was a highly visible community, much of it geographically concentrated, though not too well organized, rallying loosely around often ill-defined standards and common practices. Even today, this community constitutes the traditional core of the industry, and throughout this third edition of *Book Publishing* I have referred to it as the "mainstream."

Since I wrote the first version, and particularly since I prepared the revision in 1980, the face of the U.S. publishing industry has changed drastically. The number of firms in the traditional core has shrunk, and individual houses have grown substantially in size, due to mergers and acquisitions. At the same time there has been a vast influx of small, independent presses, so that the total number of publishers in the U.S. has increased more than tenfold since this book was originally launched.

The more than 20,000 small new imprints are far from geographically concentrated. They may be found in large and small communities throughout the fifty states. Some survive only a few months, then disappear; others engage exclusively in self-publishing their authors; yet many others have developed into important houses that are leaving their mark upon the American book scene. In consciously providing editorial and marketing alternatives to what were until recently mainstream monopolies, and in pledging to improve upon mainstream methods, the new firms often vigorously depart from time-honored traditions. In acknowledging and describing their contribution to the industry's development, I have referred to them throughout this volume as "small presses."

Because the topic of my book and the audience for it had undergone such significant transformations, and although the small-press movement had generated an extensive literature of its own (referred to in my bibliographic note on page 245), I was convinced that to fulfill its function, my text should give full coverage to the small-press phenomenon. I also wanted to provide information specifically directed to small-press readers, along with the traditional data I was passing along. Furthermore, the concentration among mainstream firms and the small-press explosion had changed my own perspective on a number of industry issues and events, which, inevitably, had to be reflected in this third edition.

Among the major additions to and changes from past versions introduced here are an expanded discussion of authors' views on publishers' contracts, a completely recast treatment of bookstores, a new analysis of employment conditions for neophytes in mainstream trade houses, and a total restructuring of the discussion of publishing accounting, which now begins with a detailed treatment of the financial experiences of a hypothetical small press during the first five years of its existence.

As was the case with the previous editions, I owe much to a number of generous individuals who were very helpful to me during the updating and revising of the text. These include Judith Appelbaum, Louis E. Auriemma, DeWitt C. Baker, Donald F. Farnsworth, James C. Giblin, Gene Gollogly, Robert T. Heller, Michael Leach, Evander Lomke, Jerry Lyons, Cameron Moseley, Jean Peters, Miriam Phelps, and Barbara Tyszka. I am greatly indebted to Werner Mark Linz, whom I am proud to call my new publisher, and whose friendship has meant a great deal to me. My wife Elaine encouraged my efforts as she has with unfailing devotion for the forty-one years of our marriage, during recent years with great gallantry in the face of a devastating, progressive illness. She knows she has my everlasting love.

As for the dear friends, many of whom have passed on, who shared their wisdom with me and contributed to my education through my more than forty-five years in the industry, I cannot name them all here individually. Like earlier editions, this version is again dedicated to them. I thank them once more and bid them au revoir—here or hereafter!

JPD

Introduction to Book Publishing

We speak of book publishing as an industry and as a profession. Both designations are certainly appropriate. Book publishing is a business conducted, for the most part, for profit. But its practitioners—at least those who do it honor—have motivations that transcend their profit interest. They know that books are no mere commodity, no mere items for consumption that leave their readers much as they find them. Books, like other vehicles of information and sources of entertainment, can change, influence, elevate, demean, exalt, or depress those who expose themselves to them. What books are and can be depends heavily on the judgment, integrity, taste, and acumen of those who select and produce them—their publishers.

Thus publishers play a vital role, not only in the marketplace, but within the culture and civilization of which they are a part, and what makes book publishing a profession as well as a business is the conscious pursuit by publishers of their responsibilities. They wield influence with pride, caution, and conscience. They make decisions with the awareness that they are injecting live matter into the cultural bloodstream. Perhaps too often they fail—tastes can be mediocre, avarice can overcome pride and conscience, even sound judgment can bow to the agitation of noisy fads. Publishing does not become a less significant calling, however, because there are sinners among the elect.

As industries go, book publishing is small, accounting for only $13 billion in revenues in 1987, according to *Book Industry Trends 1988*. Some 40% of this total, furthermore, represented sales to schools, college students, libraries, and other institutions, and only 60% ended up in the hands of general consumers.

Yet the industry enjoys an influence beyond its size because of the impact of books on the lives of their readers. That impact has been growing with the growth of book readership in recent decades. According to studies conducted in 1978 and 1983 for the Book Industry Study Group more than half of the U.S. population had read at least one book during the preceding six months, and about the same proportion had purchased at least one. However, heavy book readers who read and buy books consistently still represent a rather small minority, only 30%, of the reading age population.

Even this minority however, has been growing. There has been a general maturation of American culture in which the rise in educational level and increased affluence have played their roles. And there is reason to believe that the trends thus set in motion will continue and that books, along with other cultural commodities, will enjoy increased acceptance by American consumers.

Some observers had predicted that books and other printed means of information and entertainment would suffer a decline. Led by Marshall McLuhan, these prophets had foreseen a general conversion to audiovisual and electronic media. The very reverse has occurred. While the audiovisual scene, notably television, has of course grown dramatically, books and periodicals have also seen gains. The reason, which apparently escaped McLuhan and others seeing the matter in too simple terms, is that as the thirst and capacity for knowledge and the enjoyment of the arts increase, so does the use of the many and varied means of satisfying them. Not only do tastes and personalities differ, but the same individual, responding to different needs and moods, may find it opportune to read during one hour, work a home computer the next, then see a live play, attend a concert tomorrow, and watch some television in between. The Book Industry Study Group Surveys clearly indicate that book readers tend to be very active individuals whose leisure time occupations are highly diversified.

Reading itself, of course, is a habit that will differ greatly in nature and character from one individual to the next.

Students read and buy books because they must, although, hopefully, some will enjoy the experience and acquire the lifelong habit of doing so. Professionals—physicians, attorneys, accountants, engineers, scientists—who wish to keep up with developments in their field read and buy books in substantial numbers, as do people seeking job improvement or advancement and those engaged in continuing education.

There are hobbyists who enjoy reading about their avocations, travelers who do some of their journeying in armchairs, playgoers who relive their experience by reading a script, art lovers who visit the great galleries in books of reproductions, music devotees who deepen their appreciation by reading the lives of the composers. There are collectors who acquire books for their beauty or rarity, or even show-offs who display them out of vanity to support the appearance of sophistication. Did we say that consistent book readers and buyers constitute a minority? Not a minority—a whole host of minorities of special tastes, interests, vocations, and avocations.

In the course of this book, we shall examine the ways in which the book publishing industry attempts to satisfy these varied interests. We shall review its history briefly and examine the environment in which it functions, the qualifications required of its practitioners, the products it creates, the processes employed in their manufacture, their markets and how they are reached. We shall inquire into patterns of ownership and styles of management and into the economics and finance of the process. From this examination, we hope will emerge not only an understanding and appreciation of the massive complexity that is characteristic of this field, and of its successes and failures, but also of the important role that book publishing plays in the life of our society.

I

The Past Is Prologue

Books in History

Books in one form or another are as old as civilization. We encounter them in ancient Mesopotamia as clay tablets and in ancient Egypt as papyrus rolls. Rolls were also the form they took in Greece and Rome, where bookselling already flourished and the "scriptoria" or copying establishments plied a vigorous trade. Cities like Pergamum and Alexandria boasted of great libraries; the latter is said to have housed at one time as many as 700,000 rolls.

The format of books as we know them dates from the first century A.D. when the codex, a volume of parchment pages bound on one side, was introduced. A massive and often beautiful object, the codex remained the characteristic book of the Middle Ages. The religious and secular works then produced, mostly in monasteries, were often duplicated assembly-line style with copyists, proofreaders, and illustrators each fulfilling separate, coordinated functions.

As early as the twelfth century the stationers made their appearance as commercial duplicators and purveyors of books. Many were attached to the universities which were then being founded and taking over the publishing function from the monasteries. Later the stationers organized themselves into corporations and guilds and, like other artisans of the period, assumed monopolistic control over their own profession.

The fifteenth century witnessed two vital developments: the introduction of paper and the invention of movable type. Some bibliographers doubt that Johannes Gutenberg should be credited with the invention of type; they claim that Johann Fust and Peter Schöffer actually printed the Bible which bears Gutenberg's name, and that in any case the Constance Missal antedates that Bible as the first printed book. Be that as it may, the practice of printing books by the new method spread with great rapidity throughout Europe, and a wealth of "incunabula," as fifteenth-century books are known, survives. By 1500 books were paginated and title pages listed publishers' imprints and dates of publication much as they do today. In 1501 Aldus Manutius designed the first small book specifically intended to fit into the reader's pockets.

The Reformation and Counter-Reformation proved to be potent stimuli to reading and the publication of books. Not only were the Scriptures made available in the vernacular and widely distributed, but religious controversy found in the newly established printing presses ready means for spreading argument and counterargument far and wide. If the distribution of a great many books was thus encouraged, so was a good deal of suppression, confiscation, and burning. Censorship became a way of life. Even John Milton, who in 1644 wrote the *Areopagitica,* a ringing defense of freedom to publish, later became censor for the Commonwealth. But literacy gained ground embracing by one estimate 60 percent of the population of sixteenth-century England.

In 1638 the Puritans set up a press in Cambridge, Massachusetts, on which in 1640 the *Bay Psalm Book* was printed. It was among the first of nearly 90,000 titles which were produced in the American Colonies, mostly in English but also in German, Dutch, French, and in Indian languages. Colonial production was of course heavily supplemented by books brought to the new continent from all parts of Europe by immigrants, travelers, and merchants.

Modern Publishing Begins

During the eighteenth century the common people in the Western world shared a growing belief that they could acquire learning through reading. Women had attended the common schools and helped enlarge the audience for books. The farmer or artisan who was a man of letters was no longer a rarity. This was the era of the founding of the great encyclopedias, such as the *Britannica* in England, and the establishment of circulating libraries in many countries. The cause of authors, who had been restricted by monopolistic printers, was aided by such legislation as the British Copyright Act of 1710 which enabled them to negotiate for favorable compensation and terms.

But if book production was substantial in the eighteenth century, with two million titles issued worldwide, the nineteenth century was a period of even more significant development. Some eight million titles were published. By 1900 a best-selling novel would sell 600,000 copies in the English-speaking world. Urbanization, industrialization, and the impetus given to universal education by the growth of democratic influences were among the principal factors in this growth.

Many publishing houses still active today were founded during this period. Among imprints surviving in the United States who can trace their ancestry to the late eighteenth and the nineteenth centuries are Lea & Febiger (1785), Abingdon Press (1789), J. B. Lippincott (1792), John Wiley & Sons (1807), Harper & Row (1817), G. & C. Merriam (1831), Houghton Mifflin (1832), Little, Brown (1837), G. P. Putnam's Sons (1838), Charles E. Merrill (1842), E. P. Dutton (1852), Rand McNally (1856), Ginn & Co. (1867), Allyn & Bacon (1868), Johns Hopkins University Press (1878), and Doubleday (1897). It is noteworthy that many of these publishers specialized from the beginning in educational, professional, and religious books while others addressed themselves to the general public.

During the nineteenth century also paperbound books made their appearance, notably in Germany and France, where they became firmly and permanently established. In the United States they managed to flourish briefly during the 1830s, but an adverse postal ruling ended the experiment abruptly in 1843. They were resurrected by 1870 and had quite a vogue, particularly in the celebrated dime novel form. But so large a portion of these books was pirated from foreign editions that the copyright act of 1891 once again effectively put an end to that brief paperback era.

The Early Twentieth Century

Most of the imprints recognized in the United States today, including some of the largest and most influential, were founded in this century— some like McGraw-Hill (1909), Prentice-Hall (1913), Simon & Schuster (1924), and Random House (1925) during early decades, others like Atheneum (1959) more recently. The advent of the modern paperback was responsible for the creation of some, such as Pocket Books (1939), Bantam Books (1946), New American Library (1948), and Fawcett World Library (1950); the development of book publishing for direct mail distribution, particularly by magazine publishers, was responsible for the founding of others such as Time-Life Books (1961) and American Heritage Press (1968). New York became the center where most houses operated, but Boston, Philadelphia, and Chicago were also points of concentration.

Many of the persuasions and traditions that still move the industry today hail from the 1920s, a period of national prosperity and literary flowering, that produced great editors like Maxwell Perkins and publishing giants like George Platt Brett, Sr., and Horace Liveright. A number of industry leaders who founded or managed publishing houses during the thirties, forties, and fifties received their training during that golden age, and by their influence helped to enshrine many of its beliefs and practices as a lasting heritage. Subsequent developments—depression, New Deal, World War II, and the economic, cultural, and industry explosions that followed them—have had surprisingly little impact on that legacy.

Immediately prior to World War II the industry was, in economic terms, a minor one in the United States. Its healthiest segments, the educational, professional, and reference book areas, were able on the whole to attract sufficient capital to meet their obligations and opportunities but were not generally regarded as prime prospects for investment. Publishers serving the general consumer were often struggling to keep alive; it is no secret that in some diversified houses the educational department's income would keep the trade department in existence, and only the fascination of owners and managers with general consumer books allowed those divisions to function at all.

Salaries in the field during this period were low. Few authors could support themselves by their writing. A book could rise to the national best-seller list, particularly in nonfiction, by selling less than 50,000 copies. College enrollments, confined to a cultural-economic elite, were modest as were the textbook sales catering to them. The Great Depression intensified the limitations of what was already a minority interest in books.

Book distribution reflected these conditions. Booksellers were struggling to survive, caught in an economic squeeze that on the one hand required them to operate in expensive locations in order to maintain traffic and attract customers, while on the other hand did not allow them to sell their wares expensively enough and in sufficient volume to earn an adequate margin. Many communities consequently were not adequately served or not served at all by book outlets. Some of the great bookstores of the nation could not have kept their doors open had it not been for their used book departments, where markups were more adequate, or their rare book sections that catered to wealthy collectors.

Booksellers looked with concern on the activities of book clubs. The Book-of-the-Month Club had been founded in 1926, the Literary Guild in 1927. Undoubtedly book clubs stole some sales away from retailers, but they also reached readers who had no access to or no opportunity to visit bookstores, and they succeeded by their membership arrangements in making book buying a habit for some consumers who might otherwise have been very sporadic in their purchasing. By their promotion they created wider interest in titles they selected and in fact created new readers who subsequently proved a boon to booksellers and publishers alike. The same could be said of paperbacks when they made their appearance under the Pocket Books imprint in 1939. Though seen initially by many booksellers as a threat, they have on the whole benefited the industry beyond measure.

But these and other marketing innovations, while helpful and important in laying foundations for the future, did not then succeed in bringing prosperity to the industry. Book people, like teachers, scholars, artists, and musicians, in those days before affluence was widespread, were resigned to an existence of genteel poverty. They found other compensations. To be near books, to share if only indirectly in the literary process, to be midwife to an author's blessed event, these were exciting and rewarding. A deep commitment and dedication grew from the love of books that sustained many a publisher and bookseller despite the lack of significant financial reward.

At the same time, however, the industry—in particular its trade publishing segment—suffered from a paucity of business acumen. While there were publishers who, like Alfred Knopf, combined editorial genius with sound business sense they were unfortunately the exception rather than the rule. When an endeavor, by its very nature, attracts people who find their rewards in its nonmaterial aspects, it is not normally going to find the best talent in American business management flocking to its doors. Nor is it likely that the people whom it does attract will arrive with the persuasion that sound management ability is one of the prime requisites expected of them.

Thus many publishing houses became victims of a vicious circle: because they were not successful businesses they did not enlist the interest of good business people—with the result that they remained largely unsound from a business standpoint.

War and Postwar

World War II curtailed the industry's activities, while paper was rationed and many readers as well as industry personnel were engaged in fighting the war or in defense work. But in a patriotic and enlightened move publishers made available thousands of "Armed Forces Editions" of their books to the military in the field. Books thus became companions and solace, entertainment, and relaxation to countless individuals, many of whom might otherwise never have acquired the habit of reading. As these volumes were paperbound they also helped pave the way for the incipient paperback revolution.

The war, furthermore, resulted in the beginnings of the college explosion: the era in which higher education was to become the perceived birthright of the masses rather than of a mere elite. The veterans who flocked into college classrooms under the G.I. Bill established a precedent which has become an article of national faith and commitment. The veterans purchased a great many books with government funds, thus giving college publishing its first big postwar shot in the arm.

Shortly after the war's end the new era in paperbound books was born. The titles which Pocket Books, Bantam Books, New American Library, and others that soon joined them were disseminating were not only different in format, size, and price—they used new channels of distribution which books had never before found open to them. By making use of the facilities of national magazine and independent local distributors, books were displayed on newsstands and cigar counters, in drugstores, railroad terminals, etc. The market they created was in large measure new and previously untapped.

Mass market paperbacks spearheaded the movement that "democratized" books during the following decades. In the past books had served primarily a cultural elite; now they became common commodities that nearly everyone could enjoy or utilize in their daily living. This new, vastly expanded role for books was symptomatic of a profound cultural change then transforming American society. An egalitarian dream was being realized—no doubt imperfectly, but realized nonetheless. Improvements in the economic lot and educational attainment of the average citizen had made it possible for growing numbers of people to enjoy the civilized pursuits once reserved to the privileged few. Partaking of the cultural heritage with characteristic independence of mind, Americans created a cultural pluralism sufficiently varied to match their ethnic and religious diversity. But in the process they showed little regard for the canons of critical tradition.

This did not sit well with the cultural elite, in particular with the literary elite that had held the reins of moral leadership in the book world since the 1920s. The literati looked upon the popularization of books and the diversification of tastes as a cultural decline. But as Daniel J. Boorstin has pointed out in *The Americans: The Colonial Experience,* these developments have followed "tendencies [that] reach deep into our past":

> In modern Western European culture the most honorific use of the printed word, except for sacred religious texts, has been in the ornamental literature of its privileged classes. Such cultures are judged by their dramas, poems, novels, and essays, which like palaces and manor-houses, are the monuments of aristocratic cultures. But must we measure *our* culture by its ability to produce such monuments? Must we hope to induct an ever larger part of the American people into the mysteries of an aristocratic belles-lettres?
>
> The printed word has had another destiny in America, a role less understandable by the traditional techniques of literary archeologists. The pecu-

liarly American emphasis on relevance, utility, "reader interest," and catholicity of appeal has made of printed matter a different institution. Not the litterateur but the journalist, not the essayist but the writer of how-to manuals, not the "artist" but the publicist is the characteristic American man of letters. His readers are found not in the salon but in the market place, not in the cloister or quadrangle but in the barbershop or the fireplace of the average citizen.

Quite a different paperbound development occurred during the early 1950s in the traditional book field when trade paperbacks made their appearance. These titles of serious nonfiction and literary classics, while enjoying a certain vogue with the general consumer, found their prime markets in education. Most were used in college courses. During the late fifties, when secondary school programs were upgraded, high schools also contributed to their consumption. In fact, both trade and "mass market" paperbacks enjoyed increased educational uses until the educational slumps of the seventies, when trade paper bounds were reoriented and thereafter directed largely at the consumer.

Simultaneously with these developments several educational book publishers, noting a trend toward the use of audiovisual materials in the classroom, began to diversify their production by introducing such materials separately or in multimedia combinations. McGraw-Hill had entered the field as a lone pioneer in 1946; other textbook houses did not follow suit until several years later. While the extensive displacement of books predicted by enthusiasts for audiovisual education never materialized, multimedia publishing, later including computer software publishing, remained a factor in the decades that followed.

In fact the growth and upgrading of education on all levels that followed the 1957 shock of Sputnik had profound effects on the entire book industry. Publishers benefited from the massive infusion of federal funds that characterized the late fifties and the sixties. School classrooms, library resource centers, and college and public libraries became the beneficiaries of programs that enabled them to enlarge their holdings of books and of audiovisual and related materials which had rarely before been supported by such funding and certainly never on such a scale.

These events coincided with a consistently growing wave of affluence and also with substantial increases in enrollments on elementary, high school, and college levels (the postwar baby boom was having its effect).

The Mergers of the Sixties

By the early 1960s journalists, economic forecasters, Wall Street analysts, and other custodians of the national crystal ball began to make ecstatic predictions for the future of education, for the use of leisure time, and, by implication, for book publishing. Unfortunately their analyses were often superficial and they badly overstated their case. Nevertheless many of the factors to which they pointed were real and, for a while at least, their forecasts appeared plausible.

They succeeded in whetting the appetite of investors and corporations searching for ways to diversify their holdings. Wall Street was then, no more than later, renowned for its restraint and detached judgment; even so all the earmarks pointed to book publishing as a sound investment with future growth. Thus publishing stocks, particularly those of educational companies, became glamour holdings. And conglomerates began to woo every independent publisher whose future promised to throw off even a modest share of the forecast earnings.

The publishers being wooed were often very happy at the prospect of a merger. Few had the resources to make the growth the new markets promised a profitable reality. Some privately held companies solved the problem by offering shares to the public, though such moves often proved mere stopovers on their way to being absorbed by larger companies. Some, determined to preserve their independence, succeeded in maintaining their status quo. But a major segment of the industry found itself involved in merging, acquiring, or more frequently, being acquired.

Thus Random House was purchased by RCA after previously absorbing Alfred Knopf and Pantheon Books. Holt, Rinehart & Winston, itself the product of two mergers, became a subsidiary of CBS, as did W. B. Saunders. The Times Mirror Co. of Los Angeles made subsidiaries of New American Library, World Publishing Co., Popular Science, Harry N. Abrams, Matthew Bender, C. V. Mosby, and Year Book Medical Publishers, among others. Litton Industries acquired Van Nostrand, Reinhold, American Book Co., and McCormick-Mathers. Xerox purchased Ginn & Co. and R. R. Bowker. Meredith Corporation bought Appleton-Century-Crofts and Lyons & Carnahan. Time, Inc., acquired Little, Brown and New York Graphic Society. ITT purchased Bobbs-Merrill and Howard Sams. Harcourt Brace Jovanovich acquired Academic Press and Grune & Stratton. Encyclopaedia Britannica purchased G. & C. Merriam and Praeger. Raytheon bought D. C. Heath, and so on and so forth.

These mergers and acquisitions had a profound effect upon the book field. They made resources available without which the industry probably could not have capitalized on its opportunities and fulfilled its obligations to educational and consumer audiences alike. They brought new management and business acumen to the field which had been seriously lacking and which, in many instances resulted for the first time in orderly budgeting, forecasting, planning, and fiscal arrangements. But in many cases they also placed the power of ultimate decision and policymaking in the hands of people unfamiliar with and insensitive to books, their readers and their markets.

Boom and Aftermath

What liabilities were being engendered by these changes were not readily apparent during the prosperous sixties. These were times when books seemed to sell despite the inadequacies of their publishers, when even inferior materials were readily absorbed by a well-funded, gluttonous market. So many factors worked together to benefit the various segments of the industry that almost everyone enjoyed a slice of the pie. Research projects supported by government and foundation grants encouraged acquisition of professional books; generous federal and state budgets, bringing unaccustomed affluence to colleges, universities, and their faculties, augmented sales of scholarly materials; newly founded colleges were stocking libraries; parents eager to strengthen their children's educational resources avidly bought encyclopedias for the home; general and specialized book clubs were flourishing.

There was, in addition, the factor of growing export and foreign sales. The postwar scholarly and scientific community had embraced English as the international language, and American publishers were reaping some large benefits. Translations and the leasing of publishing rights to foreign publishers were also growing phenomena. Soon American publishers of professional and reference materials saw the advantages of founding their own subsidiary companies abroad, thus enjoying the best of both worlds.

It could not last. The 1970s ushered in some substantial reverses. General economic conditions initially declined, then recovered only sporadically. Enrollments in elementary schools, reflecting the population patterns of the preceding years, went on a downward trend. Taxpayers' revolts in many areas curtailed school budgets. College enrollments, too, began to decline even as state legislatures cut appropriations for higher education. Federal support for schools, libraries, and research were threatened and embroiled in political controversy. Home sales of encyclopedias were falling off substantially.

But if the boom era had apparently come to an end, the industry had matured and advanced significantly during this period, and many of the gains appeared to be permanent. Large numbers of new readers had come into the fold. Lower education had been upgraded and higher education expanded to a larger segment of the population with related advances in book consumption. Even if consistent readers and book buyers still represented only a minority, or more accurately a group of cultural minorities, these minorities had grown substantially, and a larger universe of occasional book buyers now surrounded the hard core of loyal devotees.

Recession and Inflation

These gains did not prevent the industry from being adversely affected by the recession and inflation of the midseventies. In fact, its very progress had made the book field more vulnerable to the impact of economic downturns: a greater number of occasional purchasers meant that more patrons could fall by the wayside during lean times. The number of consumer books sold, particularly mass market paperbacks, fell off during 1974–1975. Dollar revenues fared a great deal better, but only because substantial book price inflation set in at about the same time.

Countering a trend that had prevailed for more than a decade, when book price inflation had stayed well below general consumer commodity levels, the price dam broke in 1974 under the pressure of drastic increases in the cost of paper. Skyrocketing guarantees paid to authors, rising operating expenses, and shortsighted profit objectives set by some managements added to the pressure until book prices were inflating at rates significantly higher than the general consumer price index.

Expectably, this price inflation contributed further to the decline of unit sales as general consumers and institutions found their resources inadequate to keep up with the rapidly rising cost of books. Many schools and libraries were particularly hard-hit because their book budgets had already been cut to austerity levels.

The industry might have fared even worse had it not been for some favorable developments in the retail market where the two major chains, B. Dalton and Waldenbooks, embarked on sizable expansion programs, and where an unprecedented number of independent booksellers were entering the field. Although the rapid proliferation of these outlets led to competition for the same limited consumer dollars in many areas, expansion unquestionably arrested what might otherwise have been a disastrous decline in industry sales.

More Mergers—On a Wave of New Imprints

The late seventies brought on another round of mergers. Although the number of combinations that took place was smaller than that which had substantially changed the character of the industry during the previous decade, this series of mergers appeared to be contributing proportionately more to industry concentration. Doubleday acquired Dell, CBS added Fawcett to its holdings, Time, Inc., purchased the Book-of-the-Month

Club, Harper & Row absorbed Lippincott, and Atheneum and Scribner's joined forces. Each of the above cases involved a combination of existing publishers rather than the acquisition of a house by an outside corporation. However, there were also notable examples of outside involvement such as the purchase of Simon and Schuster–Pocket Books by Gulf & Western and of Putnam, Coward, McCann & Geogehegan, and Berkeley by MCA.

Simultaneously with concentration at the top of the industry, the 1970s produced an amazing proliferation at the bottom. According to records maintained by the R. R. Bowker Co., the number of publishers in the United States increased by 100 percent between 1972 and 1980—from 6,000 to nearly 12,000. Many of the new publishers were so-called "small presses" specializing in fiction and poetry, some with a decidedly counter-cultural cast, determined to develop alternative methods of distribution along with their "alternative" publications. Others among the new imprints were moving along more traditional lines, publishing school, college, trade, and mass market paperback titles. Still others were foreign-owned publishers anxious to exploit the U.S. market and to gain a foothold on American shores. Many of the new houses located themselves in the West and other areas distant from traditional publishing centers.

The Industry Is Reshaped

Both the mergers and the small-press expansion gained momentum during the 1980s. Paralleling events in the larger economy, where "merger mania" was creating a new generation of national and international super-corporations, publishing combinations grew larger and more multinational in character. Simon & Schuster acquired Prentice-Hall, Ginn and Silver Burdett; British-based I. R. Maxwell acquired Macmillan, which had absorbed Scribner-Atheneum and Harper & Row's school publishing division; Bertelsmann of Germany took over Bantam Books and Doubleday-Dell; Australian media magnate Rupert Murdoch, who already controlled British-based Collins, purchased Harper & Row; and French publishing giant Hachette acquired Grolier, Inc. Expectably, the industry also experienced its share of divestitures and hostile takeover attempts. RCA sold Random House to the Newhouse Corporation newspaper empire; Xerox disposed of R. R. Bowker Co. to Reed International, British owner of Cahners Magazines; and Ian Maxwell failed in a bid to capture Harcourt Brace Jovanovich. By 1988, most of the prominent houses that had led the industry for more than a century had either disappeared or lost their autonomy.

The economic pressures generated by the takeover wars intensified the prevailing profit fever and literally forced large publishers to emphasize big books at the expense of lesser titles. This led to the growing frustration of authors of "midlist" books, who found it increasingly difficult to interest agents and editors in their work. Even when a sympathetic editor accepted their manuscript, writers found that the rest of the publishing organization often failed to support their project.

Authors of midlist consumer books were particularly distressed about failures in distribution. The trade-book distribution system, which had been inadequate even in the 1920s and had remained virtually unchanged since then, relied almost exclusively on bookstores to reach consumers. Yet the vast title proliferation of the postwar era, coupled with the tendency of many booksellers to follow publishers' example in concentrating on big books, had reduced bookstore sales of midlist titles to alarmingly low levels. In desperation, some authors engaged publicity consultants or went on tour—selling more copies to lecture audiences than their publishers had to booksellers—but many others decided to publish their own books, or to entrust them to small presses.

As a result, the small-publisher universe simply exploded. Publishers could now be found in nearly every city of the U.S., in many small towns and even rural areas. Many of these ventures were operated by single individuals, by husband-and-wife teams, or by families. Many disappeared after one brief attempt, but many others survived and grew. As their success increased, so did the number of additional entrepreneurs following their example. By 1987, Bowker's *Books in Print* listed 22,500 publishers.

Most small presses cultivated special interest areas, and many created unique niches for themselves in neglected fields. They publicized their books energetically, and, following the lead of publishers of professional books and direct-mail merchandisers, effectively marketed them directly to consumers, (and, where warranted, to carefully selected, committed retailers). Whereas trade publishers had always insisted that publishing small editions for small audiences was bound to be unprofitable, many small consumer presses showed respectable profits.

In addition to the burgeoning small consumer press population, there also developed a sizable not-for-profit constituency. These were book publishing imprints of professional and trade organizations, environmental and consumer groups, trade unions and similar entities, many of them headquartered in Washington, D.C., and environs. They owed their existence to the growing conviction of their parent organizations that publishing programs in general, and book-publishing ventures in particular, were among the basic services such groups should provide for their members.

Most small presses were hospitable to new technology. Many installed desktop publishing systems to set their own type, utilizing electronic manuscripts from authors whenever possible. In fact, many were able to show a profit on their tiny operations only because of the economies they could achieve with the electronic approach. Here, too, small presses stood in marked contrast to their established colleagues in consumer publishing who had generally ignored the advantages of processing electronic manuscripts. Authors who brought such manuscripts to mainstream houses were usually asked to print them out and submit them in traditional form.

In the meantime, another consumer book boom had materialized. Defying the twilight economy of the 1980s, both adult and juvenile titles were breaking sales records. A major surprise of this period was the rebounding of hardcover books that had been losing ground to paperbounds for three decades. Perhaps publishers had been counting too heavily on the magic of the paperback format, were making too many poor editorial choices, or increasing prices too rapidly, but unit sales of both trade and mass market paperbounds slowed substantially. At the same time hardcover unit sales accelerated, particularly when Bantam Books, followed by other mass market houses, entered the hardcover field and for the first time distributed hardbounds through selected mass market channels.

The phenomenon of burgeoning juvenile sales was heartening, particularly because of its promise for the future. Juvenile publishing had experienced ups and downs in the postwar period. During the educational boom years, publishers tended to neglect the consumer market and to emphasize titles that had a strong institutional appeal. When educational funding was reduced in the 1970s, juvenile houses had to curtail their programs and some publishers left the field altogether. By the early 1980s institutional demand for juveniles had fallen so low that publishers decided to redirect their attention to the consumer market they had slighted for so long.

Their choice was fortuitous because by this time the baby boom generation, which had shown itself strongly supportive of books during its adolescence, had grown to parental age and was determined that its own children should be readers right from the start. Soon the "baby-lit" phenomenon surfaced, producing a host of titles for teaching two-year-olds to read, followed by lively successes for children's titles of all ages, from colorful flats to teen romances and mysteries. Sales were further augmented when a national campaign to eradicate illiteracy and encourage reading once more improved the funding of school and public libraries. In 1987 juvenile hardbound and paperbound sales led those of the entire industry.

By any standard the development of the book industry since World War II has been impressive. In 1947, according to government records, 648 publishers had been active; forty years later there were 22,500, an increase of 3,372 percent. Annual sales during this period grew from $464 million to

$13 billion, a gain of 2,700 percent overall, or 8.7 percent yearly, representing a growth rate 16 percent higher than that of the gross national product. Title production mushroomed as well. Between 1963 and 1987 the number of titles in print increased by 360 percent, from 163,000 to 751,000, with a net gain of 32,000 during 1987 alone, when over 50,000 new titles and new editions were released.

Bookstore growth, by national chains as well as independent retailers, has been equally vigorous. Excluding college stores (which sell textbooks primarily,) the number of booksellers increased by 111 percent between 1972 and 1987, from 8,863 to 18,719. In 1987 about half the nation's population of reading age bought books; some 30 percent, who bought more than one book a month, were responsible for 90 percent of all consumer purchases, or $9 billion. Significantly, average yearly purchases by book buyers had risen steadily, from $20.96 for 11 books in 1972, to $91.63 for 14 books in 1987, an increase of 337 percent in dollars and 27 percent in units. Overall, the biggest volume of industry growth had come from consumer books, while books for professional and work use had enjoyed the most rapid pace of expansion.

It is against this background, a generally reassuring history despite its share of difficulties, that we must take the measure of the industry in its present state.

II

A Broad Perspective

A Cultural Industry

Book publishing, as we have noted, is both a cultural activity and a business. Books are vehicles of ideas, instruments of education, vessels of literature, and sources of entertainment. But the task of bringing them into existence and of purveying them to their readers is a commercial one requiring all the resources and skill of the manager and entrepreneur.

It is appropriate, therefore, to describe book publishing as a cultural industry. The theater, film, and record businesses which share these characteristics can be similarly defined. It is important to recognize the dual character and demands of book publishing and of similar enterprises because their success depends on it. Both the environment in which they function and the qualifications of their practitioners reflect this duality; in both instances we must consider cultural *and* business requirements if our enterprise is to flourish.

A Mass Industry?

What environmental factors have an impact on book publishing? Well—certainly it is influenced by the general cultural climate to which we have already referred. Book buying, though a growing phenomenon in America, is not a consistent habit with a majority of the population. Sales figures of individual books are most revealing. When a national best seller after going through hardcover and paperbound editions sells two million copies

31

the industry rejoices and points to it with pride. Yet such a sale represents a purchase by less than 1 percent of the population. An ordinary television show on a national network will have exposure to many times that number. The same is true of the major magazines.

The average hardcover trade book published may sell up to 10,000 copies, the average "mass-market" paperback perhaps 100,000. The designation "mass market" for that paperback may be justified when comparing it with the hardcover volume—but in relation to the total potential market it is something of a fiction. In America books do not really reach the masses—at any rate not yet.

Unfortunately many editorial and marketing concepts the industry's mainstream has formulated in recent years are based on the assumption that books are a mass commodity. Thus the best-seller, which supposedly will reach a mass audience, receives major emphasis; the more specialized book, appealing to a more limited market, is given less attention. Yet all the evidence suggests that in aggregate the industry receives the bulk of its income and support from book buyers who indulge specialized interests and tastes. To the extent that the emphasis on imagined "mass" interests neglects these buyers, the industry is cutting its nose to spite its face.

It would be fair to say, in fact, that the single greatest challenge facing American book publishing today—the goal that would most enable it to reach its potential—is simply to reach effectively the people willing and anxious to buy books. This would entail emphasizing editorial choices aimed at satisfying the real interests of consumers as well as the development of adequate means of placing books into their hands. In both ways American book publishing today leaves much to be desired. Editorial emphasis is far too much on potential "mass" titles—most of which do not perform as expected. As for obtaining specialized books, such titles are rarely available in retail outlets, are often difficult to obtain even by mail, and take interminable time to arrive when special-ordered by booksellers. Uncounted book sales are lost in this country every day because willing buyers cannot find what they want on display, nor can they order most books with reasonable ease.

Publishing and Education

Closely related to the general cultural climate as an environmental factor for book publishing is the state of education. Many stresses currently trouble this field: broad public disillusionment with what are perceived to be its failures; demands for greater accountability by educators; rising costs coupled with public reluctance to meet them. Educators themselves are anxious to introduce methods that will improve performance, centering mostly around greater individuation in approach to students.

Two trends in the choice of educational materials have been challenging the traditional textbook: the use of general books, particularly paperbacks, and the employment of audiovisual and electronic media. Many educational publishers have diversified their products and are in a position to respond effectively to these trends. But industry sales figures suggest that although textbooks have lost some ground, the attrition is far smaller than the lively rhetoric would lead one to believe. If a significant trend has emerged it seems to be that in the majority of schools and colleges the textbook will remain the principal tool of instruction. Other books and other media will play their roles, of course, but they seem destined to remain secondary ones.

This is not to suggest that the textbook is not going to change as conditions change. Certainly new emphases in instruction—including, one must own, new fads—will influence the content and appearance of text materials. We are witnessing more softbound texts, more consumables (materials on which the students work directly and which they, therefore, use up), more modular packages (kits consisting of small units). What is of the essence, however, is that from all appearances printed materials especially designed for the classroom—or for individualized instruction within formal educational settings—remain the favored choice of educators and students alike.

Another factor, touching upon education in a broader sense, is receiving the attention of book publishers. The knowledge explosion, TV, and heightened career demands, among other factors, have greatly increased the thirst for continuing education which has always motivated a sizable segment of the book-buying public. (Even in the 1940s I discovered to my amazement that the best-selling books in a somewhat seedy store in New York's Times Square area were not sex manuals but College Outlines. And they were selling not to college students but to truck drivers, subway guards, accountants, and office secretaries.) Not always served effectively through normal book outlets at present, the continuing education interest can be a rewarding field for book publishers who have the imagination and skill to exploit it.

Copying and Copyright

Two other rather specific phenomena affecting the environment for book publishing need to be considered here because of their timeliness and significance: unauthorized copying and censorship.

Unauthorized copying of copyrighted materials is a problem that has become widespread since the invention of copying machines which have made it easy and relatively inexpensive to duplicate not only pages but whole chapters and sections of books. As today no self-respecting public or academic library is without a copying machine and as schools and colleges make them available to their teaching staffs, the opportunities for disregarding the legally protected rights of authors and publishers in this regard are numberless.

The present copyright law is of rather recent vintage; it became effective January 1, 1978. It was passed after years of bitter debate during which traditional allies in education, the library world, authors, and publishers became sharply divided over the issue of what copying should be permissible for research and educational purposes. Yet the battle continues, and the dust may not settle for some time to come.

In the American common law tradition, the right to literary property is considered to be a natural right, i.e., it need not be protected by statute, although its administration obviously calls for very specific and very detailed codification. The law, therefore, protects published and unpublished writings and correspondence, usually whether or not they are registered with the administering agency, the Register of Copyrights at the Library of Congress. However, in order to enjoy full legal protection, in pressing an infringement suit, for example, a work must be registered. Published books should carry a notice of copyright. The terms of copyright vary somewhat with the circumstances. For a newly created work, the term typically is the author's life plus fifty years.

The law recognizes the legitimacy of "fair use" of copyrighted materials, such as the quotation of a passage or paragraph in another published work, as well as the legality of limited photocopying, such as of a copy of a single page, for research or teaching purposes. However, it restricts extensive copying, and Congress encouraged the establishment of machinery ensuring fair compensation to the owner of copyrighted materials in instances where copying exceeds "fair use." Accordingly, publishers of books and journals have organized a Copyright Clearance Center as a means of processing payments from libraries, educational and research institutions, and others.

Libraries have been reluctant to cooperate, finding the present arrangements not sufficiently convenient or comprehensive to satisfy their needs. Educators think that the law is too restrictive; some can see no wrong in duplicating a chapter or two from a book even for the use of (and sale to) several hundred students. Researchers express alarm over the burdens of a process that requires them to pay a fee each time they want to utilize a dozen pages from a book or journal.

Yet there is ample precedent, such as in the music industry, for a universal licensing and fee collection system which is simply administered while protecting the legal rights of copyright holders. The position advocated by some librarians and educators, that information and literary property should be made freely available to all who need it, is at odds not only with the common law tradition but also with the realities of the creative process. Some authors and publishers—particularly those academic writers and presses whose income is otherwise assured—may well muster the public spirit to contribute their efforts freely to the public good. However, most writers and publishers will continue to require also a financial incentive in order to produce the publications essential to civilized progress.

Publisher vs. Censor

If the issue of unauthorized copying is volatile and controversial, that of censorship is infinitely more so. It is also far more complex.

Most authors and publishers have traditionally opposed attempts to curtail freedom of expression. Basing their position on the First Amendment, which they contend makes any restraint on publication illegal, they have fought—often courageously and at great personal sacrifice—against efforts at suppression and censorship inspired by political, philosophical, religious, and moral persuasions. Had it not been for the battles and unceasing vigilance of many authors and publishers some great works of philosophy, religion, political theory, and literature would not now be available in libraries and bookstores.

What was in the minds of those who passed the First Amendment may be more difficult to establish, but judicial interpretation has never regarded it as an absolute guarantee of unfettered expression. Libel and obscenity are among the forms of speech and writing which the courts have consistently held are not protected by the First Amendment. Nor, to recall the ever popular statement of Justice Holmes, does freedom of speech entitle one to shout "Fire!" in a crowded theater.

Some commentators point out, furthermore, that a publisher has a responsibility beyond the law when he or she makes the decision to publish. The publisher may not have the right to injure another human being without reason whether or not the libel law is sufficiently vague or vaguely interpreted to permit publication of a work filled with destructive innuendo. The public may have a right to know what is in the public interest but its hunger for sensation may perhaps not be justifiably satiated if in the process a person's right to a fair trial is hopelessly jeopardized.

Publishers Weekly, in a July 2, 1973, editorial, critical of the Supreme Court Decision which effectively places the power to determine what is obscene in the hands of local communities, states:

> . . .it may not be amiss to point out that some publishers, by their own actions in recent years, have helped to create a climate in which such a ruling can be regarded as an acceptable one by large numbers of the American people. . . This is not to say that the publishing industry deserves the new and more stringent approach the Supreme Court has taken; merely that it becomes much harder to say where a stand should be taken when segments of the industry have already gravely undercut normal publishing standards.

Novelist Anthony Burgess, in an article in the *New York Times Magazine* of July 1, 1973, entitled "For Permissiveness, with Misgivings," speaks to the literary issue when he says:

> When novels about sodomy, bestiality, multiple coition and murderous-rape-with-willing-victim cram the bookstalls, what hope has the serious and well-written novel that takes sex as merely one aspect of life? Can the present-day cinema audience watch without restiveness a film in which a couple fall deeply in love without taking off their clothes? Appetites are growing coarser and ears deafer. And there are more pseudo writers about than there should be, capitalizing merely on the freedom to be brutal or erotic or both.

The industry's well-founded case against censorship might be more persuasive therefore, and likely to gain greater public acceptance, if publishers were to exercise more consistently the responsibility that is the inevitable concomitant of freedom.

What Makes a Publisher?

If the environmental conditions to which we have referred have an influence on the publishing process, the determining factor remains the publisher's decision. It is the publisher who by his or her judgment, taste, vision, integrity, and business acumen shapes in the end not only the industry but to a significant degree the literary and general culture which harbors him or her.

What qualifications must be brought to this important role? Granting that dispositions and aptitudes vary greatly from individual to individual, there appear to be certain general traits of personality and mind that are observable not only in the giants who have left their indelible mark upon the profession, but also in those more numerous women and men who in each age have contributed solidly to its progress.

The true publisher moves with equal comfort in the world of mind and art and in the world of commerce. This may not be a common personality combination; in fact it is probably rather rare. But it appears to be an indispensable prerequisite for achievement in book publishing. Publishers who consistently disrespect the demands for quality and worth in the manuscripts they publish will, despite temporary successes, find their enterprises dying of spiritual starvation in the end; just as publishers who consistently ignore the commercial needs of their establishments will find before long that cultural opportunities are negated by bankruptcy.

Curiously in this age of often extreme ideological moralities these compatible, indeed complementary, traits have been thought to be irreconcilable. Some purists express shock at any attentiveness to solvency. The moneymen, at the other extreme, often have no patience with any concern for literary or scientific excellence. "Will it sell?" is their only question. "Will it help build and maintain the imprint so that ten years from now our books will still be received with interest and confidence, and books we published ten years ago will still be selling because of their lasting significance?" may be the question both sides should be asking.

Obviously no publisher of vision can afford to be indifferent to the total atmosphere for writers, particularly for new writers. It is a wise and honorable tradition in publishing that one should give opportunities to new talent so that such talent may eventually produce salable manuscripts. Many an author's first book is published at a loss in anticipation of substantial gains on his or her second or third book. At times publishers will even knowingly publish an author whose work they suspect will never be successful commercially simply because they assess it to be of such quality and stature that its value to civilization far outbalances any financial loss it may incur. Such publishers display enlightened self-interest for they persuade readers and writers that publishers honestly love books.

But such commitment to the future of writing must be made with sound judgment and with a shrewd eye upon the general fiscal health of the publishing venture. The truly distinguished manuscript deserving the publisher's unselfish support is rare indeed; totally aside from the fact that not-for-profit publishers (like university presses) exist precisely for the purpose of allowing material to be published that may not succeed in the commercial market. That market itself is for most literary and informative writing a simple and true test of merit: if a book cannot be published viably perhaps it is simply not good enough and should not be published at all. Vox populi—vox Dei.

This leads to a second major qualification for the publisher: the ability to empathize with public tastes. Obviously, given the lively cultural pluralism of the audience, a publisher cannot personally share its every enthusiasm, every persuasion, every perspective. But a sufficiently sympathetic imagination should enable publishers to make judgements on behalf of the tastes and interests they hope to serve. Whether it be the world of students and teachers or the complex universe of consumers, the publishers should, in evaluating a manuscript, be able to bring their needs, attitudes, and predilections to their decisions and act, as it were, as their advocates in making a choice.

Publishers are specialists in their own profession—but when it comes to learning and literature the publishers must be generalists. In fact publishing and its related cultural industries may be the last bastions of generalism in a world in which the vastness of information and the variety of available diversions are pushing most of us into narrower and narrower areas of competence.

Finally a publisher needs courage. It takes courage to place one's faith in untried authors and use one's resources on their behalf, to adhere to quality and standards in a world often addicted to mediocrity, to shoot ahead of the cultural target, and to open new paths in the hope that they may become highways for literature and knowledge.

Divisions of the Industry

The products publishers develop, the markets to which they are addressed, and the methods used to reach those markets are the principal criteria by which the industry has distinguished certain categories of its activities. Such designation, as trade, text, professional, or mass market paperback publishing have come about naturally because houses engaging in these activities share common editorial objectives and economic concerns.

I say houses but should clarify that this may, often mean a small press, or a department or internal division of a house, particularly since the days of diversification and merger when many formerly independent enterprises became parts of empires.

In defining and describing the industry's categories and, later, the various publishing functions, it becomes necessary to adopt a standard terminology. Words such as "trade books," "editorial," or "production" are generally in use throughout the industry, but they do not always have the same meaning in every establishment that employs them. Local conditions have in fact introduced considerable variation into the industry's vocabulary. Since this makes communication between publishers difficult and precise comparisons of their activities impossible, standard terms and definitions have had to be developed and are employed in the statistical surveys conducted for the Association of American Publishers (AAP). I have generally utilized these terms and definitions throughout this book.

In keeping with this approach I have also adhered to the AAP definition of books themselves. This definition includes all nonperiodical hardcover volumes regardless of length; all juveniles, hardbound or softbound regardless of length, except coloring books; and all nonperiodical softbound volumes of more than forty-eight pages. Normally a softbound nonperiodical publication of between five and forty-eight pages is considered a pamphlet, although it may be classified as a book if generally accepted as such (as, for example, a short text-related workbook or a volume published as part of a regular program by a mass market paperback publisher).

The following are major categories distinguishing books by type:

Trade books are designed for the general consumer and are sold, for the most part, through bookstores, by direct mail and to libraries. They may be hardbound or paperbound and include works for both adults and children.

Typical trade books are hardcover fiction, current nonfiction, biography, literary classics, cookbooks, hobby books, popular science books, travel books, and art books, also books for self-education, such as those in foreign languages, books on sports, music, poetry, and drama. The main distinction between trade books and textbooks is that the latter are designed for classroom use rather than for general consumption and contain pedagogical apparatus such as summaries and test questions. It does not follow, however, that trade books are not used in classrooms or for educational purposes. In fact, in recent years, increasing numbers of trade titles have been bought for use in colleges and schools. This is particularly true of trade paperbacks which are widely used in college courses.

It should be noted that juvenile trade books range anywhere from picture books for the prereading age to works for "young adults" in their late teens.

Religious books include Bibles, testaments, hymnals, and prayer books (but traditionally exclude Sunday school materials). This category also embraces other works of specifically religious content, such as theology and popular devotional literature.

Religious publishers frequently released titles which, though of interest to a religious readership, are nevertheless not specifically religious in character, as, for example, material on social work, race problems, and world peace. Such books are classified as trade books or as textbooks, depending on their content and intended market, rather than as religious materials.

Professional books are, as the designation implies, books directed to professional people and specifically related to their work. AAP surveys distinguish among three major areas of professional-book publishing: *technical and scientific books* which treat subjects in the physical, biological, earth, and social sciences as well as technology, engineering, and the trades and are addressed to practicing and research scientists, engineers, architects, technicians, mechanics, and teachers in these and allied fields; *medical books* designed for physicians, nurses, dentists, hospital administrators, veterinarians, pharmacists, et al.; and business and other professional books addressed to business people, managers, accountants, lawyers, librarians, or other professional individuals not covered under the technical, scientific and medical categories.

As with trade books, the use of professional books in educational programs is widespread. However, if the editorial character of a volume and its predominant intended audience is professional and its educational use represents a secondary market, the book is classified in the professional category. When professional-book publishers publish textbooks— for example, medical publishers' nursing texts—the textbook classification applies.

Book clubs could be regarded as a retail market channel rather than as publishers, particularly as for the most part they do not originate the materials they distribute to their members but acquire the rights from other publishers. However, traditionally book clubs have been considered to be part of the publishing industry, and as a few clubs do originate books and as all clubs prepare separate editions for their specific distribution, the classification has some rationale.

AAP surveys provide for distinctions between *consumer* and *professional* book clubs. Consumer clubs in turn involve those who cater to *general interests,* such as the Book-of-the-Month Club and the Literary Guild, which offer a great variety of titles without attempt at subject specialization, and *special interest* clubs whose members have particular subject enthusiasms, such as cooking, the outdoors, or the military, or who represent a special population group such as do students served by clubs which distribute paperbacks in the schools. Professional book clubs partake of the characteristics of professional book publishers so far as their offerings and audience are concerned.

Mail order publications are books created for large general consumer audiences and are marketed by direct mail. A careful distinction must be made here between this category, which typically includes such imprints as Time-Life Books and American Heritage Press, and the direct-mail activities of most small presses and other publishers. Nearly every publisher today utilizes direct mail to some extent, and some small presses and professional houses rely on it as their primary marketing tool. However, in industry surveys, such as the U.S. Census of Manufactures and the AAP Statistics program, these publishers are expected to report their sales as trade or professional books rather than as Mail Order Publications. The latter category was created in the 1960s to capture the activities of a unique group of major consumer magazine publishers who were marketing specially created book titles by mail to their subscribers and other mass audiences. Typically their mailings run in the millions and sales in the hundreds of thousands.

A further distinction must be made between Mail Order Publications and Book Clubs. The former are originated by the publisher who does the marketing and the publications are distributed without the specific commitments by the purchaser which characterize book club memberships. Although mail order publishers often market series or multivolume sets on a so-called continuity basis (i.e., after placing an order the purchaser receives volumes automatically unless he or she instructs the publisher to stop), the buyer incurs no obligation nor enters into a membership arrangement of any kind.

Mail order publications, too, have secondary markets consisting of trade sales through bookstores and to libraries, as well as of educational sales similar to those enjoyed by trade books.

Mass market paperbacks are softbound books on all subjects which enjoy significant distribution through "mass" channels: newsstands, chain stores, drugstores, supermarkets, and the like. Many are reprints of hardcover trade books; others are originally published in this format.

It is often very difficult to discover the differences between trade and mass market paperbacks. (Sometimes the originating publisher's imprint provides the only clue.) Generally mass market paperbacks use less costly paper and employ covers more likely to attract the "mass" audience than do their trade counterparts. Yet they, too, enjoy large secondary markets in trade outlets (book and department stores) and in educational settings.

University press books provide an instance where the content of titles and the methods used in their distribution are disregarded in their classification, and the sole criterion employed is the originating source. University presses, which are, for the most part, not-for-profit departments of universities, colleges, museums, or research institutions, publish mostly scholarly materials or titles of regional interest. However, occasionally they produce trade books and textbooks as well which are then categorized here rather than in the area which content and market would dictate.

University presses publish hardcover and softcover books. Their principal customers are scholars and libraries but many titles, particularly paperbacks, are used in classrooms. Bookstores absorb some sales, notably of trade-oriented materials.

Elementary and secondary textbooks are hardcover and softcover textbooks, workbooks, textbook-related tests, manuals, maps, and similar items all intended for classroom use and equipped with specific pedagogical features which distinguish them from consumer-oriented materials such as trade juveniles. The industry refers to producers of these materials as "elhi" publishers.

Many publishers in this field also produce computer software, audiovisual and manipulative items such as video and audio cassettes, films, filmstrips, slides, recordings, transparencies, duplicating masters, games, magnetic boards, etc. Sometimes these are combined with books or at least with printed components (cards, pamphlets, etc.) in so-called multimedia packages or kits.

Schools are the primary market. (AAP surveys consider kindergarten to the eighth grade the elementary grades and grades 9 through 12 high school.) Junior colleges often use elhi materials. Government and libraries (other than school libraries) also constitute secondary markets.

College textbooks include hardcover and softcover textbooks, pamphlets, reprints, course-related tests, computer software and certain audiovisual items such as films, slides, and video and audio cassettes. "College" here embraces all higher education (grades 13 and up), from junior college to postgraduate level. The upgrading of secondary school programs has created an interesting additional market in high schools for college publishers. Government, industry, and libraries also account for some of their sales.

It is probably more difficult to distinguish between college textbooks and trade books than it is between their counterparts on the elhi level. Some publishers have even produced trade and textbook "editions" of the same title with differences so slight (such as that the trade edition is equipped with a dust cover while the text edition is not), as to make the task of classification almost impossible.

(AAP survey practice utilizes the criterion of predominance in making some distinctions: if a book finds its principal market in the textbook area, it should be classified there, if in the trade-book area then in that categroy. Where distribution is evenly divided and two quite separate editions are actually marketed, each edition is considered to be a distinct title and classifiable in its own area.)

Standardized tests are a small industry segment closely related to textbook publishing. Standardized tests, as distinguished from "objective" tests which accompany specific textbooks and materials, measure intelligence, ability, aptitude, achievement, and other personality traits. Schools and colleges employ such tests and the evaluation services provided by their publishers, but significant markets exist also in industry and other areas outside formal education.

Subscription reference books are principally sets of encyclopedias marketed by their publishers to consumers on a door-to-door or direct-mail basis. Since this marketing pattern often involves package arrangements, other reference or self-educational materials such as dictionaries, atlases, sets of the classics, and similar publications originated by these publishers also fall under this heading. Sizable secondary markets include public and educational libraries and schools.

It is noteworthy that nearly every book category enjoys substantial markets outside its primary sales focus. This growing phenomenon is of relatively recent origin. Prior to World War II, product and market distinctions were nearly synonymous: trade books sold almost exclusively through bookstores and to libraries, elhi textbooks to schools, college textbooks to students in higher education. The advent of the mass market and of small presses, and the growing practice, in education, of supplementing texts with other books have served to blur what were once fairly precise market lines.

The industry's mainstream has sometimes found it difficult to adjust its organizational structure to these changes. Most large publishing houses have retained the product-oriented divisional and departmental arrangements of the prewar era while attempting to meet new marketing opportunities by making interdivisional sales arrangements or creating sales departments independent of their editorial counterparts. On an industrywide basis the distinctions we have enumerated continue to prevail mainly because they still provide opportunities to publishers in similar economic circumstances to compare experiences and address common problems.

The complexity of the field is such that no reliable figures are available citing the number of publishers active in each category. R. R. Bowker's *Books in Print* lists 22,500 book publishers in the United States of which approximately 2000 produced three or more titles during 1987. *Literary Market Place,* an annual Bowker publication, lists the latter individually, enumerating some of their specialties and areas of interest. Gale Research publishes the *Publishers Directory* which lists and classifies 14,000 small presses by area of emphasis. The Book Industry Study Group provides annual estimated sales figures for the categories. The figures for 1987 are shown in Table 1 including domestic as well as export sales (not, however, sales of subsidiary companies of American publishers operating in foreign countries).

TABLE 1

Estimated 1987 Book Publishing Industry Sales

Category	Millions of dollars	Millions of units
Trade (total)	$3,537.5	767.67
Adult hardbound	1,911.8	277.98
Adult paperbound	946.8	230.59
Juvenile	678.9	259.10
Religious	720.3	137.95
Professional	2,720.6	187.38
Mass market paperback	1,014.1	607.24
Book clubs	645.7	106.22
Mail order publications	587.2	118.49
University presses	120.5	10.42
Elementary and secondary text	1,684.3	219.08
College text	1,679.3	123.53
Subscription reference	216.3	.53
Total	$12,925.7	2,278.51

Source: *Book Industry Trends—1988*

Publishers' receipts are not identical to consumer expenditures. Many books are sold by publishers at a discount to bookstores or to wholesalers—who in turn market to bookstores and other retail outlets—and bookstores and wholesalers must have their markup on the merchandise before it is sold to the consumer. Only in cases where the publisher sells directly to individuals or to libraries and institutions (which then makes the library or institution the consumer), is the publisher's sales income identical to the consumer expenditure.

Book Audiences and Industry Markets

Given the vast range of subjects books cover and the diverse approaches they take in doing so, it is apparent that audiences for books are nearly limitless in number and awesome in their complexity. However, for practical purposes, book audiences can be segregated into three major areas: general consumers, professionals/scholars, and students. Recognizing that particular individuals may belong to more than one area, we observe that consumers read primarily for their own satisfaction, professionals/scholars read to succeed in their work, and students read to learn. Consumer book purchases tend to be discretionary, while work-related purchases are often mandatory or made by the employer, and student purchases are involuntary insofar as texts are assigned by the instructor or supplied by the school.

As we have seen, publishers serve these audiences directly as well as through intermediaries such as retailers, wholesalers, and jobbers. More specifically the major domestic market areas may be described as follows:

General Retailers include bookstores; book departments in department stores; shops selling religious, stationery, and gift items; museum stores; chain stores, supermarkets, and drugstores; and newsstands, among others. Professional books are often sold in medical and engineering supply stores, hobby books in hobby stores, art books in art supply stores, etc.

Of the above, book, department, and other stores which have traditonally handled books for the general consumer are thought of as trade outlets. Chain stores, drugstores, supermarkets, and newsstands comprise the so-called mass market.

College stores are often classified separately since they provide the principal channel for books utilized in higher education. However, they also account for substantial noneducational sales to the students and faculty whom they serve.

Publishers may deal with the above retail outlets directly or through *wholesalers.*

TABLE 2

1987 Estimated Domestic Consumer Expenditures on Books

Category	Millions of dollars	% of total
Trade	$5,810.1	35
Religious	1,242.4	7
Professional	2,910.0	17
Mass market paperback	1,580.0	9
Book club	627.4	4
Mail order publications	606.4	4
University press	116.1	1
School (elhi) text	1,620.9	10
College text	1,952.1	12
Subscription reference	188.1	1
Total	$16,653.3	100 %

Source: *Book Industry Trends—1988*

Libraries and institutions include public, college, and university and special (i.e., industrial, research, or special interest) libraries. School library sales are usually classified with sales to schools and institutions. Some library sales are consummated by publishers directly; however, most are supplied through the facilities of *library jobbers,* i.e., specialists in supplying the library trade.

Schools comprise school systems, districts, depositories, classrooms, resource centers, libraries, and school stores, as well as other educational institutions public or private from kindergarten level through grade 12.

Direct to consumer transactions are those in which the publisher or book club markets directly to the individual by mail or door-to-door and include sales to industry and government.

Other sales include transactions, such as to premium users, sales of book overstock at sacrifice prices ("remainders"), as well as other marketing efforts outside the normal pattern.

Table 3 shows estimated 1987 consumer expenditures and unit sales for the market categories just described.

In addition to these domestic markets publishers enjoy *export sales* to foreign bookstores, libraries, and individuals. Sometimes they make arrangements with foreign publishers for the sale of an entire edition of bound books or of unbound sheets which the foreign publisher then markets under its own imprint. A number of American publishers operate subsidiary companies abroad to which they export books and sheets but which also manufacture indigenous editions and originate titles in their own territories.

Finally, publishers gain important income from the marketing of domestic and foreign *rights.* Book clubs and paperback publishers will purchase the right to reprint books, as may magazines for certain portions of a book or for serialization of the whole. Foreign publishers will buy translation or reprint rights. Motion picture and TV rights, though often controlled exclusively by the author, are also occasionally a source of revenue for the publisher. "Subsidiary" rights as the industry terms them are of particular importance in the economics of trade-book publishers.

Figure 1 illustrates the structure of the U.S. book industry. Book categories are shown at left, followed by blocks for audiences, wholesalers, and markets. Each block shows the percentage of book category sales realized in the audience or market segment indicated. (Sales of rights are not included.)

The Publishing Process

The basic functions of the publisher involve the selection of manuscripts or the planning of projects; the preparation of manuscripts for

FIGURE 1- STRUCTURE OF THE U.S. BOOK INDUSTRY

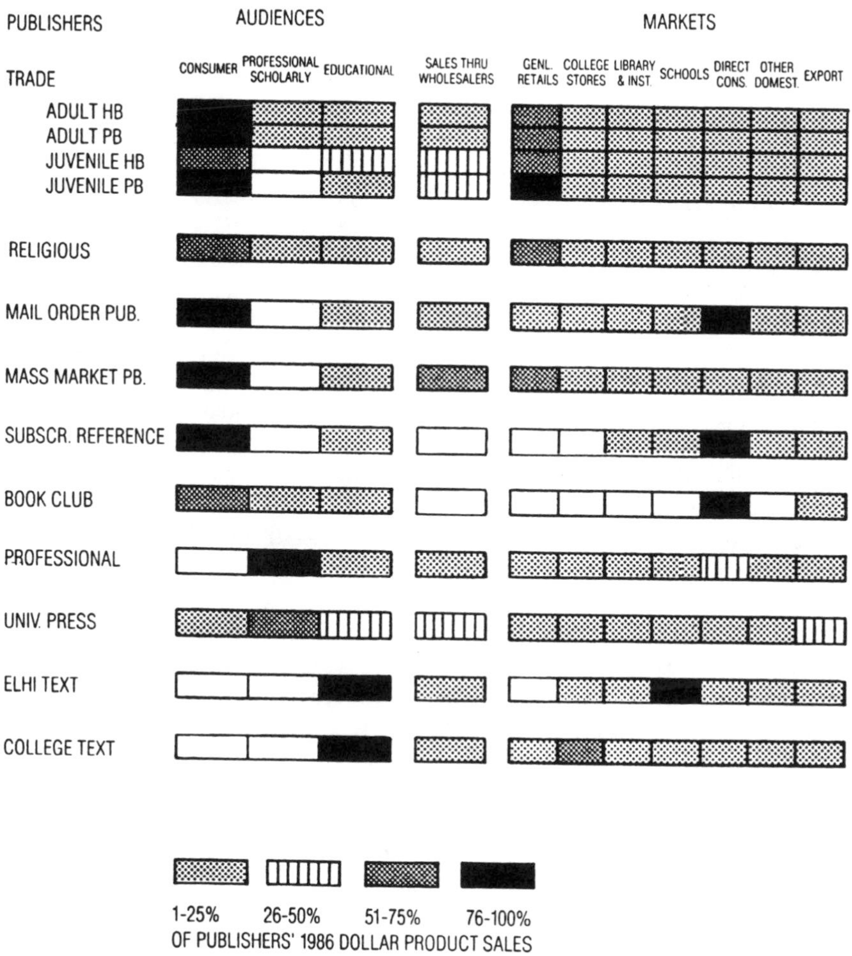

PUBLISHERS	AUDIENCES					MARKETS

AUDIENCES: CONSUMER | PROFESSIONAL SCHOLARLY | EDUCATIONAL | SALES THRU WHOLESALERS

MARKETS: GENL. RETAILS | COLLEGE STORES | LIBRARY & INST. | SCHOOLS | DIRECT CONS. | OTHER DOMEST. | EXPORT

TRADE
ADULT HB
ADULT PB
JUVENILE HB
JUVENILE PB

RELIGIOUS

MAIL ORDER PUB.

MASS MARKET PB.

SUBSCR. REFERENCE

BOOK CLUB

PROFESSIONAL

UNIV. PRESS

ELHI TEXT

COLLEGE TEXT

1-25% 26-50% 51-75% 76-100%
OF PUBLISHERS' 1986 DOLLAR PRODUCT SALES

Source: Book Industry Trends 1988

TABLE 3

1987 Channels of Domestic Book Distribution

Channel	*Estimated consumer expenditures*	
	Millions of dollars	*Millions of units*
General retailers	$7,543.4	1,100.89
College stores	3,026.2	265.47
Libraries and institutions	1,452.7	99.43
Schools	1,955.6	244.76
Direct to consumer	2,373.2	289.94
Other	302.3	121.30
Total	$16,653.3	2,121.80

Source: *Book Industry Trends—1980*

typesetting; the supervision of the book-manufacturing process; marketing and publicizing; the processing of orders; the warehousing and shipping of inventory; and the necessary financing, accounting, and housekeeping tasks attendant upon the preceding obligations.

From these fundamental responsibilities evolve the functional areas of publishing: editorial, production, marketing, fulfillment, and administration. (See also the organization chart on page 156).

Editorial. The editing task is basically twofold: the selection of manuscripts and their preparation for publication. In its first phase editors choose or recommend a manuscript after being satisfied that it has the merit and salability that warrants placing it on the list. Or they may conceive of a project and find an author to undertake it. In the second phase editors will work with the author to ensure the best possible presentation of the subject and material. Because the process is varied and complex it encourages a certain amount of specialization in large houses, where there may be editorial readers (who do nothing but give first readings to manuscripts), procurement, or acquisition editors (who visit authors to solicit their work), creative editors (who dream up projects and subsequently find writers to undertake them), and copy editors (who are experts on grammar, punctuation, and language usage as well as demons on accuracy). Most editors combine two or more of these functions in their daily tasks and small publishers may perform them all. All editors are, or should be, master diplomats, for they must constantly work and negotiate with that most temperamental species, *Homo scrivens.*

Production. The AAP definition of production involves the supervision of the manufacturing process. This includes the planning and designing of the physical book, choice of materials for it, and the selection of and relations with suppliers throughout its typesetting, printing, and binding.

Marketing. This function includes personal contact selling, direct-mail advertising, promotion, and publicity.

Fulfillment. This area covers order processing, invoicing, handling of accounts receivable, payments and collections, credit control, shipping and warehousing, and the maintenance of sales and inventory records.

Administration. Fiscal, personnel, and general business management, including the accounting function, fall under this heading, as do in larger firms, corporate organization, policy, and planning.

We shall be discussing these publishing functions in detail, as they are exercised in various categorical settings, in the succeeding chapters of this book.

Industry Activities and Associations

The record of the book field in dealing with its common problems is a strangely mixed one. Some mainstream publishers groups have maintained good information services and statistics for many years, and textbook publishers in particular have established effective joint relations with national and local governments. Consumer publishers have often united in battling censorship, and one small-press association has instituted a vigorous marketing program. But although nearly forty organizations now serve the industry, their efforts are on the whole fragmented and ineffectual and, with some exceptions, weak in the areas of professional education and development that are usually given top priority in other industries. They have also failed to play an effective role in addressing the industry's most critical problems, such as inadequate distribution.

Book people are often known and admired for their rugged individualism, which stands them in good stead when they must make difficult editorial decisions. Unfortunately the same staunchness of spirit often makes them less than wholly receptive to the needs and possibilities of cooperation. Here even small presses, which have generally shown themselves to be more alert and venturesome than their established colleagues, have displayed remarkably little vision.

Serving principally mainstream firms, the Association of American Publishers has been in existence since 1970 when it was created by a merger of the American Book Publishers Council and the American Educational Publishers Institute. Although it began as a lively federation of semiautonomous divisions that placed great emphasis on professional education, it has recently curtailed the divisions' scope and educational programs and has given primary weight to political lobbying activities. Its composition of some two hundred publisher members, to which a group of affiliated manufacturing members has lately been added, has been little affected by the small-press explosion. However, AAP sponsors a valuable statistics program which invites participation from nonmembers.

More diverse in its makeup is the Society for Scholarly Publishing, a professional association that serves 1,100 individuals and firms, among them a number of mainstream professional houses, university presses, imprints recently founded by professional societies, academics, researchers, museums, printers, and librarians. SSP sponsors a limited number of educational programs aimed principally at senior executives.

Most of the associations serving small presses are small, regional groups with limited funds and intermittent programs. Among the few national in scope is the Publishers Marketing Association (PMA) which sponsors cooperative sales campaigns, exhibits and catalogs, and related educational programs. However, PMA's membership is limited to publishers of nonfiction with bookstore potential.

A number of groups serve specialized publishers, among them the Children's Book Council, the Association of American University Presses, and the Evangelical Christian Publishers Association. Publishers with interest in data base, software, and other electronic publishing may join the Information Industry Association. Book industry firms committed to research may affiliate with the Book Industry Study Group, which sponsors the annual statistical compilation and forecast *Book Industry Trends* and other occasional consumer and distribution studies. A number of worldwide organizations serve publishing interests, such as the International Publishers Association. Extensive lists of publishers' organizations may be found in Bowker's *Literary Market Place* and in *The Independent Publisher's Bookshelf* by John Kremer (Ad-Lib Publications).

Also noteworthy in this context are organizations serving authors, publishers' suppliers, booksellers, and others with whom publishers deal. Prominent among authors' groups are the Authors League of America and the American Society of Journalists and Authors. The Book Manufacturers' Institute serves the country's larger manufacturing firms. General booksellers support the national American Booksellers Association as well as a number of regional groups. College stores rely on the National Association of College Stores. Independent wholesalers of magazines and paperbacks sponsor a number of regional associations who together have formed the Council for Periodical Distributors Associations. Book designers often affiliate with the American Institute of Graphic Arts. Book reviewers are served by the National Book Critics Circle. These and similar organizations are listed in *Literary Market Place*.

Although some of the industry's organizations have formed liaison committees to dialogue with each other, their primary tendency has been to concentrate on the narrow concerns of their particular constituencies. One looks in vain for effective displays of public spirit or visionary statesmanship aimed at solving the industry's most pressing common problems. Given the role of books in society, this stance appears alarmingly shortsighted. As a cultural industry, the book field is far too dependent on public attitudes and public policy to afford its members the luxury of autocratic isolation.

III

How Books Are Created

ADULT HARDCOVER TRADE BOOKS

As long as there is popular interest in a subject writers will write books about it and publishers will publish them. The horizon for trade books is therefore practically unlimited, and the topics they cover are legion.

There is fiction. Since the days of Thomas Deloney in the sixteenth century the novel has been an institution in the English language. At times reports of its imminent death have been circulated which have proved, however, to be greatly exaggerated. Perhaps the novel no longer plays as central a role in popular diversion as it did in Dickens's day when it appeared in installments which so gripped their readers that people would crowd the dockside of ships arriving from England and shout to the captain inquiring whether Little Nell was still alive. Perhaps the tragedy is that many novelists today lack Dickens's genius or at least his discipline and vision. But no one can look at the popular consumption of novels in both hard and soft covers and persuade him- or herself that the medium is biting the dust.

On the contrary, the cat has had kittens, with historical fiction, romance, mystery fiction, science fiction, and gothic fiction among the offspring. Occasionally we even sell a collection of short stories, proverbially a tough nut in publishing experience.

There is topical nonfiction: books dealing with the issues of the day. There are biographies, ranging from Alexander the Great to Willie Mays. There is history—American, Asian, Australian, and Afghanistanian. There are reference works: encyclopedias, dictionaries, and atlases. There is the whole range of "how-to" books on bridge, gardening, cooking, modern languages, various crafts, hobbies, and sex. There are popularizations of science and scholarship. There are books on art, drama, and poetry and on travel and leisure time activities. There are the cartoon, picture, and novelty titles which the trade's snobs nobly refer to as "nonbooks." One marvels at the ingenuity of authors and publishers in satisfying, stimulating, and occasionally even inventing topics of interest.

When publishers think of the market for their titles they recognize that some will have a short life, others may go on selling for years. Most fiction is likely to fall into the first category, as will probably topical nonfiction, whereas a good biography or work of history, a basic reference title, a helpful how-to book, or a sound popularization is likely to become part of what the publisher calls the "backlist": titles that consistently contribute to income year after year.

Whether or not a book becomes a best seller may have little to do with its life expectancy, however. A successful novel may sell half a million copies in two years (after which it will probably enjoy another life cycle in paperback), but subsequently disappear from the publisher's list. A work of philosophy or science on the other hand may become a best seller at its beginning yet continue its career for decades thereafter. And of course the large majority of backlist titles never come even close to making the national best-seller list.

On some titles hardcover trade-book publishers may earn income from subsidiary rights. If a book appeals to a wide audience the publisher is likely to sell reprint rights to a mass market paperback publisher. If it could enjoy application in school or college classrooms the publisher will place it in his or her own or another publisher's trade paperback program. The major book clubs may choose it, or at least make it available to their members, if its prospective audience is broad; if more limited in appeal it may be selected or listed by one of the numerous special interest book clubs. And for many books there is the opportunity of publication abroad or translation for release in other languages.

Agents and Their Role

While small presses tend to deal with authors directly, most trade books placed with mainstream publishers arrive through literary agents. Although a few established houses still read manuscripts submitted directly by authors—"unsolicited" or "over the transom" in trade parlance—the actual record of acceptance of such manuscripts is small, even diminutive, in comparison with the number which reach publication after they have had an agent's attention.

The agent's role has been augmented over the years for a number of reasons. As book markets have grown, both successes and failures in mainstream trade-book publishing have begun to involve much larger commitments, expenditures, and risks. The professionalism which agents represent in scouting for and screening manuscripts, advising authors on their writing, and negotiating on their behalf with publishers has been welcomed by both sides. Agents seek out authors—at writers' conferences, in academic institutions, by scanning magazines for promising talent, and among celebrities—encouraging them and guiding them to produce publishable manuscripts. They sift submissions by hopeful writers, discouraging the presumably untalented or unfashionable, while working constructively with those who appear to have potential. By the time an agent submits a manuscript to a publisher it has presumably passed a rigorous test and is in such shape as to warrant that publisher's serious consideration.

Should the publisher be interested, the horse trading begins. Royalties, advances, and guarantees against royalties, author's shares in subsidiary rights—all must be worked out to mutual satisfaction. Most authors feel neither qualified nor temperamentally inclined to struggle with the publisher over these matters; yet, as very substantial sums are often involved they are happy to have an agent's services and counsel in settling them. Furthermore, with an agent in the picture, motion picture, TV, and foreign rights are often reserved to the author exclusively, and the agent undertakes to make arrangements for and negotiate these contracts as well.

In fact, though publishers often stoutly refuse to admit it, agents have taken over some of the traditional functions of mainstream trade-book publishers: manuscript screening, finding new writers, conceiving book ideas and recruiting authors to produce them, working with the author in shaping up the manuscript, and negotiating on his or her behalf for certain subsidiary rights. However, publishers continue to pursue these tasks on their own, thus paralleling, supplementing, and occasionally duplicating agents' efforts.

The Selection Process

Small-press entrepreneurs are likely to choose manuscripts for publication themselves, but at larger firms, screening, creating projects, and assisting the author are the roles of editors and their supporting staff. In houses where unsolicited manuscripts are welcome they are often given a first reading by a junior staff member who prepares a report which together with the manuscript is reviewed by a staff editor. Such a report addresses itself to the significance of the work, its subject matter, the quality of the writing, and its market potential, and it recommends either further consideration or rejection. The staff editor on the basis of the report and his or her own examination of the manuscript will then decide whether the material should be declined or further examination is warranted. In cases where an outline or sample chapters are submitted the procedure is much the same.

Except for a manuscript that appears to warrant an immediately favorable decision—such as a spectacularly well done novel submitted by a reliable agent—a promising work is given additional readings within the house or by outside experts. If the manuscript treats an established subject, inquiries are made into existing or previously published books and their performance in the marketplace. Is the new title really needed? Will it contribute enough to command the support of its intended audience? Can sufficient copies be sold to ensure a profit? Or barring this possibility are there vital cultural considerations, such as the discovery of a major new talent, or possibilities of favorable returns on future books to warrant the investment? It is only after inside readers and authorities in the field have answered these basic questions affirmatively that a title is likely to be recommended for publication.

The procedure is modified if the house has taken the initiative in approaching the author or agent or in generating the project. In such cases a proposal may be drafted by the author or the initiating editor which must be approved before a contract can be signed. Such a proposal may be sent to outside experts for comment unless the merits and nature of the project are sufficiently persuasive to make such a step unnecessary. Similar methods are employed in the consideration of a hardcover edition of a title originated by a paperback house, of a foreign manuscript for translation, or a foreign publisher's title for publication in this country.

Money and Auctions

When a title with major marketing possibilities is under consideration and its appeal to a mass market paperback publisher is a foregone conclusion, the trade publishers may well explore possible reprint arrangements and the mass market paperback publisher's likely commitment before a decision is made. They will do this not only because the subsidiary income will loom large in their own profit projections but because the publisher will be asked to pay a very steep price (millions of dollars in some cases) by the author and the agent for the acquisition of the manuscript. In fact major books are often "auctioned off" among publishers, i.e., literally sold to the highest bidder.

It is not unusual to pay several hundred thousand dollars in guarantees (nonreturnable advances) against royalties for a top novel. Superior nonfiction may demand $100,000. A celebrity writing his or her autobiography with the help of a collaborator may command $250,000 or more. True, the average good novel or nonfiction manuscript may bring no more than $25,000, and first novels only $7,500. In fact the generally high cost of literary property has often worked against the interests of new writers who were left by the wayside while mad auctions for obviously more salable properties were going on. Yet one can hardly regret the fact that some writers at least are receiving sufficient reward for their labors to provide them with a decent livelihood.

The problem is, however, that many of the auctioned books are not earning their advances. In fact, very often such books have turned out to be dismal failures whose value was more perceived than real and which benefited from the ability of a plausible agent to sell the big sizzle on a small, tough steak. The reason the auctioneers succeed is that some mainstream publishers—both paperback and hardcover—have ample resources, and are willing to pay inflated prices, thus forcing others in the industry to go along if they are anxious enough to lay their hands on the auctioned properties.

The Endangered Midlist

While books with potentially large audiences have received increasingly generous attention from mainstream houses, less popular and specialized titles have not fared nearly as well at these establishments. Because economic pressures induced corporate managements to raise the profit goals of their publishing subsidiaries to ever higher levels, mainstream editors were forced to turn their backs on books with small markets. They may have regretted doing so, but were left no choice: given existing mainstream marketing methods, only small profits, or no profit at all, could be realized from distributing specialized titles. Whenever enthusiastic editors did sign up such titles, marketing staffs tended not to support them.

Dubbed "midlist" by the industry (to distinguish them from the big sellers that presumably top publishers' lists,) these titles have become an endangered species at mainstream establishments. At the same time, they have become bread-and-butter and raison d'être to small presses. Midlist authors disenchanted with their mainstream experiences have increasingly turned to small houses as viable alternatives. One such author, Todd

Walton, whose earlier novels, *Inside Moves, Forgotten Impulses,* and *Louie & Women* had been published successfully in hardcover and paperback by New York houses, placed *Night Train* with a West Coast publisher. In a "My Say" column in *Publishers Weekly* of July 11, 1986, he explained that "the New York method of publishing a novel, the 'adversary technique,' is no longer acceptable to me." Tired of battling to have his manuscript accepted, of "duelling" with editors who were in constant fear of losing their jobs, of "crusading" for promotional money, and "screaming" for decent distribution, he opted for the small-press alternative:

> The advantages of going to a smaller house are numerous. Such a publishing company cannot survive if it is divided against itself. Each book purchased is a significant investment. The author must be treated with respect, since money is not the primary bond. It is a mutual effort, a mutual sacrifice for the book. At a small house, the creation itself is usually the highest priority, not the system. If the book succeeds, everyone gains. It's a dance, not a race.

In *The Complete Guide to Self-Publishing* (Writer's Digest Books) authors Tom and Marilyn Ross cite many titles that were successfully self-published after they had been rejected, or published with little commitment, by mainstream houses. According to the Rosses this approach benefits even literary works:

> Literary contribution is an important facet of self-publishing. As trade publishers become more and more preoccupied with celebrity books and sure bets, good literary writers turn more and more to self-publishing. . . . Some have spent arduous years submitting and having manuscripts returned, cutting and rewriting and sending again, vainly trying to please an editor, any editor. Often those few who do sell find their work whittled and changed beyond recognition. Even more frustrated are those with a strong belief in their work, who have not been willing to alter it and have thus found themselves without a market.

THE AUTHOR'S CONTRACT

The document that charts the course of author-publisher relations, at large houses as well as at small presses, is the author's contract. In this instrument the obligations, rights, and privileges of author and publisher are defined, and the manner and extent to which they will share revenues is specified. Commonly covered in a contract are the delivery date of the manuscript, the conditions under which the publisher may accept or reject it, guarantees by the author respecting the originality and legality of the contents, conditions binding the publisher in editing, producing, and marketing the book, the royalties, advances, and other income shares to be paid to the author, and the term and termination provisions of the contract.

Authors and authors' organizations often complain that mainstream contracts are one-sided, favoring publishers. They note, for example, that in some contracts authors are required to deliver a manuscript within six months or a year, yet publishers are free to delay publication of the book for as long as they please, a year or two in some cases. In many instances, publishers are able to reject contracted manuscripts at their discretion, without any compensation to the author who, on the contrary, is obligated to pay back any previously received advances. Therefore, if an author has been given a contract by an enthusiastic editor who has left the firm by the time the manuscript is delivered, a new editor, who may not care for the project, is free to reject it out of hand. Since editorial turnover is very high in mainstream houses, and since mergers and acquisitions frequently alter even the firmest publishing plans, some authors favor arrangements that allow them to retain at least part of the advance when a publisher wishes to back out of a contract.

Another cause for contention are clauses that obligate the author to guarantee that a manuscript is free of libel, and to assume the costs of legal defense on behalf of the publisher in case of suit. Murray Teigh Bloom, for many years chairman of the Editor-Writer Relations Committee of the American Society of Journalists and Authors, believes that all publishers should cover their authors under their umbrella libel insurance policy (some houses already do), and that publishers' house counsels should review every contracted manuscript for libel, rather than place the burden on authors who are rarely qualified to make competent judgments in these matters.

To authors who take pride in their work a clause like the following, taken from an actual contract is hardly appealing:

> The Publisher hereby agrees for itself, its successors, representatives, and assigns that it will, after delivery to it of the manuscript as aforesaid and its approval by its editors, proceed at such time as it determines that conditions are suitable, to publish the Work in suitable style as to format, packaging, title, imprint, and at a price such as, in its sole judgment, best meets the requirements of the market, using the customary means to market the said Work. The Publisher shall reprint the Work as it deems the demand for the same may require. The Publisher shall have the right to make such editorial changes in the Work as it deems desirable and necessary, but the Author may approve any such changes which are substantial, which approval the Author shall not unreasonably withhold or delay.

Most authors would object to language providing that they "may" approve of changes which they believe it is their right to approve or disapprove as they see fit. After all, it is their literary property that is being licensed temporarily to the publisher and they must have the ultimate disposition of it. But many authors would take exception also to the absolute powers the publisher here assumes over other aspects of the publishing process, insisting that under the contract they should be consulted regarding the design, cover, advertising copy, and other sensitive aspects of the book's launching. Furthermore, they would demand that they be kept apprised of developments, be supplied with copies of reviews and advertisements, be told when the book ran out of stock or out of print, or was being reprinted. To many authors a participatory voice in the publishing process is as important as the money they hope to earn. To the objection publishers often voice to such demands—that authors are not well enough informed about the process to exercise effective judgments about it—writers reply that they are often more sophisticated and experienced than the publishers' employees with whom they must deal, and that in any case their ownership of the intellectual property being published entitles them to have a say in the matter.

Another concern authors often voice is over substantial payments of shares for paperback reprint, book club, and other rights which, contracts provide, are not paid to authors when monies are received but often months later, in conjunction with semiannual royalty settlements. Here Murray Teigh Bloom suggests either prompt payment or, should book-keeping complexities prevent that alternative, the holding of amounts above $10,000 in interest-bearing escrow accounts.

Many authors also believe that when a publisher has allowed the stock of a title to be depleted and has not arranged to reprint it, or when sales fall below an agreed-upon annual minimum, the contract should automatically terminate and all rights revert to the author.

As for the royalty provisions of contracts, rates currently begin at 10 percent of the list price, graduating upward to 15 percent, or even 20 percent in rare cases, with increasing sales. A reduced royalty structure commonly applies to such sales as disposals of overstock at less than manufacturing cost, sales of entire editions to foreign publishers, and direct-mail sales. While lower royalties may be justified on "remainder" sales, bulk sales abroad and other transactions that earn substantially lower gross margins for publishers, the same cannot be said for direct-mail transactions which are demonstrably more rather than less profitable for most trade publishers.

Income from subsidiary rights—paperback, book club, translation, foreign publication, and the like—are shared between author and publisher,

50–50 percent at a minimum, 60 percent in favor of the author on books with significant potential, or in some cases, on a graduated scale that begins at 50–50 percent, turns to 60–40 percent at $100,000, culminating at 70–30 percent at $200,000. A model contract developed by the Authors League recommends 50–50 percent on the first $10,000, 60–40 percent on the next $10,000, and 70–30 percent above $20,000.

Cost Considerations

If publishers are thorough and dedicated to intelligent financial planning, they will, prior to making a publishing decision, carefully examine the prospective investment and return on every project. Anticipated sales income and earnings from subsidiary rights must be weighed against advances and royalties payable, manufacturing cost, promotional expense, and overhead. This calls for establishing a realistic profit objective and pricing structure based on market potential, as well as carefully prepared estimates of sales and manufacturing costs. Once price and optimal printing are decided, including provisions for anticipated reprintings, the financial prospects of the title can be forecast.

Prudent publishers will therefore not make decisions until they have consulted various experts on their staff: the sales manager, the subsidiary rights manager, the production manager, the business manager, and the manager of financial planning. Strangely enough the traditional editorial meeting—a revered ritual at many publishing houses at which a good many decisions to publish are still made—often excludes production and financial representation, a sad indication that, from a business standpoint, some trade publishers are still flying by the seat of their pants.

Critics who claim that business consciousness inhibits editorial integrity may be reassured by the following inspiring yet down-to-earth statement. In *What Is an Editor? Saxe Commins at Work* (University of Chicago Press), Dorothy Commins quotes from a letter the renowned Random House editor wrote in 1944:

> In my book, the first principle of publishing is the communication of ideas. Let the economic determinists cry from now until doomsday that the profit motive is paramount; I still insist that the printed word is a living, sacred thing. . . .
>
> But this is not to say that publishing can exist outside the frame of our time and the limitations it imposes. Above everything it is essential to be a practical publisher and, if you like, a commercial one. And I hold a very strong brief even for the commercial publisher. He serves his function in the very real world and helps to shape, perhaps in a small way, the future our children will know. This is not vague idealism; it is the ultimate reality, and

the only reality I know. I like to believe that good books, by your definition and mine, can make or lose as much money as bad books can make or lose. The notion that commercial success is the result of compromise is a cheap fallacy. Once the principle is established that both good and bad ideas are marketable and either may prove financially rewarding or penalizing, the choice, it seems to me, is obvious.

Why Books Fail

The excessively intuitive character of many publishing decisions provides a clue to the very high rate of failure among trade books and to the fact that trade-book publishing is among the least profitable categories in the business. The sad fact is that most mainstream trade editors rarely talk to readers. Therefore, these editors scarcely have the opportunity to learn at first hand what readers' reading habits and interests are, what they like and dislike, their views of books previously read, and their unfulfilled desires.

Why do editors not talk to readers? Because of the way they are trained. Traditionally, editors are selected from among the thousands of college graduates who eagerly flock every year to large publishing houses in search of editorial work. Usually they begin in minor clerical positions, and although some candidates have prior knowledge of publishing from college courses or summer institutes, the vast majority are expected to learn the basics in their lowly positions.

After a while such hopefuls may be asked to undertake first manuscript readings or assist in routine editorial tasks. If in the judgment of their superiors they show promise, they may be offered junior editorial positions with further on-the-job training. In choosing new blood, senior editors look for candidates with editorial intuition—that special inner sense that supposedly recognizes publishable writing instantly and can measure its worth by the degree of enthusiasm an editor feels.

Note the emphasis placed on intuitive, subjective judgment rather than on the use of objective criteria in making editorial decisions. One would imagine that editors would want most of all to find out what makes readers tick, spend time with readers, and consult them before making costly editorial decisions. Not so. Most trade editors voice nothing but disdain for market research and consumer testing.

Perhaps this attitude becomes more comprehensible when we recall the literary roots of the trade-book tradition; literary discovery is, after all, a largely intuitive exercise. Sociologist, and onetime Knopf editor, Elizabeth Long provides a similar, if subtler explanation in an analysis in *Book Research Quarterly* (Winter 1985–86):

The people who work in trade publishing have continued to be recruited from the middle and upper middle class. Publishing is thus not staffed by a group that represents the broader audience books reach. Even within the middle class, publishing is an insular world. People who work in major New York houses—those responsible for most best-sellers as well as high-culture books—are bookish, and tend to be liberal, secular, and middle-to-highbrow as well. Therefore, publishers stand at a certain distance from many members of the audience for books, even within the middle and upper-middle class.

In the real world, where trade publishers are expected to serve a vast, complex, pluralistic constituency, the mainstream industry has been paying a heavy price for its editorial subjectivism. Another editor, Ann Orlov, eloquently described the intellectual cost of insularity in the September 1975 issue of *The Annals of the American Academy of Political and Social Science:*

> There is an offensive lack of hard data about virtually every area of publishing. On the other hand, there is no shortage of seductive myths and random impressions. This is not a correlation, but a simple matter of cause and effect. In the absence of facts—which would have to be rigorously collected and rigorously analyzed—we are as much at the mercy of assorted fancies about why certain things take place and others do not as are all authors and publishers, booksellers and book buyers, reviewers and other interested parties.
>
> Whether these myths reveal or conceal the truth, some are based on assumptions about the real world and some are only normative judgments. Most operate as self-fulfilling prophecies; some are essential to the practice of the profession; some embody a necessary standard for publisher and author. All should be examined in detail at some point.

Small-press editors tend to be less isolated from their readers than mainstream editors are, because they often specialize in subject areas in which they have a personal interest and enjoy personal contact with other aficionados. But all editors are occasionally guilty of faulty judgments. Sometimes editors are overly impressed by an author's previous record; or fail to do their homework by not obtaining sufficient expert opinion on the manuscript or by choosing the wrong reader. Their own enthusiasm or that of the agent may get the better of them. Or they may be under management pressure to fill a quota—in many large houses editors are judged and rewarded according to the number of manuscripts they bring in—and may be reaching for a borderline property which had better be left alone. As trade-book editor Steven Frimmer suggests, an editor may also be guilty of a simplistic approach to success, trying to imitate last year's best seller with a book which, by the time it is published, will be badly out of fashion.

The house's marketing efforts may also be ineffectual—although as every publisher knows no amount of advertising will turn an obvious failure into a success. A major reason why trade books fail—even some excellent titles that deserve a better fate—is sheer numbers. There are simply too many books published, certainly far more than there is room for in bookstores and libraries, far more than can be noticed and reviewed, far more than the hard-pressed editorial, marketing, and fulfillment staffs of large publishers can handle efficiently.

Take fiction. The better bookstore or library can probably make room for a few hundred new titles each year. In 1987 publishers whelped no fewer than 5,647 new fiction titles upon these defenseless outlets, by conservative estimate five times as many as they could have successfully absorbed.

This is not a new story. O. H. Cheney, in his lively and revealing *Economic Survey of the Book Industry 1930–1931,* listed the flood of titles as one of the business's main problems. That too many books are published is a subject on which it is possible to elicit agreement from many publishers, no matter how much they may differ on other matters. Why, then, does the deluge continue?

There are a number of reasons, some of which were implied earlier: unwarranted editorial enthusiasms, overly persuasive agents, the lazy urge to imitate success and to flood the market with carbon copies of yesterday's money-maker. There is the desire to keep people on the payroll occupied; since we published 400 titles last year we must publish 400 titles this year, even if some are not too good. There is even what passes superficially for corporate planning which may commit a house to a given size program simply to meet its projection, an approach that may work in the hardware business but hardly in a cultural industry.

But by far the most significant factor in overproduction is what may be described as the buckshot approach to publishing, the lightning-will-strike theory, playing the lottery, or the gold-rush syndrome. The idea is, says the trade publisher who subscribes to this suicidal concept, that trade books are unpredictable because the public is unpredictable. Fickle is the word—they take the "sleeper" to their bosom while turning up their noses at the hot prospect everyone swore would make millions. The answer? Place as many entries in the stakes as possible, take a flyer on as much material as seems to hold promise and you can afford—lightning may strike some of it. And indeed lightning seems to have struck enough of it from time to time to have permitted the practice to survive (although a good many publishers who operated this way have disappeared from the scene, bankrupting their imprints).

It is not difficult to rationalize the choices that are made in this chaotic process; even marginal books can be described as a "contribution to learning and literature." Furthermore the habit of thinking in this way, reinforced by predetermined size lists and editors' quotas, becomes a sacred ritual in time: carried on behind handsomely paneled walls on which hang autographed photographs of best-selling authors, it assumes full respectability and even, superficially, the aura of success.

Occasionally talk is heard about birth control—from retailers who plan to cut back on their new title purchases, from publishers who are convinced that careful selectivity, sound market research, and wise planning can make a few titles far more successful and profitable than buckshot-style whelping ever could. Not until the industry as a whole is convinced, however, or at least until its major producers are persuaded of this wisdom, can the average title published receive a fair and equitable chance in an honestly and efficiently managed market.

The American consumer is, unfortunately, obsolescence-prone. Though serious book buyers may be less so than others, they too have often been conditioned by publishers and book clubs to go hungrily searching for the latest rather than the best. The simple fact is, however, that a cultural experience such as reading is only very superficially dependent on novelty—Henry Fielding still reads better than most novels on the best-seller list, and Spinoza has it over the conventional wisdom any day. It is difficult to understand why publishers have permitted themselves to become so fervently trapped in emphasizing the new—it's so much less costly to sell backlist items on which development costs are paid and which require hardly any promotion and often not even any royalty payments. Furthermore, since the quality of most backlist titles—which have had to establish themselves by survival—is far greater than that of most new items, the satisfaction of readers and their appetites for buying more will be more consistent if they are urged to partake of such proven and established titles among available books. From every standpoint, cultural as well as economic, publishers would be well advised to exercise greater care in their new title production.

Editing the Manuscript

Once a manuscript has been accepted for publication it becomes the subject of further editorial ministrations. The editor who has taken special responsibility for it will now work with the author to help him or her achieve the best organization, the most appropriate emphasis, the right tone, the optimal length, and the proper slant for the work. This editor may be assisted in the task by a staff or free-lance copy editor—a specialist on grammar, punctuation, and English usage who will also check facts, quotations, and citations for accuracy.

Editors are often accused of overediting. Yet without their fussing many a manuscript would go into print with contradictions and inconsistencies, tiresome repetition, glaring errors, awkward constructions, and tortured phrases. Many an author has been saved from the wrath and scorn of critics and readers by the alertness and punctiliousness of the publisher's editorial staff. Editors *do* overedit, of course, when they substitute their own taste, their own approach, their own view of a subject for those of the author. Nowhere is the essential midwifery of publishing more apparent than at that point when the editor must literally inhabit an author's soul and whisper as though from within, seeing the world and the subject with the author's eyes and hearing the cadences of language with the author's ears.

There are celebrated cases of editorial empathy, like that of Maxwell Perkins, who became Thomas Wolfe's literary mentor and without whose labors Wolfe's novels would never have become possible. Such instances of intimate collaboration may be rare; yet most good authors have words of praise for their editors and pay tribute to their understanding, skill, and diplomacy.

Imprint Editors and Packagers

Various incarnations of the editorial processes that we have been describing exist in the industry; two of these deserve particular mention because of their growing importance: the imprint editor and the packager.

The imprint editor is basically a publisher within a publishing house: a renowned editor with a faithful following of authors whose name becomes part of the book's imprint. The editors' arrangements with the publishing house usually include an equity interest or financial stake in the list of books they sponsor, making the editors effectively partners in the programs which bear their names. Such arrangements benefit all parties: the editors enjoy a greater degree of autonomy and earning power than as publisher's employees, yet need not assume the cares and burdens of managing their own houses, while the publisher enjoys the editorial and financial advantages of collaboration with a distinguished and successful entrepreneur.

Packagers enjoy similar advantages. Operating independently, they ready a book for publication, then sell the complete "package" to a publisher. Often packagers initiate the idea for a book, then find an author to write it, but in any case will supply the editing and production know-how, commission the necessary artwork, or perform whatever other tasks may be necessary to enable the purchasing publisher simply to turn the completed project over to a printer. Packagers may be compensated by a flat fee or by royalties, which they in turn will share with their authors in a variety of arrangements.

ADULT SOFTCOVER TRADE BOOKS

The beneficial effects of the paperback revolution are all around us. Hardly a segment of publishing has failed to be touched by it; from potboiler to modular textbook the economics, convenience, and fashionable popularity of the soft binding have created new markets, new audiences, even new uses for books. One does not have to embrace the extreme position of wild paperback enthusiasts, who would have us believe that their product will ultimately replace the hardbound book entirely, to acknowledge the appeal of paperbound books.

As the cultural maturity of Americans deepens—a maturity manifested in significant degree by the reading population which grows not only larger but in some ways more discriminating—the softbound book continues to be both a major cause and effect of our advancing civilization. Nowhere has this been more apparent than with the paperbacks published by trade publishers.

The numbers of trade paperbacks are smaller, and their prices generally higher, than of books conceived for the mass market. In 1987 some 607 million units were sold by mass market paperback publishers at an average cover price of $2.93, while trade publishers sold 231 million units at an average list price of $7.29. And, although these distinctions, like all others, are becoming less precise as the entire paperback phenomenon continues to gain momentum, trade paperbacks are generally more handsomely designed and printed on better paper than most of their mass-oriented counterparts.

They had different "inventors" as well. Robert de Graff, who founded Pocket Books in 1939, is credited with initiating the mass market entity; Jason Epstein, who persuaded Doubleday & Co. in 1953 to launch Anchor Books, is considered to be the father of the trade version. It was Epstein who realized that growing college enrollments, scarcity of copies on university library shelves—particularly of out-of-print works of scholarly importance—the tendency to widen the range of collateral reading coupled with decreasing reliance on the core textbook (particularly in humanities and social science courses), would all work together to provide a ready market for reprints of significant writing in these fields. The general public, furthermore, was ready to respond to more serious paperbound offerings than those which the mass market publishers had generally been able to provide (even if some titles, like the Mentor Books published by New American Library, had paved the way for several years for a higher level dimension to the revolution).

The early development of trade paperbacks was a wonder to behold. Out-of-print titles that had slumbered quietly on the discontinued lists of university presses and scholarly societies and which in their lifetime had sold perhaps 1,500 or 2,000 copies were suddenly resurrected and began to enjoy sales of 3,000, even 5,000, copies in the new format, not to speak of a few which sold in the tens, even the hundreds, of thousands. Soon backlists and out-of-print lists were feverishly combed by publishers hoping to sell rights and by publishers hoping to establish paperback imprints. From an academic standpoint the concept was highly successful; in fact it accelerated the move away from a unique emphasis on textbooks and toward a broadening of general book use in college courses. Characteristically it also led to overproduction and a serious surfeit of titles so that some publishers who had entered the field suffered damaging economic reverses.

The time has long since passed when an out-of-print title may readily be found for successful incorporation in a paperback program. Titles planned for original trade paperback release, a phenomenon evident even at the beginning of the era, are more common now, even though publishers still reprint a good many of their own and other publishers' books in maintaining their paperback lists. Occasionally a title is released simultaneously in soft and hard covers largely to gain critical attention because some review media are still reluctant to notice paperback originals. The availability of a hardbound edition is also an accommodation to libraries.

The selection process is usually placed in the hands of editors who specialize in this field and includes, as it does in the hardback area, screening and creating projects. Royalty rates are traditionally lower than in the hardback field; paperback lines pay author or originating publisher (who then shares the income with the author according to contract) 5 to 8 percent of list price. Advances are generally modest, reflecting anticipated royalties from a first printing of 4,000 to 10,000 copies. Of course top sellers may be reached far more eagerly and may even be subject to auction by the originating publisher or agent. When rights are licensed by the originating publisher the contract term itself is limited to seven or even five years after which it expires. Some contracts are then renegotiated and renewed. The originating publisher usually insists on a delay of a year or more in the appearance of the paperback in order to protect the hardcover market during that time.

The number of outlets for paperbacks has grown. Most booksellers devote more than half of their display space to them. Bookstores specializing in paperbacks have also increased in number. In consequence, trade paperback publishers, who at one time relied almost exclusively on the college market, now produce most of their material for the general audience, including the youth audience which, they have discovered, is particularly receptive to their medium. There have been some remarkable successes, where even oversized, high-priced paperbound volumes have outsold nearly everything else in sight.

At the same time the notion that almost any title will sell substantially better in paper than in hard binding has proved to be a costly error. The public is apparently persuaded that paperbound books should continue to be significantly cheaper than hardbounds, and has steadily resisted paperback price increases, which have occurred at far above average rates. Furthermore, the performance of many specialized books publishers have paperbacked has not been materially better than that of hardbounds, resulting in lost revenues for publishers and authors who would have fared better if the market had been supplied with higher-priced hardbound copies. The public's lukewarm response to overpriced specialized and even popular paperbacks, coupled with overall growth in the book market, has resulted in the reversal of the thirty-year-old trend whereby paperbound unit growth had outpaced that of hardbounds. In the last few years, hardbound unit sales have increased at a faster rate, particularly after hardbounds were successfully introduced in the mass market.

JUVENILE TRADE BOOKS

The consumer boom in children's books has been the big success story of the 1980s.

A solid juvenile consumer trade existed before and immediately after World War II. It featured mostly traditional and modern classics in a variety of formats and editions. However, when the educational and library markets exploded with the infusion of federal funding during the late fifties and sixties, many children's book publishers reoriented their programs to serve these markets. While it lasted, institutional prosperity proved to be a real boon to publishers, persuading even houses that had only rarely published juveniles before to get into the act.

The books that libraries and schools acquired were generally too educational in character and too expensive to appeal to consumers. As a result, most juvenile houses, preoccupied with gorging the seemingly insatiable institutional monster, increasingly slighted consumer interests. Soon juveniles fell behind the pace of growth adult books were enjoying in bookstores. In the mass market, on the other hand, a significant new development had occurred when a few enterprising houses launched series of inexpensive hardcover "flats" for young children. Little Golden Books, which had been introduced in the 1940s, and similar titles were soon selling in unprecedented numbers.

After the school and library bonanza came to an end in the seventies, the fortunes of juvenile imprints began to wane. A number of publishers left the field and those who remained curtailed their programs. As institutional budgets continued to shrink, however, some juvenile houses, faced with virtual extinction, turned their attention once again to consumers. First, following an earlier lead set by mass market houses, several launched children's paperback programs which, while highly successful with the public, were at first not very profitable for publishers because of the high cost of color printing. Nevertheless, the genre has grown mightily, several additional publishers have entered the field, and sales volume has virtually exploded.

Next a number of juvenile houses launched paperback series of romances and choose-your-own-adventures for young adults that likewise found a ready audience. Also at about this time the "baby lit" phenomenon came to prominence in response to the determination by baby boomer parents to teach their children to read at a very early age. The surge in board books for toddlers ushered in a new era that soon benefited books for children of all ages. When budgets began to ease for public and school libraries, they, too, demonstrated their enthusiasm for the new, consumer-oriented materials. Today juveniles are the industry's best-selling category.

Although there is quite a diversity among the houses publishing children's books, in general their method for selecting manuscripts and the terms they extend to authors are much the same. At most only a third of the books are handled by agents; except at the mass market houses, few are created or planned by their publishers; most arrive over the transom. Since children's manuscripts, particularly those for the lower age groups, are short (many only five or ten typescript pages), the burden of examining them is not excessive even though the acceptance rate may be as low as 4 acceptances in 1,000 submissions.

(Commenting on the mass of manuscripts submitted, children's book editor James C. Giblin wonders why aspiring authors do not acquaint themselves better with what is being published—by examining books in their local library or bookstore, for example—thus avoiding so many false starts and efforts doomed to disappointment.)

Many of the picture book manuscripts arrive with illustrations. Often these cannot be used, however, even if the manuscript is publishable, and the publisher must find experienced and competent illustrators. Among the titles published three fourths are designed for children under 12 and the remaining fourth for ages 12 and up, including so-called "young adults." Of course these days adult books are read by "young adults" as much as, or even more than, titles classified as juveniles, just as many young adult titles published by juvenile houses are also listed as adult titles in promotional literature to libraries.

Royalty advances in this field are relatively modest. On a picture book the author and illustrator may each receive $2,500 to $5,000 against royalties to each of 5 percent of the list price. Books for the intermediate and upper age groups may bring the author $3,000 to $5,000, while the illustrator, whose contribution probably consists only of some ten line drawings and a jacket design, may receive a flat fee of $2,000 or even $3,000 if he or she enjoys a major reputation. Royalties to the author might be as high as 10 percent; should the illustrator receive royalties rather than a fee these might be 2 percent. Better established authors may command a graduated royalty such as 10 percent on the first printing, or 7,500 copies, and 12½ percent thereafter, in rare cases rising even to 15 percent at perhaps 20,000 copies. Conversely once a book is established and enjoys a steady but slow sale, royalties might be renegotiated downward to make it economical to keep the book in print.

First printings on picture books vary with their complexity and cost. (The greater the initial fixed manufacturing cost the greater is the tendency to print in larger quantities in order to distribute that cost over a larger number of units—a tendency which is not always sound from a financial viewpoint.) A two-color volume might enjoy a first printing of 7,500 copies. A four-color or full color book may be printed in the 12,000 to 15,000 range or even in the 20,000 to 25,000 range if the illustrator is well-known and the book is thought to have bookstore appeal. Printings in the 8–12 age group normally run 6,000 to 8,500 copies and in the 12-and-up bracket 5,000 to 7,500.

Since much of the market for juveniles is still institutional and since many libraries have particular binding requirements, the publisher may prepare a specially bound library edition or sell sheets to a "prebinder," a firm specializing in binding books to the particular specifications of their library customers.

Needless to say, printings, royalties, and advances go up substantially if one is dealing with a highly popular author whose following embraces consumers in addition to institutions. As for mass market titles, those in hard covers are often classics in the public domain and therefore not subject to royalty, or they represent repackaged titles on which a reduced royalty has been negotiated.

Somewhat the same is true of paperbound juveniles, most of which are reprints of hardcover items. As many of them sport color illustrations and carry low list prices, large printings (30,000 to 50,000) are the order of the day. The paperbound format in children's books has also been a success in the student book clubs operated for some years by such firms as Scholastic Magazines. These firms purchase book club rights from publishers and prepare their own editions which are then marketed through the classroom, with teachers acting as agents for the clubs. When such arrangements are concluded they usually provide for 6 to 8 percent royalty based on the club price which the publisher then shares on a 50–50 percent basis with the author and/or illustrator. Hardcover children's book clubs, on the other hand, some of which work through schools and teachers while others reach their members directly, will generally make arrangements paralleling those in the adult field.

MASS MARKET PAPERBACKS

Compared with other mass media, books with their 100,000 to 200,000 average sales do not usually reach audiences of a size deserving the "mass market" descriptions. Still no other development in twentieth-century book publishing has contributed as much to their wide dissemination as that which Robert de Graff launched with Pocket Books only five decades ago. Occasionally a softbound best-seller does roll up very impressive sales figures: eight million, ten million, twelve million, or even more copies. And if such sales reach less than even one tenth of the population, one can be encouraged by the fact that each year best-seller figures appear to grow larger—a happy indication that the paperback is indeed becoming more of a mass commodity all the time.

An interesting characteristic of the mass paperback field is that it embraces a relatively small number of publishers. Fewer than twenty houses produce any significant volume of sales. However, the growth of this industry segment continues to attract new entries to the field and is likely to continue doing so in the future.

Anyone investigating the possibility soon discovers that the potential rewards may be equaled or even exceeded by the hazards, however, which may explain why relatively few publishers have braved the waters. For one thing the sheer investment—in guarantees to authors, in printings, in publicity campaigns—can be staggering. For another, market conditions border on the chaotic and only a solidly established, editorially shrewd and extraordinarily capable sales and fulfillment organization can even begin to cope with them effectively.

A Problematic Market

Nearly half of mass paperbacks are distributed through fewer than 500 independent news wholesalers throughout the United States who serve some 90,000 outlets most of which are newsstands and drugstores, but which also include bookstores, department stores, college stores, and schools. To reach the independent news wholesalers, publishers employ the facilities of a national magazine distributor or their own sales organization, often a combination of both.

The ability and sophistication of independent wholesalers in serving their book customers vary drastically from one to the next. Some have developed excellent techniques for selecting, warehousing, and delivering books which have proved to be efficient and profitable; some even operate retail outlets of their own. Others unfortunately approach the task haphazardly and with varying degrees of confusion. The consequences of these conditions are quite staggering: more than half of all books shipped to wholesalers remain unsold, and while some are returned to the publisher whole, most are discarded after the covers have been torn off and affidavits have been submitted for credit.

In fairness to wholesalers one must recognize the publishers' share of responsibility for these conditions. In 1987 mass market publishers produced some 3,900 new releases, or an average of 325 titles monthly, according to *Publishers Weekly*. Even some of the better outlets served by wholesalers cannot accommodate even one-third of such releases; they may have 90 to 100 pockets for display, some of which should be devoted to best-sellers and backlist items that will produce more revenues for the retailer than will certain of the new titles. For the relatively few establishments served by wholesalers that can support a larger selection, there are many more whose facilities are even smaller than the average. For the market as a whole to display adequately the mass titles being produced each month is a physical and mathematical impossibility.

Publishers have come to recognize this, and those who are well organized and responsible have made attempts to deal with the problem both individually and by participating in industry dialogues with wholesaler representatives. The most important step, greater selectivity in publishing new releases, is apparently being implemented by some publishers. Other problems, notably the inability of many wholesalers to select salable titles from the flood and to serve their outlets intelligently and efficaciously, remain largely unsolved.

One solution publishers have favored—though wholesalers are often grieved by it—is to intensify their direct selling efforts to retailers and trade jobbers. Here selectivity in buying is greater and merchandising ability is often superior, and the results show it. Returns from bookstores, college stores, department stores, supermarkets, chain stores, and trade jobbers amount to only some 28 percent of shipped goods, not an ideal situation perhaps but certainly a much better one than the wholesaler percentage (55 percent) and no worse than the experience of trade publishers in the same market. Furthermore, direct sales are usually more productive in maintaining best-sellers exposed and a solid backlist title on the shelves—again because the customer is often a more sophisticated, efficient merchandiser of books.

The mass paperback industry's total marketing pattern is quite revealing in this respect: some 49 percent of all units are shipped to wholesalers but only 35 percent of units actually sold are so channeled. Direct transactions (including export to overseas markets) account for only 41 percent of shipments but for 49 percent of actual sales. The balance—1.6 percent of shipments and 16 percent of sales—is accounted for by so-called "special sales," such as bulk shipments to industry for premium purposes.

The Best-Seller Emphasis

One consequence of the difficult wholesaler market has been that some publishers have placed extraordinary, even excessive, emphasis on best-sellers. A publisher who produces such a best-seller becomes a welcome supplier to the wholesaler; a publisher's list that consistently contains best-sellers may be perceived as worth stocking month after month, certainly in preference to a list which cannot boast as many best-sellers.

Soon the publisher's anxiety to capture a best-seller for the list becomes intense; the stakes are certainly thought to be high enough. If one is a smaller publisher wishing to establish oneself more thoroughly in the market the need to have a best-seller may be regarded as essential. In consequence competition for top books becomes more intense and the guarantees offered go up and up—millions of dollars is no longer an unbelievable or unheard of figure. Soon the titles of the second rank or titles with outside best-seller potential are caught up in the inflationary spiral and guarantees for them reach six figures. And the title which used to be available for $15,000—and still is hardly worth more in real terms—is bringing $40,000 or even $60,000. Only routine acquisitions are still likely to command the once common $5,000.

Not everyone in the paperback field is happy with these developments. Oscar Dystel, former president of the industry's leader, Bantam Books, has warned his colleagues against the shortsightedness and steadily diminishing returns of a policy favoring swollen guarantees. Nor does every publisher in the field regard the competition for best sellers as the only path to editorial success. Ian Ballantine, for example, whose gifts for innovation have earned him the reputation of being one of the major pioneers in the field, developed new concepts and new series and discovered new titles and new authors which became successful without the burden of drastic overpayments in guarantees.

The Selection Process

Most mass market softbounds are still reprints leased from hardcover publishers for five to seven years (after a waiting period of a year or so). And in sheer numbers titles still predominate that appeal not to the reader of best-sellers but to buyers with specialized tastes: romance, science, western, mystery, or gothic fiction addicts, sports fans, astrology buffs, fanciers of witchcraft, war history enthusiasts, people looking for self-help and self-improvement. And since some 25 percent of all sales reach the educational market, there are long lists of classics, reference titles, serious nonfiction on all levels, and children's books. As Marc Jaffe, a renowned mass market executive, has said, "There are many mass markets."

Original paperbacks have been with us for a good many years, but paperback houses have more incentive than ever to take the initiative in developing titles. Guarantees can be somewhat smaller if one deals with the author directly rather than through a hardcover publisher; in fact, why not have the hardcover publisher pay a guarantee for the privilege of launching the title initially or simultaneously? Or even better, why not publish the hardcover edition oneself? As there is often a respectable sale in hard covers—to libraries if to no one else—and as review coverage is often nonexistent unless a title appears in the traditional way, there is a strong incentive to proceed in this fashion. Indeed, a number of major paperback houses operate their own hardcover programs.

But in certain genres, notably romances, westerns, mysteries, science, and gothic fiction, and so-called "instant" books on current events, there may not even be a sufficiently large sale in hard covers to justify that effort and many today appear in soft covers only. Thus the editorial activities of most mass market paperback houses parallel those of the hardcover trade firms: they screen, procure, and create titles with the best of them, even while they are in constant touch with the hardcover houses for reprint rights.

As for royalties, rates range from 6 to 15 percent of the cover price in rare cases even 20 percent. Some modifications have been introduced by publishers who have developed more trade-type programs where the marketing effort is more selective, the returns lower, waste smaller, and the royalty structure more in keeping with that employed by trade paperbound publishers. Of course the printings in such instances are also smaller, amounting perhaps to 50,000 to 75,000 in contrast to the 200,000 characteristic in mass title instances.

The growth of original title including hardcover production, the ever rising demands of authors and agents, the blurring of mass and trade paperback distinctions, all have worked together to introduce new concepts and techniques as well as new problems into this fast developing field. Hardcover and paperback publishers have found new ways of working together, jointly sponsoring and developing new titles and series. Because of the distinct though overlapping markets reached by hardcover books and by trade and mass paperbacks, some titles go through three formats beginning with a hardcover edition, going next into mass market for a limited time to satisfy the broad consumer interest, and finally arriving in trade paperback format for a long-term career as an educational and select consumer item. As small presses have been playing an increasing role, instances of cooperation between them and mass market houses are multiplying as well.

RELIGIOUS BOOKS

For reasons only vaguely related to those which brought prosperity in the sixties, an erratic recession in the seventies, and recovery in the eighties to certain other industry segments, the religious book field underwent a significant cycle of its own. In large measure it paralleled the fortunes of organized religion itself during these decades.

There was the postwar religious boom, when peace of mind and soul were offered in national best-sellers and when optimistic churchmen could speak of a religious revival in American society. A nation seeking normalcy and security, shaking off the aftermath of depression and world conflict, living under the shadow of nuclear annihilation, and nobly articulating its public and international responsibilities was a scene in which religious practice and religious publishing could flourish. Not only the traditional denominational presses and religious publishing houses but the large general publishers, several of whom founded or expanded existing religious departments, were busy catering to the growing interest. Traditional editions of Bibles, hymnals, devotional volumes, and prayer books sold in substantial numbers. Inspirational works in hard covers and in paperback reached thousands. Church-sponsored educational programs consumed carloads of books.

Was it affluence, the civil rights struggle, Vietnam, the Vatican Council, the youth rebellion of the sixties, the sexual revolution that changed it all? Or was it a combination of these and other factors? God alone knows. The fact is, however, that as liberal denominations conceived of their religious responsibility increasingly in terms of social issues, the specifically religious character of their concerns was no longer apparent. Many "religious" books became indistinguishable from other works on peace, race, poverty, and civic involvement, just as church membership lost some of its distinguishing character and could be subsumed in political and social action.

The mood of the nation generally had certainly changed enough to outdate the once successful inspirational volumes with their emphasis on personal salvation. Action, involvement, ecology, public morality—these were now the fashionable subjects for religious reading. These changes coincided, furthermore, with organizational and liturgical reform in several faiths. The easing of traditional rigidities within Catholicism brought about by Vatican II, for example, and the far-reaching changes in ritual which it decreed, had a profoundly depressing effect on the sale of missals, prayer books, and other perennial standbys. Ecumenism, accepted by most mainline denominations, caused a lessening of emphasis on any, including liturgical, practices that advanced strictly denominational interests, therefore also causing a drop in the demand for denominational hymn and prayer books. And of course both laity and clergy were defecting from Catholic and some mainline Protestant churches at a rate that would have been unbelievable just a decade before.

This fate was not shared by evangelical and fundamentalist Protestant churches. On the contrary, during the early seventies an evangelical revival took place that attracted large numbers of Protestants, led to the founding of scores of new publishing houses, substantially expanded the religious bookstore universe, and created an impressive surge in Christian book sales. Theologically and politically conservative, the movement emphasized a return to basic values, Bible study and private and public morality.

Many Christians flocked from liberal churches to the new, nondenominational evangelical congregations that were springing up everywhere. Christian bookstores moved from backstreets to malls and other high-traffic locations, while their inventories took on a lively, contemporary look and stressed topics of current interest. For a good part of the decade the evangelical book boom more than compensated for the volume lost by mainline Christian publishers. By the early eighties, however, the revival began to lose momentum and sales growth slowed. Yet even as the evangelical sector was cooling off, mainline Christian publishing showed strong signs of recovery.

There were indications, furthermore, that like the revivals of the eighteenth and nineteenth centuries, the evangelical movement would leave a permanent impact on American Christianity. This becomes evident from the lists of mainline denominational and other established imprints which had recovered much of their former, distinctly religious character.

The market for religious books remains sizable. The R. R. Bowker Co. lists 5,169 stores handling religious titles. Ecumenism has advanced and that there is a good deal of publishing and selling across denominational lines. The Christian Booksellers Association, a group enrolling mostly evangelically oriented Protestant stores, numbers over 3,000 members. General and college bookstores handle some of the most popular titles, and direct mail is a common method of distribution employed by both publishers and certain booksellers. A number of book clubs serve both the professional and lay segments of the field.

Religious publishers' lists fall generally into one or more of four categories: Bibles and devotional manuals; inspirational books for laypeople; materials directed to the professional clergy and theologians; and textbooks for use in religious education programs. Needless to say, particularly during the present era of blurring distinctions, serious theological works may sell to laypeople (although perhaps not as readily as they did two decades ago), and some titles, such as those on Eastern religions, will circulate far beyond a strictly religious audience. As has always been true, the publishing of theological works and of religious scholarship may require a financial subsidy which is one reason why denominational houses that are not organized for profit can devote themselves to it. Such support may come from Bible sales or similar income which then may also be used to market certain devotional or inspirational books at or near cost in order to give them the widest possible dissemination.

Very few religious authors come to publishers through agents. Their manuscripts either arrive over the transom or are obtained by procurement (or acquisitions) editors at conferences and meetings; or the authors may come to the attention of the house through their writing, through their teaching or their preaching. Royalties conform to conservative textbook standards; advances are modest if paid at all. First printings are often considerably smaller than those common in the trade field; it is characteristic for a religious book to get off to a slow start but, once established, to enjoy a long and solid existence. Of course if a title has trade-book character, because the author is a celebrity, for example, the terms it commands may well be similar to those of a strong trade book as will be its printing and sales pattern. By implication somewhat the same is true of religious textbooks, particularly those which find wide use in adult and youth parish education programs.

Bibles and devotional manuals are, of course, in a class by themselves. Most editions are well established and have predictable sales year after year. The commissioning of a new translation or edition, often shared these days by several denominations, is a major undertaking consuming a number of years and sizable endowments by the sponsoring group. The sales of a successful Bible are, then, often quite spectacular, with some editions soon running into millions.

PROFESSIONAL BOOKS

Professional-book publishing ranks with the most profitable categories in the industry, a record which even the winds of change, blowing as lustily here as elsewhere, have been unable to shake. Recent growth in certain areas, such as health and computers, has shown particularly encouraging patterns.

Professional books are fundamental tools of work. The best titles are indispensable to their purchasers; certain reference volumes promulgating standards or data universally utilized in a profession have almost totally predictable markets strictly related to the number of individuals practicing or teaching or the number of companies active in a field. A publisher who is fortunate enough to have such a work on his or her list—and some run to several volumes and command substantial list prices—and who can count on a continuously active response as updated and revised editions are published, is indeed fortunate. Of course the investment and the expertise necessary to create and publish such books are also substantial.

The reverses that have buffeted some of the professions have of course been felt by publishers. Curtailment of federal research grants, cutbacks in the space program, the ecology crisis and related disenchantment with technology particularly among the young, and the financial crunch in higher education have contributed to the flat performance of some categories in science and technology. Disciplinary shifts also trouble publishers. Professionals like other people "move with the money" and a former physicist might be found working on a biophysical project which is both academically and practically popular. The creation of new disciplines or subdisciplines requires extraordinary alertness on the publishers' part as they must publish for tomorrow, not yesterday. It also makes marketing more difficult, as some people who could be reached with relative ease a few years ago through membership rosters of professional societies and subscription lists of disciplinary journals are becoming more elusive.

A related phenomenon, that of increasingly narrowing specialization brought about by the refinement of research and the knowledge explosion, was aptly termed "twigging" by the late Curtis Benjamin, former McGraw-Hill president and chairman. As the various scientific branches grow more numerous twigs, and the twigs in turn do some twigging of their own, the number of subjects for books grows proportionately but the audience for them tends to shrink. Also, since research in many fields moves very rapidly, practitioners cannot wait to communicate with each other by the traditional methods of journal or book publication, but must resort to less formal and time-consuming techniques, such as sharing mimeographed notes or electronic mail. Twigging has on the whole been beneficial because of the opportunities it has provided for significant books to come into being, but everyone agrees with Benjamin's contention that contracting markets are creating economic problems of serious proportions. Publishers have attempted to reduce the costs and speed up the process of book publication in some cases by virtually eliminating copyediting, design and typesetting, and simply reproducing the author's manuscript prepared electronically, or in hard copy, to publishers' specifications. However, in many instances, audiences are so limited that even these economies cannot solve the problem. When one adds to this the difficulties publishers are experiencing because of unauthorized photocopying, which tends to diminish their marketing opportunities even further, one recognizes that some books whose appeal is extremely narrow can no longer be published profitably despite their obvious merits. Publishers of professional books, like those in other fields, feel an obligation to their constituents to publish some titles of superior quality despite the certain knowledge that they will create losses. However, given the hard economic realities, they must forego publishing some less extraordinary though worthwhile items in the hope that scholarly societies or university presses will take up the slack.

Paradoxically professional-book publishing suffers from overproduction just as other industry segments do. Of course the concentration is on the "popular" subjects rather than on the very narrowly specialized, and the pressures that create a title surplus—attempts to duplicate yesterday's successes, ill-considered editorial decisions, the feeling on the part of small houses that they must grow rapidly to gain sufficient recognition in the field—are very similar to those pertaining elsewhere. There are the added hazards resulting from the need to anticipate developments in the professions themselves.

One of the most critical problems plaguing the professional-book publisher is the inadequacy of existing distribution facilities. Bowker lists 1,503 stores carrying technical and 582 stocking business books, few of which provide an adequate selection and could be described as satisfactory outlets. Many dealers lack well-trained staff; they are uninformed about new publications; and do not know their own inventory or keep adequate controls over what they sell. Often a book is sold within a week of its arrival at a store but then not reordered until six months later when the publisher's sales representative pays the next visit. One cannot help but contrast this state of affairs with the impressive expertise and efficiency of European professional booksellers who bring to their enterprise knowledge, sophistication, and initiative—in other words a professionalism of their own—that makes them notable instruments in the progress and dissemination of knowledge.

Because retail outlets are so often unsatisfactory, direct selling has been one of the principal marketing tools of publishers. Medical and law houses usually maintain sales forces calling on private practitioners, law firms, and hospitals. Scientific and business publishers cannot usually justify such arrangements economically and therefore engage extensively in direct mail promotion. The direct-mail effort has been complicated somewhat, however, by the consequences of disciplinary shifts and twigging. Furthermore, most professional customers would prefer to examine a book before buying it, and opportunities for so doing are simply nonexistent in many cases. It is impossible to estimate the sales losses to publishers resulting from these conditions.

On the bright side has been the success of American professional books abroad. Since English has become the international language of science and scholarship, and American technology and management techniques have in the past been regarded as advanced over those of most other countries, American books in these fields have found ready acceptance overseas. More than 12 percent of professional publishers' income currently results from export sales. Of course American preeminence in many areas is being successfully challenged by Japan and some of the highly industrialized European nations.

Most professional manuscripts result from the publisher's editorial initiative. Many title ideas originate with house editors who often themselves are competent in a discipline and become aware of the need for treating a certain subject from their contacts with the field. In many cases—since specialization makes it impossible for a house editor to deal with equal effectiveness with every subcategory of every discipline—the house retains a competent scholar or practitioner to act as editor for a series in his or her specialty. Such editors, chosen for their ability to deal with other professional writers, to originate ideas, and to keep abreast of their special fields, are usually responsible for most of the book ideas in their series.

House editors carefully scan technical, scientific, and medical journals as well as periodicals in the management, accounting, data processing, and computer fields for ideas and potential authors. They attend professional and scholarly meetings where they often make contacts directly with authors or gather useful suggestions for book topics and for writers who might develop them. Occasionally they find it advisable to involve two authors in a volume: an outstanding authority in a field who may be, however, not too effective a writer and an individual of perhaps less celebrated standing but able to communicate clearly and effectively the great authority's ideas and knowledge. Some publishers even have a staff of house writers available to collaborate with authors.

In other cases editors may encourage the preparation of a multi-authored book. This is usually germane where a massive reference tool requires the competence of many hands; it is also pertinent when a relatively new and fast-moving subject needs to be rapidly treated and no single author would be able to find the time or be able to work rapidly enough to do it justice. It isn't easy for a busy professional to sacrifice many hours and normal income to write an entire book; such a person is often able, however, to prepare an essay or a chapter. In any case, be it complete book or contributed essay, many professional authors would not even be writing but for the encouragement of publishers' editors.

In all, some 80 percent of professional books are generated through in-house initiative, and only 20 percent arrive over the transom. Agents are only infrequently involved. Advances are paid occasionally but are rarely sizable. Royalties may be 10 percent of the list price or 15 percent of the publisher's receipts (which are less than the list price since discounts are extended to retailers and institutions and even occasionally to individuals such as teaching faculty), except on direct sales where they may be as little as 5 percent (the rationale given being the supposedly greater cost of direct marketing, a not altogether persuasive argument). Contributors to multiauthored volumes are often paid a flat fee per page instead of a share of royalties. Where one of the small but important professional book clubs selects a title, publisher and author will share equally in the royalty which usually represents 10 percent of the club price.

Most authors of professional books, like most authors in other areas, are not likely to amass fortunes as the result of their writing. They are not usually motivated by the prospects of gain in any case but by professional pride, considerations of prestige, the urge to communicate significant findings to their peers, and to serve their disciplines. However, authors of major handbooks, reference works, or leading work tools in their field have at times seen their royalties exceed their regular income, and a few have become quite affluent thanks to their publishing successes.

In recent years a number of professional publishers have added products in other media to their programs: software, microfilm, microfiche, data banks, slides, films, video, and audiocassettes are among the items one now finds on many medical, law, technical, and business lists. Such products have significantly rounded publishers' offerings and augmented their income without displacing or even diminishing their book production. It is noteworthy that the demand for such nonprint products seems to be a parallel to rather than a substitute for books; in fact, in many cases where publishers have offered microfilm or fiche as an alternative form of acquiring a book in print, libraries and individuals have continued to select the book, passing up the alternative.

SCHOLARLY BOOKS

Scholarly books are published for the most part by not-for-profit, subsidized enterprises: research institutions, university presses, museums, and learned societies. The reason is basically simple: audiences for scholarly books are small. Consumers of such books are reluctant to pay the very high prices which would result from normal profit markups on high unit costs dictated by small printings; therefore—with a few notable exceptions—commercial publishers do not usually find it possible to undertake the production of scholarly materials.

University presses, which account for a major portion of scholarly title output, have had an interesting history. Still numbering probably less than one hundred in the United States—an exact count is difficult to establish since small publications programs exist on many campuses which may or may not be classifiable as university presses—they have, however, nearly tripled their numbers since World War II. Several causes have contributed to this proliferation: the growth of higher education itself, the greater affluence of universities during the fifties and sixties, and the unique role which publication plays in the academic process. Budget cuts have snuffed out the life of some of these enterprises and threatened a few more, and nearly all have been forced to curtail their programs. Nevertheless the majority have weathered the storm, and some are enjoying considerable success.

Most presses owe their existence to a genuine need for making scholarly works available, and their lists bear eloquent testimony to the importance, both qualitative and quantitative, of their contribution. Others, however, appear to have been called into being less from real need than from such academic pressures as an exaggerated emphasis on institutional prestige and a faculty promotion system that gives undue weight to a scholar's list of publications irrespective of their value. To operate a press has become a status symbol at some institutions of lesser rank, as well as a hope for ready access to print for certain second-rate academic authors whose chances for salary increases and advancement are dependent on their ability to present a publications list to a promotions committee.

Given these pressures and the unfortunate wastefulness of some universities, particularly since their boom years, academic publishing presents a somewhat checkered picture even today. Ill-disguised dissertations, hastily compiled symposia, and excessively esoteric monographs still find their way into print even under some very prestigious labels. Economies have served to reduce this tendency as have contemporary alternatives to book publication—microfilm and fiche and photocopying—through which materials can be made available that have limited value but not sufficient merit to warrant book publication.

A potent force for setting and advancing standards in the field has been the Association of American University Presses (AAUP) which by its admission policy and various programs has kept the goals of excellence before its sixty-odd members. Reflecting unquestionably the commitments of the majority, it has preached rigorous selectivity, meticulous copy editing, attractive design, and high quality in production. As a result several university presses have become industry pioneers, and some significant innovations, notably in design and production, were first introduced on academic campuses.

University presses to some extent partake of the characteristics of trade, professional, and textbook publishers. While most of their titles are addressed to specialists, particularly faculty in higher education, some are aimed at a wider audience, usually a regional one, of general consumers. As many presses are attached to state universities, they have naturally assumed the obligation to publish books about their state and region for a local readership. Some have also published textbooks, usually of an experimental type or designed for highly specialized graduate level courses where enrollments are small and commercial publishers find the risks unduly great. Many presses have paperback programs with titles that are often found on college and graduate course reading lists. Very occasionally a university press book even becomes a best-seller, a major book club selection, or a widely adopted text. These instances are rare however because presses are not normally equipped, editorially or through their marketing machinery, to select, develop, or distribute materials for large commercial markets.

Most manuscripts reaching academic publishers are unsolicited. The campus on which a press is located is probably its prime source for submissions, although many presses prefer to limit the number of books by campus authors, just as some scholars prefer to be published by off-campus presses. The reasons given by both, that seeking off-campus associations lessens the danger of a faculty becoming "captive" to its press and the press to its faculty, is not however persuasive to all practitioners in the field. Agents are hardly ever involved. A few presses employ procurement editors traveling to other campuses, often competing with a press located there or with other presses similarly engaged in procurement. Some press directors have noted, however, that they believe such a practice to be in conflict with stated objectives of service to scholarship and the nonprofit status of university presses.

A key problem in scholarly publishing is the evaluation of manuscripts which in most cases can only be undertaken by other scholars in the field. Great care must be taken to select readers whose judgment will be both competent and impartial; academic rivalries and disciplinary disputes must not be allowed to influence objective scholarly assessments. Most presses will obtain three favorable reports before they decide to recommend a work for publication. Such recommendation is then usually made to a faculty committee, representing the parent university, with whom rests the ultimate power of decision to publish.

Arrangements with authors vary. A royalty of 10 percent of the list price is common although in some cases such a royalty is deferred until certain costs are met or a minimum number of copies, possibly 1,000, are sold. Some contracts provide for a royalty of 15 percent of the press's income from the book which, with the usual discounts, may amount to less than 10 percent of the list price. Occasionally a particularly costly volume may be published without a royalty or the author may be paid a flat sum. And in certain cases, when development expense of a title is expected to be very large and its market particularly narrow, a subvention may be required before the press can consider publication. Such a subsidy may be furnished by a grant or a fund but most presses will not accept subventions furnished personally by the author as such a practice smacks too much of vanity publishing. (Vanity publishing is the industry's term for an arrangement wherein an author pays the entire publication costs to a publisher who specializes in such work.) Presses with paperback programs usually provide for lower royalties (5 to 7 percent) on softbound editions.

The largest market for scholarly books is libraries: academic, special, and public. College bookstores absorb a significant portion as do general retail outlets. Domestically some 9 percent are sold by mail directly to scholars, reflecting the effectiveness of direct mail promotion which also accounts for much of the university library sale since these libraries often respond to requests from faculty who have been circularized. Other promotion includes advertisements in scholarly journals and, less commonly, in general review media as well as exhibits at scholarly meetings. The trends that have benefited the foreign sales of commercial publishers have also augmented the overseas activities of university presses to the point where some now operate foreign distribution offices of their own or jointly with other presses. In 1987 some 28 percent of all university press sales were export.

The greatest problem facing academic publishers is money. The parent institutions, which traditionally have supported their publishing enterprises with cash subsidies and free services, are themselves struggling with tight budgets and are seeking acceptable ways to limit their expenditures. The press is often a vulnerable entity because it is not readily understood to be related to the university's teaching or research role.

Nothing could be more shortsighted, however. Often the only way in which some of the most significant teaching and research taking place on a campus can be disseminated to the scholarly community at large is by means of adequate, competent book publication. Because the scholarly community is small—most university press editions do not exceed 2,000 copies—commercial publishers cannot assume the burden should universities decide to disclaim it. On the contrary, current pressures in the commercial field are if anything intensifying the need for well-managed, able and alert not-for-profit publishing enterprises. If the better presses now on the scene are not adequately supported, everyone—but most of all the academic community itself—will be severely impoverished.

Some institutions and some press managers are tempted in these difficult times not to confront this issue but instead to imagine that it can be solved by presses engaging in activities that might show a profit such as the publication of textbooks and trade books. Totally aside from the possible conflict this might create with commercial publishers who would rightly wonder why they should be subjected to competition from tax-exempt institutions, this appears to be a self-defeating strategy also from a practical point of view. Even commercial publishers are hard put to keep up with changing conditions in consumer and educational markets; even with large-scale procurement efforts, sizable capital resources, and ambitious marketing programs—which university presses could never hope to match—commercial houses often find it difficult to gain representation in the overcrowded and intensely competitive areas of textbook and trade-book publishing. If university presses attempted intensively to enter these fields one suspects that they would quickly and fatally increase their losses.

No—the answer is what it has always been: a firm, reliable commitment by the parent university to its press because it recognizes that along with its other teaching and research programs its publishing effort represents a unique and irreplaceable contribution to knowledge and culture.

In recent years some significant innovations have been introduced by commercial publishers that were subsequently also taken up by some not-for-profit imprints. Arguing that communication and economy were more important than cosmetics of style or appearance, pioneers like Frederick Praeger, the renowned publisher of Westwood Press of Boulder, Colorado, have advocated that monographs be subject to little or no editing or design. Accordingly, they have encouraged authors to prepare manuscripts that could simply be reproduced, or to encode their work on word-processing disks from which type could be set inexpensively on publishers' in-house computers. This approach has made it possible to publish many titles that might otherwise never have been written or received public circulation.

SUBSCRIPTION REFERENCE BOOKS

Few achievements in the publishing world are as impressive as the compilation and production of a multivolume, major, general encyclopedia. When such a work is developed on a level of high quality and competence it represents both a rich fruit and a significant tool of civilization. In a world of exploding knowledge it also constitutes a publishing challenge of unrivaled proportions.

The challenge is of course a perpetual one. The well-established reference sets, which have justly earned their reputation, are subject to continuous revision. Reprinted annually, they attempt to incorporate as much updated and new information as possible. Their publishers also issue annual supplements or yearbooks so that sets purchased in previous years may continue to be useful to their owners.

In the eighteenth century, when they were first created, encyclopedias served the entire literate population. As differentials in educational levels became more significant and as encyclopedias were recognized to be valuable tools in the education of children, publishers began to issue sets for various levels of age and sophistication. Today, among the dozen or so leading sets published by American houses are works aimed at elementary-school-level children, at those attending high school or readers with a secondary-level education, and scholarly sets that are intended to serve college and university students or graduates.

The development of a new set, or the major overhauling of an established one, represents a multimillion dollar investment. Scores of house editors and researchers, hundreds of contributors, and many consultants in specialized fields must collaborate on the text, to say nothing of the illustrations and maps commissioned or located for the purpose. In every case selectivity of material and authors, level of detail, and the nature of the presentation figure importantly in a managing editor's plans and decisions; in the case of children's encyclopedias, reading level and vocabulary limitations are additional considerations.

The same complexities, albeit on a more limited scale, figure in the task of perpetual revision although computerization has facilitated the task in recent years. Constant decisions must be made regarding the incorporation and the extent of treatment of new facts and developments, the need for change in previous articles and entries, and the illustrations and maps that support the text. Special editorial problems arise from the limitations of existing format and length into which revisions and additions must be incorporated. All this must be done under the pressure of inflexible deadlines; it is proverbial in the field to speak of next year's revisions even as the pages for the current edition are going to press.

Domestically encyclopedia publishers market the major portion of their product directly to homes and businesses; nearly 95 percent of their sales in the United States are consummated through large staffs of field salespeople or by direct mail. Such sales usually include an arrangement for the automatic supply of yearbooks and may involve package deals which include other reference materials, series of classics, globes, slides, viewers, etc. Other domestic marketing efforts comprise sales to libraries and schools, covered also by sales travelers, as well as intensive mail order programs which in recent years have sometimes branched off into book club and similar operations marketing other publishers' titles to the consumer. During the last decade a number of publishers have also converted their sets to electronic data banks, marketing them in that format as well.

The last development was inspired in part by the fact that domestic encyclopedia sales fell off drastically—by approximately 30 percent during the seventies—and publishers looked for ways to take up the slack. The reasons for the sales decline are probably several, among them the economic recession, the "saturation" selling in which publishers engaged during the prosperous sixties, consumer criticism of and resistance to high-pressure or deceptive sales techniques, editorial weaknesses in the products themselves, declining birth rates, and readier access to reference works provided to children in school libraries and resource centers. The sales declines leveled off during the eighties.

But although domestic sales had declined, foreign sales had grown at an impressive rate—nearly 65 percent during the seventies. Foreign sales represent some export but mostly the indigenous revenues of subsidiary companies overseas where English-language as well as adapted translations of American sets (in addition to locally originated products) are marketed. So important has this foreign production become that some 46 percent of encyclopedia revenues of American publishers are generated abroad, making this segment of the industry the most international of any in character.

ELEMENTARY AND HIGH SCHOOL TEXTBOOKS

Schoolbook publishers constitute the second largest industry segment on the basis of revenues; they are also among the divisions which have traditionally operated in the most businesslike fashion. By its very nature, elhi publishing has always demanded long-range planning, sizable investments, carefully designed marketing strategy, and fiercely competitive selling. These circumstances have discouraged the excessively intuitive decision making that has characterized some of the other areas of the book publishing world. Paradoxically, however, recent developments have loosened the very rigidities of the adoption process which have hitherto conditioned the nature of this field.

At one time nearly every state in the union exercised strong central control over the textbooks used in its classrooms. Usually only one title or series per subject and grade level won the approval of the state selection board; such an award was a rich plum indeed and publishers would work feverishly—sometimes even unscrupulously—to gain and retain it.

Changing educational and political forces have eroded this monolithic structure. Only 22 states now retain some control over the selection of textbooks, and even the most authoritarian will approve four or five titles per subject and grade level, permitting districts to select from the list at their own discretion. In the remaining states, districts, individual schools, or even individual teachers are at liberty to choose with almost total freedom from whatever may be available for their needs.

The impetus for this development has come from both the teaching profession and the public. Teachers, serving communities with differing needs and character, have exerted pressure for greater discretion in the choice of materials that would suit their circumstances, be they urban, suburban, rural, advantaged, or disadvantaged. The public, often highly critical of educational performance (why can't Johnny read? why can't he add?), has supported these efforts, seeing in the trend toward individuation some hope that children would derive greater benefits from the national investment in the educational process.

On the other hand, the selection process is often dominated by fads or special pleading to which publishers must bow if they wish to capture an adoption. When textbooks become pedagogically weak in consequence, an outraged public is wont to point a finger at publishers, accusing them of being shoddy or mercenary for allowing standards to deteriorate. It is difficult to see, however, that publishers have much choice so long as adoption authorities continue to force them into compliance. Textbooks reflect the preferences of educators, not of publishers, and if materials require improvement, it is reform of educational theory and adoption procedures, rather than a futile censure of publishers, that would have to bring it about.

Much has been made of the fact that in introducing diversity into the materials selection process, the educational community has toppled the traditional textbook from its once unique position. Not only are many more textbook titles now in use than in earlier days, thus fragmenting their impact, but nontextbooks, notably paperbacks, and nonbook items such as card kits and periodicals have replaced the old textbooks in some instances. Audiovisual materials, computer software, manipulatives, and other nonprint products, furthermore, abound and are sometimes said to be on the verge of replacing books altogether.

The shift may be more apparent than real, however, and journalistic enthusiasm coupled with the faddism which periodically grips the educational scene may have served to create an exaggerated impression. No doubt the iron hold which a few books once had on the materials market has disappeared, probably forever. No doubt more general books, paperbacks, periodicals, kits, audiovisuals, software and other materials will continue to take important shares of that market. But schools and publishers are reporting, and industry sales confirm, a strong adherence to textbooks as basic teaching tools—not the textbooks of yesterday, but new textbooks—many of them paperbound, many modulized, many designed for individualized instruction, and many of them reflecting the conviction that the innate fascination of knowledge and learning, rather than a rote emphasis, should be conveyed to their young users.

This discrimination and perceptiveness is reinforced by the pressure for accountability. Maybe learning should be fun, say the advocates of accountability—it should certainly be basically absorbing and respond to that innate curiosity which is a fundamental human trait—but it should also stick. After being exposed to it for the required number of years, assuming a minimal willingness to learn which he or she must bring to the process and without which any school is totally powerless to teach, the youngster should have something to show for the investment made in education. If despite a reasonably good disposition on his or her part, the student is found to be incapable of functioning and surviving in the contemporary world, the schools have failed. These days school boards and parent groups are often demanding a demonstration of the school's effectiveness, of teachers' competence, and of the value of the materials acquired at public expense.

How Elhi Titles Are Developed

Ideas for the overwhelming majority of elementary and secondary textbooks originate with their publishers. Salespeople, consultants (i.e., teachers who are employed to demonstrate products to other teachers), editors, and managers all travel, attend national and regional meetings, and are constantly alert to new trends and developments in the field. Authors already on the list are also valuable sources for suggestions which are then explored and investigated.

Such exploration assessing the market, evaluating existing and competitive materials, curriculum trends, and other factors likely to affect the success of a new book or series, is vital. The lead time from idea to finished product may be two or more years, the investment may run from one to several million dollars. The risks, particularly in today's volatile markets, are therefore very high. Only a carefully analyzed income and cost projection strongly indicative of a profitable return on a project will encourage management to undertake such risks on behalf of its stockholders.

Once a project has been decided upon, authors are sought who can undertake it. A school publisher often develops authors by stages and over a period of time. Usually they are teachers who have established a reputation for effective teaching and writing, who ably communicate with today's youngsters, and who have demonstrated their ability to motivate them to learn. Many are innovators or pioneers in curriculum development. Their thinking is likely to be representative of a sizable segment of their profession, and they are usually good speakers, for they must serve as the principal advocates of the new product before their peers.

Authors come to the publisher's attention through salespeople and consultants—the publisher's eyes and ears in the field—through editorial contacts and on the recommendation of other authors or teachers. They may have written articles for journals or delivered papers at meetings. The publisher may initially assign an author a small task such as writing a supplementary bulletin for an existing text; later the author may be asked to prepare a workbook or to conduct tests on a new product. In this manner the publisher determines whether the author can write effectively, to age level. Often more than one author will finally be selected for a textbook; in some series where several grade levels need to be served as many as fifteen authors may be engaged in the development of a project.

It is remarkable, given all these efforts, how poorly most school texts are written. Dull, plodding, and uninspiring, even books about exciting historical events, great technical achievements, and vital dimensions of modern life often manage to make their subjects sound uninteresting. One wonders how children can be drawn to learning when their encounters with it are made so unattractive.

Many textbooks are dull because the task of writing them is so over-regulated that spontaneity and life are driven out of them. Textbook authors are confronted by a benumbing mass of rules: readability formulas drastically limiting the vocabulary they may use, structural formulas dictating their writing strategy and approach, pedagogical formulas aimed at making things easy for teachers, and nondiscrimination formulas designed to pacify even the most sensitive protesters. Inhibited by such a smothering array, even the most creative talent will be emptied of the vibrancy it needs to produce good writing.

The curiosity that leads to knowledge is stimulated by the fascinating world around us. Destroy that fascination and you destroy the natural motivation for learning. All the world's readability formulas, classroom projects, collateral activities, resource guides, and teacher's manuals will not replace it. If educators prefer that children want to learn—as opposed to being cajoled into doing so—they will have to restore a sane, non-threatening environment to textbook authorship.

Authors' basic royalty rates of 2 to 6 percent of publisher's income for elementary materials and 5 to 8 percent for secondary titles increase with sales volume. Workbooks and supplemental items may carry a royalty or may be paid for under a flat fee arrangement. Advances if paid at all are small and designed to help the author meet expenses such as typing of the manuscript. However, even though unit prices of schoolbooks are usually not very high (in 1987 they averaged $6.49 for elementary and $10.31 for secondary hardbound and paperbound texts and workbooks combined), the sheer sales volume of some titles can result in handsome incomes for their authors, considerably larger very often than their regular salaries as teachers.

In recent years, an alternative to both in-house development and outside authorship that has found increasing favor with publishers has been the use of packagers. Such packagers assume the responsibilities and costs of product development, turning a project over to the publisher when it is ready for manufacture. The growing popularity of this approach, which parallels a similar trend in the trade and other publishing areas, suggests that the mainstream firms are placing increasing emphasis on the marketing and investment facets of the enterprise while reducing their creative involvement in the process. Given present realities, this is probably a logical and not necessarily a detrimental development. The trend has, in fact, created new opportunities for smaller entrepreneurs to contribute creatively in their areas of strength while leaving problems of capitalization and mass dissemination to giants better equipped to deal with them.

Validation and Testing

Testing materials in the field, thereby discovering their weaknesses, if any, and making needed changes before publication, is a recently established practice with many school publishers. Some testing has always been done, notably by authors with their own students; recently, however, some state adoption requirements, economic considerations, and the general trend toward accountability have intensified publishers' efforts in this direction.

Testing, if well designed and implemented, will establish the workability of a program in a variety of geographic and cultural settings. It will enable the publisher to present a more convincing case to adoption authorities, whether or not they require such testing. It will also provide protection for the publishers against failure of a project in which they have invested substantial time, energy, and money.

Testing can take many forms and can be conducted on various levels of sophistication. One can, for example, measure reading ability before and after the application of a program that purports to teach children to read. The test criteria and methods of measurement then become important considerations. More frequently, however, testing may simply involve having the author and selected teachers use page proofs of the book in actual classroom situations. "Bugs" discovered in the program can then be identified and removed, and gaps in its effectiveness can be noted and filled. Computer programs have been developed to check reading levels, and computers generally are used on a wide scale in various testing procedures.

The "show-me" attitude manifested by accountability indicates a determination to have education perform or reform. But one doubts that it is a sign of American disenchantment with education itself; if anything, the prevalent disillusionment is the reverse side of a coin of excessive expectations. Perhaps the educators who have contributed to both exaggerated hopes and overwrought disappointments by promising more for education than it can possibly deliver would be well advised to introduce a new realism into their discussions with the public.

COLLEGE TEXTBOOKS

For awhile, during the restless sixties, it seemed as though the traditional college textbook was doomed. Spurred on by the general relaxation of standards and requirements in higher education, college instructors turned eagerly to nontextbook materials, notably trade and mass market paperbacks, for primary, as distinguished from supplemental, use in course assignments. The practice became particularly widespread in humanities and social science courses offered by elite schools. .

Today, the college textbook is back in its preeminent position, though changed somewhat in character and approach. Common now are text "packages" which include, in addition to the core book, tests, solution manuals, study guides, workbooks, computer software, and teaching aids for the instructor. While the bonanzas of yesteryear, when a major textbook would sell 200,000 copies annually, no longer occur, a successful text package can roll up an annual volume of 100,000, particularly when it covers a basic subject on the freshman-sophomore level. Less basically oriented titles and packages may post annual sales of 20,000 copies. Supplemental materials, though still important, are playing a lesser role.

New Publishing Initiatives

Although textbooks have regained their status in higher education, the publishers' task in developing and distributing them has grown more demanding than in the past. For one thing, the publishers must keep in closer touch with the many fields of study, observe rapidly changing trends, anticipate developments, and make available what is likely to be in demand tomorrow, not what reflects the abandoned concepts of yesterday. This forces them to rely more intensively on their own judgment and to do more homework. In the past, college publishers would characteristically approach a distinguished teacher or scholar, inquire into his or her writing activity, try to persuade the author to place a book with the house, and rely almost totally on the writer's familiarity with the field to produce a viable and successful work. While some publishers did engage in market research, few looked sufficiently into such questions as existing competition, satisfaction and dissatisfaction with books being used, and expressed needs and preferences by those likely to adopt the materials. In some cases even such factors as total enrollment and potential market share were only imperfectly guessed at. In consequence, like other industry divisions, college publishing suffered from serious overproduction.

Today, with success or failure dependent on a multiplicity of small decisions, the correct answers to these market questions are vital. Nor can any publisher afford to disregard the impact on sales of the significant used book trade carried on by college stores and among individual students.

So the college publisher must plan. What is needed in both basic and supplemental texts? What features should the material offer? Who is best equipped to write it? The publisher may still rely on the sales travelers to maintain contact with the faculty, to bring back ideas, to report trends and developments. But it is the editor who must conceive the project and work more intensively than heretofore with the author in shaping it into an effective teaching tool. The market researcher must provide reliable data on its competition and market potential.

The role of the faculty author or adviser is accordingly changed, perhaps in some ways diminished. What may matter less than a distinguished reputation is the competence and intelligibility with which the material is presented so that students will regard it as acceptable. Publishers are more willing today to employ less established yet imaginative and able writers. Should they encounter a great man whose ability to communicate fails to equal his disciplinary competence, they are more anxious than ever to find a collaborator for him—perhaps even a staff writer—so that prestige and wisdom may be matched by intelligibility and efficacy.

College textbook authors' royalties are in the 10 to 18 percent of receipts range. Occasionally on a book of considerable potential an escalating royalty formula may be employed. Advances are made to help an author meet out-of-pocket expenses, such as permissions fees on a book of readings, but such advances are rare and normally modest.

A number of college publishers have entered the audiovisual and electronic fields to produce software, films, slides, transparencies, records, and cassettes. As in other publishing areas, notably elhi, such products have made their way and have become significant sources of income for their originators. Generally however they have supplemented and complemented rather than competed with the book programs of their publishers.

IV

How Books Are Manufactured

The soul of a book—its ideas and contents—must be housed in a suitable body. Thus from their beginnings books have enjoyed the attention of master designers, illuminators, and artisans. The great manuscript books of the Middle Ages are precious museum treasures. Since the Renaissance outstanding typographers have designed the typefaces in use to this day. Some of the world's greatest artists have illustrated and designed books: Daumier, Matisse, and Picasso come readily to mind. The custom of collecting books for their beauty has been established for centuries.

It is not likely, or even desirable, that every book published should be a great work of art. But every book should offer to the reader a functional attractiveness that makes the content fully accessible and that conveys by its arrangement and appearance the purposes of the author. Text should be as easy to read as possible. Illustrations should be well reproduced and appropriately integrated with the text. Binding should be as durable as required by the character of the book and the reader's needs.

Good functional design helps to sell books. The reader browsing in a bookshop may not have the slightest inkling of what constitutes good book design, but if the package he or she holds is visually inviting, the reader is more likely to buy it. How clearly the pages are laid out, how readable the type is, how striking the illustrations are, and how well they are coordinated with written matter may well have a bearing on the decision. This is particularly true of professional, educational, hobby, craft, and how-to titles. Sheer beauty of design is bound furthermore to have an influence on people with discriminating literary tastes who are likely to be more sensitive than average to aesthetic factors.

Within a publishing house the responsibility for creating the book as a physical entity lies with the production department. Very few publishers own their own printing facilities, so this responsibility normally involves dealing with commercial typesetters, printers, and binders. A small press entrepreneur or, in a larger house, a production manager and his or her staff are therefore involved in the following basic steps as the physical book is brought into being: planning, cost estimating, scheduling, design, selection of suppliers, purchase of paper and cover materials, and the supervision of typesetting, printing, and binding.

What the production staff does is a great deal more comprehensible when one has a basic acquaintanceship with the technical areas with which that staff must deal: typesetting, printing (including book papers), and binding.

Type and Its Characteristics

Anyone who has ever played with a rubber type kit, or used a typewriter for that matter, is acquainted with the rudiments of typography. There are, to begin with, certain basic differences between typefaces. The most common variety of letters employed in printing (including the type in which this book is set) is some version of the letters used by the ancient Romans:

ABCDEFGHIJK

These letters are characterized among other features by the cross strokes at line endings which are known as "serifs." There are other styles of typefaces which lack these serifs and which are therefore known as "sans serif":

ABCDEFGHIJK

Roman faces are generally considered to be more readable than sans serif and are therefore more commonly used for setting text. Sans serif faces are occasionally employed for body type but are more often used in setting headings, captions, and tabular material.

Within the families of roman and sans serif there are many typefaces of which some of the most popular are shown in Figure 2. Each face is available in the capital letters of the alphabet (caps or uppercase), usually in two sizes (large caps and small caps), as well as in the small letters (lowercase), in addition to numerals, punctuation, and certain symbols (such as the asterisk). There are also items such as superior numbers ([1]) used in references to footnotes. Most faces are available in a slanted version known as "italic" which is used for emphasis, notes, or captions. Typefaces usually are available in a variety of weights: light, demibold, and bold. Most text composition employs light weight exclusively, with the bolder weights reserved for headings. (Figure 3 shows variations of regular and italic faces in different weights.) A complete set of letters, numerals, punctuation marks, and symbols in a given slant or weight is known as a "font."

An important factor in type selection is size. In typography a special system of measurement is employed based on "points." A point is a shade less than $\frac{1}{72}$ inch; 12 points make a "pica" which is therefore a little less than $\frac{1}{6}$ inch. A foot is equivalent to approximately $72\frac{1}{2}$ picas. The size of a letter is predicated on its height; when it is measured, however, it is not the letter itself but the "body" on which it is mounted that determines its size (see Figure 4). As a result, because of design variations, there may be noticeable differences in, say, the 12-point size of different typefaces.

There are also considerable differences in the width of fonts. Some are set narrow and close together (condensed), others are more rounded and spread (extended). Some faces are even available in condensed and extended versions. These features not only have an effect on legibility but they can seriously affect the "measure" (width) of a line containing the same number of "characters" (letters). Consequently they will affect also the length of the entire book.

Legibility is the major consideration in the choice of type. Preferably a line should not exceed in measure one and one half alphabets (or 39 characters) since the eye has difficulty maintaining focus on a larger number of letters. Smaller than 8-point type is difficult to read in most fonts; notes might be set in 6-point but one should avoid so small a size for the body of the text. Usually the upper limit for adult books is 12-point type; of course volumes for younger readers will often be set in much larger sizes.

White space on a page is also important. Adequate margins rest the eye and prevent that crowded appearance that often makes reading a strain. Even more significant is the spacing between lines known as "leading." A

Baskerville

ABCDEFGHIJKLMNOPQRSTUVWXYZ
ABCDEFGHIJKLMNOPQRSTUVWXYZ
abcdefghijklmnopqrstuvwxyz
1234567890$

Bodoni

ABCDEFGHIJKLMNOPQRSTUVWXYZ
ABCDEFGHIJKLMNOPQRSTUVWXYZ
abcdefghijklmnopqrstuvwxyz
1234567890$

Century Expanded

ABCDEFGHIJKLMNOPQRSTUVWXYZ
ABCDEFGHIJKLMNOPQRSTUVWXYZ
abcdefghijklmnopqrstuvwxyz
1234567890$

Times Roman

ABCDEFGHIJKLMNOPQRSTUVWXYZ
ABCDEFGHIJKLMNOPQRSTUVWXYZ
abcdefghijklmnopqrstuvwxyz
1234567890$

Folio Light

ABCDEFGHIJKLMNOPQRSTUVWXYZ
abcdefghijklmnopqrstuvwxyz
1234567890$

Helvetica Regular

ABCDEFGHIJKLMNOPQRSTUVWXYZ
abcdefghijklmnopqrstuvwxyz
1234567890$

Univers #45

ABCDEFGHIJKLMNOPQRSTUVWXYZ
abcdefghijklmnopqrstuvwxyz
1234567890$

Figure 2. Commonly used typefaces. The first four, Baskerville, Bodoni, Century, and Times Roman, are roman faces; the last three, Folio, Helvetica, and Univers are sans serif. Shown for each face are large caps, lowercase letters, and numbers. Small caps are shown in the roman faces, but are not available in sans serif.

critical factor in eye fatigue is the jump from the end of a line to the beginning of the next; the eye has difficulty locating the succeeding line if the spacing is insufficient so most composition allows for a point or two of leading.

A typesetter who encountered the following instructions on a manuscript:

Set body in 10/12 Garamond × 24 picas

would know that the text should be set in 10-point Garamond, with a distance of 12 points from the bottom of one line to the bottom of the next, thus providing for two points of leading. The measure, or width, of the line would be 24 picas.

In addition to faces suitable for body copy there are others known as display type which are particularly appropriate for headings or title pages. These may be quite elaborate and are available in sizes larger than those in which text faces are customarily furnished.

How Type is Set

There are four basic methods by which type can be set: by hand, on Monotype machines, on Linotype machines, and through computers.

Type is still set by hand, as it was in Gutenberg's day, for some title pages and jackets, or where display type is involved. Some publishers of gift editions set entire books this way. Needless to say, the practice is rare in this mechanized age.

In hand-setting each letter—which presents an appearance such as that shown in Figure 4—is placed in line individually, and spacing between words and lines is inserted by means of metal slugs or strips. (Line-spacing metal contains a good deal of lead, hence the term "leading.") The spacing between words is subject to skillful adjustment so that lines may end evenly ("justified") at right-hand margins.

It is in the art of spacing words and letters that the typographer's craft comes to the fore, whether the type used is on metal, drawn by a letterer, or generated by a computer. When spacing becomes uneven and awkward, when lines, paragraphs, and pages are poorly balanced or riddled with unsightly blank streaks ("rivers"), it is a sign of poor craftsmanship.

Almost as rare as hand-setting is the use of Linotype machines. Utilizing a keyboard not dissimilar to that of a typewriter, the compositor sets one line at a time. As the compositor presses the keys, matrices (molds) of letters and spaces are assembled which occasionally must be adjusted by hand to achieve the proper balance and justification of lines. Each line is then cast individually in hot metal.

Univers #46 Italic

ABCDEFGHIJKLMNOPQRSTUVWXYZ
abcdefghijklmnopqrstuvwxyz
1234567890$

Bodoni Italic

ABCDEFGHIJKLMNOPQRSTUVWZYX
abcdefghijklmnopqrstuvwxyz
123456789$

Bodoni Bold Italic

ABCDEFGHIJKLMNOPQRSTUVWXYZ
abcdefghijklmnopqrstuvwxyz
1234567890$

Century Bold Italic

ABCDEFGHIJKLMNOPQRSTUVWXYZ
abcdefghijklmnopqrstuvwxyz
1234567890$

Times Roman Italic

ABCDEFGHIJKLMNOPQRSTUVWXYZ
abcdefghijklmnopqrstuvwxyz
1234567890$

Folio Light Italic

ABCDEFGHIJKLMNOPQRSTUVWXYZ
abcdefghijklmnopqrstuvwxyz
1234567890$

Helvetica Semi-Bold Italic

ABCDEFGHIJKLMNOPQRSTUVWXYZ
abcdefghijklmnopqrstuvwxyz
1234567890$

Figure 3. Some typeface variations. Note the slant of the italic face when compared to its regular equivalent in Figure 1. Also note the differences in weight, such as between Bodoni and Bodoni Bold in the second and third examples.

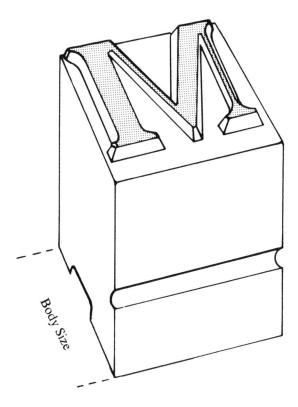

Body Size

Figure 4. A letterpress type character, showing the mounting of the letter on the body.

In Monotype composition, which is generally more costly than Linotype, a keyboard is also used, but letters and spaces are cast individually rather than in complete lines. Because this provides for greater flexibility both for copy and spacing within the text, Monotype is still occasionally employed for complicated technical composition.

In all methods of metal type composition, lines of type are assembled in long trays known as "galleys" from which proofs, appropriately designated as galley proofs, can be pulled. Editors and authors use them to indicate text corrections. In hand-setting and Monotype, the compositor makes corrections by removing the faulty individual letters or words and making the needed substitutions. In Linotype the entire line in which an error has occurred must be reset. This creates the possibility that a new error may be made in another part of the line even as the first mistake is corrected and necessitates a new reading of the entire line to ascertain that it really corresponds to the specified copy. Extensive corrections going beyond typographical errors and involving changes of words, phrases, or even sentences usually require the resetting of entire paragraphs since every line must be rejustified.

Once galley proofs are corrected, the compositor breaks the galleys into pages in accordance with the desired number of lines per page. At that time the typesetter also inserts page numbers ("folios"), placing odd numbers on right-hand pages ("recto") and even numbered folios on left-hand pages ("verso"). At the same time chapter headings are inserted as well as "running heads" (the lines at the top of pages that identify chapter or section and often repeat the title of the book itself).

Certain pages may not carry folios or running heads, for example, blank pages facing chapter openings, the title page, or so-called "half-titles," i.e., pages such as the recto preceding the title page, or the parts of a book on which title or names of parts are shown in sizable, sometimes decorative type. Often a different folio sequence, of Roman numerals, is provided for so-called "front matter": preface or foreword, acknowledgments, and table of contents. From the made-up pages are pulled the "page proofs" which serve publisher and author for a final check of the entire setting.

Modern Typesetting Methods

The various computerized typesetting systems—though they may employ a variety of electronic methods, such as encoding on tape or disc, machine printout, or projections of entire pages by cathode ray tube—have one thing in common: they attempt to automate a significant portion of the work that would otherwise have to be performed by human minds and hands. Word breaks are an example. A good typographer is sufficiently familiar with the language to make the proper word separation at the end of a line. Programs have been written—not always with total success—which attempt to undertake this chore. Another example is justification. Often adjustments are needed because a line runs slightly over or under when standard interword spacing is employed, which the skilled typographer effects either on the keyboard or by hand. Complex programs have been written to automate this task as well.

Fundamentally, there are three program levels in computer composition: the basic systems program which involves general factors like word breaks and justification; an intermediate level program which contains general instructions for the particular setting—font, spacing, leading, indentations, style features; and, finally, the specific keyboard instructions which are part of the encoding. It is possible, therefore, to effect changes of intermediate level features such as size of font without having to make changes in the encoding itself. It is also possible to have type set by a person with relatively little training: for example a good typist in a publisher's office may be able to encode the manuscript on tape which is then forwarded to the compositor.

Characteristically, instructions for paging the book are part of the intermediate level program; consequently, proofs are furnished in page form. This presents challenges and problems to editors, authors, and production people. For example, it is considered desirable when reading proof to eliminate dangling single words or a very short line at the end of a paragraph or at the top of a page ("widows"). However, proofreading is followed by a correction pass against the original encoding (including any instructions for eliminating widows), and the entire book is then reset from the corrected encoding. As a result, paragraphs and pages may shift in the resetting and new widows may be created. It is wise, therefore, to wait for the last proof before undertaking such cosmetic changes; even then, one must look ahead carefully at the full effect of each and every change.

Significant advances, which thus far have been more widely adopted by newspaper, magazine, and small presses than by larger book publishers, are editing-composition and desktop publishing systems. These installations combine the function of effecting editorial changes with those of setting type. In the process, an original manuscript is electronically encoded and then displayed on a video terminal in sections or page by page. Editorial changes are made electronically—although hard copy printouts may be employed to share proofs with the author—and reproduceable (camera-ready) pages constitute the final product.

Authors are increasingly resorting to the use of word processors in preparing their manuscripts. Some publishers have discovered that effective advance coordination with such authors enable them to employ the machine-readable output of the author's word processor (e.g., a floppy disk) in their own editing-composition or desktop publishing systems, thereby allowing them to copyedit and typeset the manuscript electronically without ever setting pencil to paper or printing out proofs. What is disappointing is the indifference, even hostility, of many large publishers toward these technological advances. Authors are often disappointed when they expect that their use of word processors will be welcomed and effectively exploited by mainstream publishers. In marked contrast, many small presses operate on a totally electronic basis.

So-called cold type—a term originally designed to distinguish certain methods of composition from those employing hot metal—can utilize equipment ranging from a simple typewriter to automated installations. In its most primitive form—on an ordinary typewriter with a carbon (onetime) ribbon—the text will be set without proportional spacing and with unjustified right-hand margins. Common typewriters do not space letters proportionately because each key is the same width and the machine is constructed to move ahead by the same distance as each letter is used. But of course the letter "m" is wider than the letter "i," and in metal typesetting the body on which each letter is mounted varies proportionately in width with the letter itself. Electronic typewriters furnish proportional spacing, and are able to justify lines. Desktop publishing and automated systems, such as Atex and Compugraphic, provide proportional spacing, justification, and page makeup; however, quality and appearance are less satisfactory than in more sophisticated systems, such as Videocomp usually employed in setting mainstream titles. But the simpler processes are more economical and have been widely successful.

Printing and Its Methods

There are three methods of printing in use today: letterpress, offset (or lithography), and gravure.

Letterpress is the traditional process, basically a continuation of the way books were printed in the fifteenth century. In this method ink is applied to raised surfaces which impress their image on paper (see Figure 5). While some printing of hand-set books is still done directly from type, the use of plates molded from type is more common.

There are two types of letterpresses: flatbed presses, which hold the type or plates on a plane and print on sheets of paper, and rotary presses, which bend the plates over cylinders and print on sheets or rolls (webs) (see Figure 6). Rotaries work at far greater speeds than flatbeds and are therefore more economical for commercial runs, such as for mass market paperbacks.

An important variation is the Cameron Belt Press in which plastic plates are carried on a continuous belt, and impressions are made in sequence on a continuous roll of paper. This system permits economies on shorter runs but its uniqueness requires that a book be planned especially for the process.

Since World War II offset printing has practically replaced the letterpress process, and most books today are printed by this method. Offset is basically photographic, although laser and electronic beam technology are also employed. Type and illustrations are photographed, and from the negatives thin metal plates are made which are bent over cylinders. The to-

Figure 5. Diagrams showing four stages of printing production. The first picture symbolizes original images, the subject matter of printing. The second shows how original images appear on a printing-image carrier for relief printing, letterpress, for example. The third picture shows the ink image on the image carrier, and on the fourth picture you see the final printed image on a sheet of paper.

be-printed images have been etched slightly into the surface of the plate, and the ink adheres to the etched areas. Adjoining the drum on which the plate rotates is another cylinder covered with a rubber blanket onto which the plate offsets (hence the name of the process) these images. The rubber-covered cylinder in turn rolls against and prints on the paper (sheets on a flatbed, or a web on a rotary press).

One of the major advantages offered by offset is the greater facility it provides in preparing illustrations. In fact, it would be fair to say that the offset process has made possible the use of illustrations in books which could not possibly have included them when only letterpress was avail-

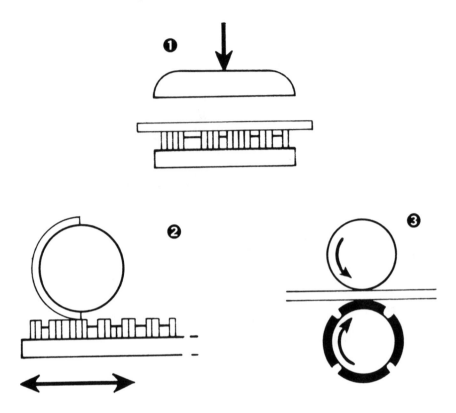

Figure 6. In platen presses (1) the platen and the bed are flat; in flatbed-cylinder Presses (2) the bed is still flat but the platen is replaced by an impression cylinder; in rotary presses (3) the plate cylinder takes the place of the flatbed, and both members of the printing unit are cylindrical.

able, and it has substantially simplified and reduced the production cost of illustrated books in general.

There are basically two types of black-and-white illustrations: those involving line only (without shading of any sort) and halftones where shadings or tones occur. An example of a line illustration is a geometric diagram or a pen-and-ink drawing; photographs are examples of halftones.

Regardless of the printing process used, all illustrations, be they line or halftone, must first be photographed or scanned electronically. In the case of line illustrations this process is relatively simple. When it comes to halftones, however, it becomes more complicated. Halftones are reproduced by means of small dots, often indistinguishable to the naked eye and only clearly visible under a magnifying glass. These dots are larger and appear closer together where a dark area is desired; they are smaller and seem farther apart where a picture is lighter. The dots are created by a screen of crisscrossed lines: where the picture is darker, larger dots result, where lighter, their density is less. The greater the density of the screen (i.e., the greater the number of individual dots per given area) the better the quality of an illustration will be. In letterpress the maximum density of screen that could be used with good results was 110 lines to the inch; in offset finer screens can be used: 130 to 150 lines per inch are common. In consequence the fidelity, contrast, and tonal quality of offset illustrations are superior.

The same may be said of color printing. Color illustrations are prepared in one of two ways: either the colors are preseparated by the artist, or they are separated electronically in what is known as "process" color. Pre-separation is certainly logical where only two colors are involved: the artist simply prepares two separate versions of the picture, each showing the area in which one of the colors is to be used. Each color is then applied in a separate impression on the press, although two or several simultaneous impressions can be run on certain large color presses.

When it comes to full (multi) color, the printing process takes advantage of the fact that not only can the eye not distinguish small dots individually, but also that it tends to mix primary colors (yellow, red, and blue) into the full range of the spectrum, provided the printed dots are effectively arranged.

A good artist, conversant with the graphic process, can so preseparate colors and so instruct the plate maker as to achieve astounding variations, combinations, and richness in color illustrations. Where photographs or paintings are to be reproduced, however, process color is usually employed. An electronic scanner extracts the primary colors—red, blue, and yellow—from the original, and for each color a plate is made, with a fourth plate, for printing black, added to strengthen outlines, shadings, and contrasts. The dot arrangements employed are highly elaborate and ingenious and require computerized controls to insure correct color values.

Photogravure printing is a rather expensive process occasionally employed for art books and other heavily illustrated volumes. Also known as "intaglio" printing, it is celebrated for its soft halftones and pleasing color work. Unlike letterpress, where the printing surface is raised, and offset, where it is practically flat, in gravure it is indented. Plates are made by etching the indentations into metal, a process that traces its origins to the engraving art of the Middle Ages and the Renaissance.

Gravure presses may be sheet-fed or web-fed. Papers used must have a high absorbency level as the stock must literally blot the ink out of the indentations. Before offset printing developed to its present state and provided such satisfactory halftone and color work, gravure was the only process that offered a mellowness of tone not achieved by letterpress. Like letterpress, it has had to give way to the steadily advancing offset supremacy.

Paper

Book papers come in many weights, sizes, and colors. The intended use of a stock will determine its desirable features and the grade that will be selected.

In regard to quality, there are three classes of book papers: permanent papers, so-called free sheet, and groundwood stocks. Permanent, or more technically "neutral PH" papers, the best and most costly commonly used, are free of acids and are guaranteed to last for more than a century without deterioration. Libraries have been urging publishers to utilize such papers on all books of lasting significance. Books printed decades ago on paper containing acids have been disintegrating, and the Library of Congress, for one, is currently forced to spend millions of dollars on the preservation of its holdings.

The pulp used in "free" sheet is free of groundwood and has been bleached and chemically treated (with acids among other ingredients,) to maintain its color. However, it will deteriorate after some years. Groundwood papers, used for mass market paperbacks, for example, tend to be somewhat grayish in color and to turn brown after some months. Some groundwood stocks are coated and therefore present a better initial appearance. Some papers milled have rag content; they are used in better Bibles but only rarely for other books because of their high cost.

Within the above classes available papers vary in substance weight, bulk, finish, color, and opacity. Weight is determined by basis ream weight; a 50-pound paper is one of which a standard ream (500 sheets, 25×38 inches in size) weighs 50 pounds. (There are occasional variations in standard measurements which are noted in manufacturers' specifications.) Bulk is shown by indicating the number of pages to the inch after the paper has been "smashed," i.e., air trapped between the pages has been squeezed out.

The combination of weight and bulk is a major consideration in the choice of stock as it will affect the overall appearance of a book. Many weights are available in standard and high bulk, the latter resulting from whipping more air into the pulp as the paper is milled. Of course some papers are characteristically low or high bulk to begin with, depending on their fiber content and the manner in which they were milled. Most adult books are printed on papers ranging in substance weight from 45 to 60 pounds. Children's books are often printed on 70- or 80-pound stock.

Opacity is an important factor. A paper with poor opacity will allow the text or illustrations from the reverse page to show through which makes for very unsatisfactory reading. The chemical titanium, when added to book paper, increases its opacity. Finish is similarly significant. Antique finish, which is velvety in character, is usually employed for trade books. Coated papers are used for certain art books and scientific and medical texts, although advances in offset printing have reduced the demand for coated papers which at one time were essential for printing letterpress illustrations. Some papers are "calendered," i.e., they are run between metal rollers at the mill in order to provide them with a smoother finish. Machine-finish and English-finish papers, often used in text and reference books, are of this variety.

Paper colors range from blue-white to various shades of cream. A great deal of experimentation with nonglare papers has been done and even some coated stocks are available today with low-glare characteristics. Grain is also a factor. As paper runs off the milling machine the fibers flow along the length of the paper. It is desirable to have the grain run parallel to the binding edge (vertical) of a book when printing because subsequent folding and trimming will then occur with, rather than against, the grain and make production easier while resulting in a more attractive product.

Binding

The binding process involves folding the large press sheets down to book size, gathering the folded pages in sequence, sewing or gluing them together, and attaching endpapers and a cover to them. If desired a dustcover or jacket can be placed over the binding.

Press sheets hold a multiple of pages, the number—usually divisible by four—depending on the sheet size, the book-page size, and the size of the press. As many as 128 pages are common today, but 64, 32, and 16 pages per sheet are not unusual. Since most papers will not fold well if the sheet contains more than 32 pages, and as the handling of very large sheets is cumbersome, the sheets are usually cut to 32-page maximum size as they come off the press.

At the bindery—which may be located either in the same manufacturing plant or at some distance from the printer—the sheets of 32 pages (or less) are folded to individual page size. Depending on the type of folding machine employed, the binder will have instructed the printer to arrange ("impose") the pages in a certain order so that they will come out in correct sequence after folding. What results are uncut booklets known as "signatures."

The signatures are arranged in proper sequence in a process called "gathering." Once gathered they can be bound together in a variety of ways. The traditional method is "smyth-sewing," by which a special sewing machine threads the pages of each signature together and all the signatures to each other. This process is still employed for large art or reference books, for titles that are expected to receive very hard use, and where superior quality of product is desired.

The more common process today, however, is adhesive binding. In this method the back folds of the gathered signatures are ground off and a very strong, highly elastic adhesive substance is applied to them. On hardcover books, and some better paperbacks, a version of the process used is known as "burst" or "notch" binding, wherein the backs of the signatures are ground off only superficially, and the adhesive penetrates the pages through holes or notches made during folding. This leaves the signatures largely intact and permits books to lie nearly flat when open. On mass market and other less costly paperbacks, in a version of the process known as "perfect" binding, the backs of the signatures are ground off completely before the adhesive is applied. Thanks to the development of excellent glues, perfect binding is proving to be as lasting and as satisfactory as sewing.

Some books are "side-sewn," i.e., the stitches, instead of penetrating the backs of signatures, are taken through the side, making for a very tight and secure binding able to withstand extraordinary punishment. Booklets of 64 pages or less are often saddle-wire stitched, i.e., held at the backs by metal staples. One can also employ side-staples, thereby providing a sturdier hold and one that can accommodate a larger number of pages.

At this point the cover is ready to go on. If it is a paper cover, it is simply held by the adhesive of the perfect binding, or adhesive is applied to the backs of the sewn or notched signatures and the cover affixed to them. (Note that paperbacks are square-backed.) As a final step in paperback binding, pages and cover are trimmed together to specified size.

If the book is to have a hard cover ("case binding") the cases must first be made. They consist of "boards" over which the cover materials—made of cloth, plastic, or treated papers—are folded and glued. Sometimes the cover design has been printed on the material in advance; more commonly the cases are stamped with ink or foils.

Endpapers are then attached to the sheets. (They are the heavy pages at

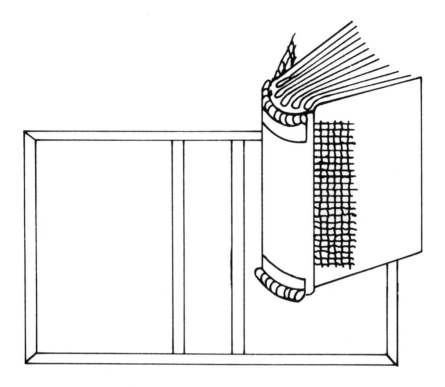

Figure 7. Diagram of the rounded and backed book and a binder's case prior to casing-in, or combining the book and its cover.

beginning and end, sometimes decorated or of colored stock, glued on one side to the case.) The entire set is then trimmed to size. Most books are cut evenly on all three sides; however one may leave the front and bottom untrimmed for a "rough front and foot" (also known as "quad open") which is quite stylish and attractive. If the top is to be colored ("stained") this is also done now. Mounted on the back, which is forcibly rounded as a rule, is a broad strip of reinforced gauze ("crash") to which the so-called "head- and footbands" (usually made of brightly colored threads) adhere at top and bottom. Finally the case is attached by gluing the overlapping crash and endpapers to the inside of the boards (see Figure 7). So-called "building-in" machines season the cases in a few seconds. Dustcovers, be they craft wrappers or colorful jackets, go on last.

A significant departure from the usual printing and binding process is the Cameron Belt Press which not only prints but folds, collates, and perfect-binds, all in one operation. It is for this reason that its use requires special planning; it is certainly difficult to convert a project to the Cameron process after planning to produce it by another method or to change to an alternative approach once a book has been designed for production by the Cameron system.

Planning and Design

Like every aspect of book publishing, production does not and cannot work in isolation. At one end it touches upon the editorial process, at the other upon the marketing program, and throughout it must be conscious of costs and the dictates of sound capital investment. In a large house, when a production manager and staff plan and produce books, they must coordinate their efforts with their editorial, marketing, and financial colleagues.

Hopefully the production staff will have become involved in a project from its very beginning, even before the manuscript was accepted for publication. It will then have an opportunity to provide early cost estimates, to note any special manufacturing problems, and to communicate effectively with editors and the sales department as overall plans for publication of the book were formulated. As soon as possible after the acceptance of the manuscript the production department likes to design the volume, make plans for its manufacture, and formulate a schedule for the various stages of the process. Often this is done from a duplicate manuscript even before it is copyedited (although it is advisable in that case to have the editorial department indicate in some detail the nature and extent of the editing anticipated).

A preliminary step in designing the book requires that the length of the text be established by means of a "character-count," a quite precise determination that enables the designer to anticipate the number of lines of body type that will have to be set. The designer then lays out the volume. Title page and other front matter may be drawn specifically; chapter openings and headings and the overall scheme for paragraphs and pages may require only a general layout and/or specifications. Included will be trim size (i.e., page size, exclusive of binding), typographical instructions for body type, notes and headings, running heads and folios, instructions for margins and spacing, depth (number of lines) of page, and placement of the various elements on the page.

Illustrations must be sized (i.e., their dimensions must be specified), they must be marked for reduction or cropping if necessary, and their placement on pages must be indicated. A heavily illustrated volume may require more extensive and detailed layout.

In planning the layout the designer realizes that the book must come out ("cast off") to "even forms," i.e., the total number of pages must fit exactly on the large sheets utilized in printing; if they do not, several blank pages may be left over and look awkward at the back of the volume. To achieve an even castoff the designer must carefully estimate space that will be consumed by text and illustrations, taking into account partially blank pages (at the ends of chapters, for example), blanks, and half titles. Designers have a good deal of flexibility—in choice of type, depth of page, sizing of illustrations, and allowing for blank pages—and can usually achieve this objective without too much difficulty. Of course the more complex a volume, the more difficult the task. In certain cases final determination of some elements is not possible until pages are made up, with the designer dummying up the more demanding projects.

Paper must be specified next. The designer, knowing what paper the publisher stocks at various printers, or what the printer is able to furnish or even purchase on special order, will make a selection with the character of the book and its particular printing needs in mind. A designer must also be conscious of special standards or requirements which, in the case of elhi books, for example, are quite rigidly defined for both paper and binding.

If the volume is to have a hard binding, the designer will also provide instructions for endpapers, top stain, head- and footbands (if any), boards, and cloth or other binding materials. He or she will, furthermore, design the printing or stamping to be applied to the case. He or she may or may not design the jacket, or the paper cover in case of softbound volumes, as this task is sometimes left to special cover artists. Generally speaking, the book designer who is on the publisher's staff is likely to prepare simple typographical covers but leave more complex artwork, requiring original paintings or photography, to outside specialists. Freelance book designers are usually retained with the understanding that they will furnish jacket or cover art as part of their service.

Not every book needs to be fully designed. Many publishers employ standard designs for series and for certain types of books, which then require minimal attention on the designer's part—perhaps in laying out front matter and sizing illustrations only. This approach is sound from both an economic and an aesthetic standpoint: there is a desirable logic in having books in series or by the same author bear an identifying re-semblance.

Unfortunately designers are often stout opponents of standardization. Their resistance is a symptom of an even more serious and fundamental shortcoming that is an occupational hazard in book design: overemphasis on the aesthetic and corresponding failure to meet the functional demands of their task. Obviously good design is essential in the production of books, but good design means first and foremost good *publishing:* clarity, readability, ready communication, inviting appearance, service of the reader and of the author's purposes. The designer who sacrifices readability to "arty" typographical devices, who lays out pages that may look superbly balanced but set the text too small or in confusing arrangements, who lets illustrations bleed off the page (i.e., run to the very edge) but permits important details to be cropped off in the process, is not truly fulfilling a designer's function. Self-expression may be a legitimate aim in any artistic endeavor, but in functional design it must become subservient to and accept the limitations of the objectives which the designed product seeks to serve.

Production managers often complain that designers develop ideas that are difficult and costly to implement, consume unnecessary time, and yet add little to the usefulness and value of a book. Designers when confronted with such criticism then often murmur about the "crass commercialism" of publishers and their failure to appreciate real talent. Interestingly enough the truly great designers, who have left their impact on the development of the book as an objet d'art, have been those who have served with equal effectiveness the aesthetic and the functional requirements of their profession.

Selection of Suppliers

Choice of suppliers begins with decisions about process. Shall we use sheet-fed or web-fed presses? Case-bind or paper-bind? Adhesive-bind or smyth-sew? Character of the book, consumer expectations, level of quality in production, size of printing and anticipated reprint needs, scheduling, and related economic considerations will figure prominently in such decisions.

A good production manager knows the suppliers, knows their equipment capability, the speed with which they work, the efficiency and quality of their workmanship. Is cost a major consideration? The manager may find typesetters and printers with low rates but busy schedules and plan a longer production cycle in order to save money. Is speed a major factor? The publisher may be willing to pay a somewhat higher price for prompt service. Is quality the predominant consideration? The house may be willing to sacrifice both time and money to achieve it.

Some production plans can become very complicated. Sometimes type is set abroad—particularly where complex scientific and technical composition is involved—with reproduction proofs (special pulls of the setting which are perfect enough to be photographed for platemaking) flown stateside where offset negatives are made from them. Because a particular printer offers economical and efficient offset facilities, the printing may be done by that firm, which in turn will ship flat sheets to a bindery whose prices and capability for case binding are similarly favorable. In other instances an integrated book manufacturer, offering complete typesetting, printing, and binding facilities, may be awarded the entire job.

For certain projects the number of alternative facilities capable of doing good, prompt, and economical work may be limited. For certain specialties foreign sources may be preferable; for example, on large, economical, high-quality process color runs, overseas printing may be more advantageous than domestic manufacture. Because of dollar devaluation and cost inflation abroad the economic advantages of foreign printing have been greatly diminished, and as American technology and skill in color printing have improved, domestic manufacturers find themselves in competitive positions.

Speed in producing a book or the ability to deliver a fast reprint is often a vital consideration, particularly where a book may be a potential bestseller. Similarly the economics of ganging up books in series or of like format—original printings together with reprints—will argue for placing jobs with certain manufacturers. Paper must then be in supply at such plants, and one of the most demanding logistical problems confronting a production department is the need to have the right paper in the right place in the right quantity at all times. Cost-conscious and efficient publishers have learned to help solve this problem through standardization—in the variety of papers they will use and the number of trim sizes they will normally employ.

Estimating Costs

To determine costs of manufacture in advance is vital, not only as a control over the process and as a guide in making decisions regarding methods and suppliers, but also because for some publishers these costs are significant factors in the setting of retail prices. In fact many publishers use unit manufacturing costs of first printings as bases for price decisions; a popular traditional formula in trade-book publishing, for example, places prices at from five to six times that cost.

Such formulas may have some utility, although far more sophisticated and effective methods, which set a profit objective and measure total publishing cost in relation to total income based on projected price and subsidiary revenues, can and are being employed. But in any case, manufacturing expense remains a major factor in the pricing structure.

Choice of process and supplier and cost estimates are obviously interrelated and interdependent, and production people must often weigh several alternatives before making the optimal decision. Of course with many, perhaps most, titles pricing and process decisions will be routine; such titles may be part of a series or conform to established patterns which can be safely and advantageously followed.

The basic cost unit in typesetting is the "em"; i.e., charges are predicated on the space consumed by the lower case "m" in a given font and the equivalency of "ems" represented by a particular setting. Since there is more to typesetting than straight body type, however, and since even text composition is sometimes highly complicated, involving mathematical symbols and scientific formulas, estimates are usually based on costs per page which take into consideration the nature and complexity of the entire setting.

Costs per page in turn are contingent on such factors as size, capacity of the page (i.e., the number of characters or words that can be accommodated—see Table 4), the complexity of setting body type, notes, and headings, and the method of typesetting employed. Normally straight text composition in trade-book formats will run at $7 to $10 per page; a scientific monograph or a reference volume may run $30 a page or even more in certain cases. This includes an allowance for author's alterations (AA's) for which there is a charge. Printer's errors (PE's) are corrected at no charge.

If the publisher has assumed the responsibility for furnishing illustrations—more commonly the author's concern—the cost of producing these in-house or on the outside must be calculated. Sometimes even if the author has provided illustrations they require touching up or further work which, unless it can be charged to the author, will have to become part of the estimated expense. The publisher normally commissions cover art which likewise is added to the projected total.

Printing cost estimates usually involve negatives and/or plates. Here the process used and the number and type of illustrations included will significantly affect totals. Color work, particularly process color, is far more costly than black-and-white. Presswork costs, on the other hand, will depend on the length and complexity of the book (halftones add also to presswork expense as does, for example, so-called "open matter," i.e., extensive occurrence of short lines such as in poetry, drama, or narrative dialogue) and the number of impressions in the run. Of course negatives and plates will cost the same regardless of the number of copies printed; presswork however will vary with the size of the printing, including any ganging up with other books that may be possible.

A strange logic appears in many cases to determine the size of first

TABLE 4

Average Words per Printed Page for Certain Book Trim Sizes[a]
(10/12 type size)

Trim size (inches)[b]	Type area (picas)	Approximate number of words
5⅜ × 8⅜	24 × 40½	450
6 × 9	27 × 44½	550
6½ × 9	29 × 44½	600
6⅞ × 10	32½ × 52½[c]	650
7½ × 9¼	37 × 48[c]	800
7½ × 9¼	36 × 48[d]	575–595
8½ × 11	37½ × 53½[c]	830

[a]The estimates shown in this table were compiled by Dennis Hudson and reflect design practices in use in 1973 in the College Department of John Wiley & Sons.

[b]To allow for illustrations and tables, assume that in the first three trim sizes one half page would be used per unit; in the next three sizes, one third page per unit; in the last size, one fourth page per unit illustration or table.

[c]double column

[d]single column

printings. Some publishers argue that since fixed initial manufacturing costs (typesetting, art, negatives, and plates) will involve a lower investment per unit if the number of units manufactured is larger, therefore as many copies should be run at the beginning as possible. This kind of reasoning seems to stem from the practice of basing list price on a predetermined multiple of manufacturing cost and literally concluding that a lower price can be justified or a higher total of fixed cost tolerated simply because more copies are being printed.

What matters is not the unit cost of a first printing in relation to price but the total lifetime earnings of a book in relation to its total lifetime costs. To concentrate one's income planning on the first printing and ignore both the cost and earnings from likely reprints is unrealistic. On the other hand to run a sizable first printing in order to lower unit cost and in the process acquire excess inventory is altogether foolhardy. Cash is unnecessarily tied up, warehouse space is needlessly occupied, administrative costs in controlling the surplus inventory are needlessly incurred without having any real advantage to show for the effort. In most cases a printing, be it original or reprint, should represent a supply for no longer than a season (six months) or at most a year. Should the economics of the case not warrant a printing small enough not to last beyond this period, then the book should probably not be published or reprinted at all unless strong secondary motives exist for doing so or the sponsor is a not-for-profit publisher performing a service for scholarship or culture.

What usually makes sense then is a modest first printing, permitting the publisher to watch a title's performance before making a larger commitment with well-laid plans for running a fast reprint when and if it becomes needed. If, as so often happens, a book sells well below expectations, such a first printing may then be just sufficient or at least it will not be a major disaster which would only aggravate the losses already incurred on the fixed publishing expenses of the project.

Part of the loss that can be thus prevented would involve paper. In estimating paper consumption, the number of forms (aggregate of pages printed on one side of a press sheet) must be calculated, divided by two (as there are forms printed on each side of the sheet), and then multiplied by the number of planned impressions. As some of the stock will be wasted in printing and binding, an allowance for spoilage must be added in accordance with specified industry standards. Tables furnished by paper houses show ream weight of papers in various grades and sizes, and as paper is sold by weight its costs can be calculated accordingly. Permanent paper and free sheets are more costly than groundwood, coated papers more expensive than antique- or machine-finish stock, paper with rag content the most expensive of all.

Most book papers run in the 45 to 50 cents per pound range. Savings are realized in buying paper by the carload. If the printer is asked to furnish the paper a markup of 5 to 10 percent is added to the firm's cost of the stock. Smaller publishers who cannot command sufficient purchasing power to work advantageously with the paper houses directly may find it worthwhile to deal with paper merchants who represent several mills.

When it comes to binding cost, the biggest portion lies in folding, gathering, sewing, or adhesive binding, not in casing-in, i.e., attaching covers. For this reason—and since printing costs remain the same irrespective of the type of binding employed—the variable manufacturing costs (paper, printing, and binding) of trade paperbacks is almost as great as that of hardbacks. (Only the fact that they can be sold in larger volume and carry a reduced royalty and often a lower fixed cost makes it possible, therefore, to sell such paperbacks profitably.)

Smyth-sewing is more expensive than notch or perfect binding. Case binding varies in cost with the cover materials employed, with high-grade cloths like buckram involving far greater expense than plastic or impregnated paper substitutes. Little luxuries like top stain and head- and footbands also add to the budget but do enough to dress up a book so that they are usually employed in quality production. Two-color jackets or covers are cheaper than three-color and certainly far less expensive than four-color process covers. Lamination of covers is more costly than the application of an ultraviolet coating while on the press; however, the use of coated coverstocks with high ink absorbency often makes even the application of UVC unnecessary.

As a compromise measure some publishers succumbing to the temptation of overprinting a title's initial run hold some of the printed sheets, binding only a portion of them. While this method may have some advantages over binding up an excessive inventory in its entirety, it may be better still not even to print the extra sheets. To begin with, sheets that are held flat on skids (i.e., stacked on movable platforms) are often damaged in transit or storage. If they are partially bound (folded, gathered, and sewn with endpapers attached) the largest portion of the binding cost will have been incurred anyway and little saving realized.

In the terminology of the trade as defined in AAP surveys, fixed or nonrecurring manufacturing costs (typesetting, artwork, negatives, and/or plates and binding dies) are known as "plant costs." Those that recur in reprinting (paper, printing, and binding) are called "running costs." (Offset plates that are used only once for a particular printing are considered to be running costs; deep-etched plates that can be used repeatedly are classified as plant costs.)

Scheduling

The production of a book from edited manuscript to finished product may take as long as a year. Trade books usually take no more than seven or eight months, but complicated texts and professional and scholarly works necessarily consume more time. There is the exception of the "instant" book of course: a topical work on a "hot" subject which can be manufactured on a crash basis in one or two months. To do so requires very special and costly arrangements, however, which would not be possible except under very special circumstances.

Why does it take so long? Because of the series of cumbersome steps that must be taken before the book is ready for sale. The process begins with the designing of the book and, often, the ordering of sample pages from the compositor. The design must be reviewed and approved, decisions must be made regarding processes and suppliers, and a definite schedule must be prepared. This schedule will allow for the time needed to set the text and prepare any missing illustrations, for first proofs to be read by editors and author, for corrections to be made by the compositor, for final proofs to be read by editors and author, and for the index to be prepared. Only then can reproduction proofs be furnished. Negatives and plates need to be made, arrangements for paper must be completed, all before the presses can roll. Press time itself is not always easy to come by, particularly if one has in mind to use certain equipment, and there are long waiting lists for some presses. Finally books must be bound and jacketed. In the case of trade books, an allowance of up to two months must be added before publication date to permit the distribution of review copies and allow shipments to reach bookstores.

It is a lot easier to prepare a schedule, furthermore, than to keep one. When the manufacturing timetable is first formulated, the production department will agree with the editor on the specific dates by which proofs are to be furnished and returned. The editor in turn will advise the author and elicit a commitment from him or her regarding these dates. Predicated on these firm promises, press and bindery schedules are set and manufacturers reserve time on their equipment for the title in question. Far too often, however, editors and authors fail to live up to their commitments. The result is that the book loses its turn on the manufacturer's docket, must be rescheduled, and a delay of days in returning proofs can lead to a delay of weeks in getting on to a printing press or into a bindery.

Some editors and authors appear to have little sense of time and to remain insensitive to the pleadings of production and marketing managers about the absolute necessity of keeping schedules. Authors particularly, though they may be vocal about what they regard as the unconscionably long periods it takes to move their manuscripts into print, fail to realize that their own sins of commission and omission are often the chief instruments of demolishing a carefully worked out timetable. The bane of a publisher's existence are authors who insist on rewriting a book in proof. Though the contract usually specifies that any alteration costs in excess of 10 percent of the original setting expense will be charged to the authors, they may ignore this item and make such extensive changes that the time required to correct—really to reset—the proofs is totally beyond any reasonable allowance that can be built into the schedule.

There are other reasons why schedules fail, such as delays in receiving ordered paper or binding materials, failures by printers and binders to meet their commitments, and inefficiency on the part of production people themselves. In any case, sales departments and booksellers tend to view announced publication dates with skepticism, and delays often have unfortunate effects on promotion plans and on the market success of the books in question.

If industry performance on routine schedules is sometimes less than enviable, the virtuosity, skill, ingenuity, and determination of publishers who produce instant books are therefore all the more admirable. Such events call for total rapport between author and editor, superlative planning by the production manager, perfect coordination of the manufacturing process, and all the cajoling and sweet-talking of suppliers that may be needed and that long-established and valued personal relationships make possible. Sometimes the editor takes up residence at the typesetter to work on proofs as they come off the machines and to check any necessary changes with the author by telephone. A special emissary from the production department may stand by the presses as the books runs to lend moral support and to emphasize the stake the house has in the crash program. The process is costly—but it works. And perhaps it teaches us something about ways in which even normal schedules could be improved.

Imports

Not every book published in this country is manufactured here. We alluded earlier to the occasional desirability of printing certain books abroad. In addition economies can be achieved by joining a foreign publisher in its pressrun (sharing rather than duplicating its fixed manufacturing costs, in other words), thus making even a small import economically feasible. Many trade, professional, and scholarly publishers import titles which have been printed for them abroad, sometimes acquiring fully bound and jacketed books, at other times sheets which are then bound stateside.

V

How Books Are Marketed

No matter how carefully selected, meticulously edited, or attractively produced a book may be it will not achieve its purpose nor will a publishing house achieve its goal unless the book reaches its intended consumer. What the publisher does in marketing and distributing the product is as vital to success as the editorial and production efforts.

Myth and Reality

Marketing has long been the industry's weakest link. This has been true less of textbook and professional publishing, where markets are on the whole clearly defined, accessible, and well developed, than of consumer publishing where the audience is vast, complex, fragmented, and dispersed. In the consumer field a great potential has remained largely unrealized because mainstream publishers—particularly trade houses—have not been able to rise to the challenges posed by today's pluralistic marketplace.

Traditional publishers have failed on two counts: first, by neglecting to inform themselves adequately about the highly diverse, rapidly changing consumer universe; and second, by failing to employ the contemporary techniques and tools available for reaching fragmented audiences. In both instances publishers were inhibited from pursuing the proper course by "seductive myths and random impressions" inherited from the 1920s, which as Ann Orlov rightly observed often "operate as self-fulfilling prophecies."

When publishers believe that marketing consists simply of persuading as many booksellers as they can to stock as many of their books as possible, other aspects of the complex task of bringing book and interested reader together are bound to be neglected. There will be little discrimination about the enormous diversity of titles and markets, about the substantial differences that characterize various booksellers, or about the advantages of alternative approaches, such as direct mail. When publishers believe, furthermore, that to publicize books all they need to do is distribute review copies and run a few ads in national review media, numberless opportunities for gaining the attention of the specialized audiences that buy most books are lost.

Publishers substituting myth for reality not only neglect to engage in consumer research themselves but tend to ignore research done by others. In 1978 and 1983, the Book Industry Study Group sponsored major Consumer Research Studies on Reading and Book Purchasing which inquired into the leisure-time, reading, and book-buying practices of Americans. While far from exhausting the subject, or even adequately making up for nearly a century of neglect, these studies did furnish a valuable statistical framework on which marketing strategies and further research could be based. Yet they appear not to have had an appreciable impact on mainstream trade-marketing theory or practice.

The BISG studies confirm the existence of a vast number of small consumer markets. The complex interaction of readers' native endowments and interests, cultural backgrounds, occupation, financial circumstances, and social ties create such diversity as to make every reader almost unique. Readers do share interests, of course, some broadly popular, others quite narrow and specialized. Commonly the same reader will entertain a number of interests. A woman executive may read books on management to advance herself professionally, books on health for her well-being, books on political and social issues out of civic concern, books on music and art to satisfy her creative interests, books on tennis to improve her game, books on rearing children in her role as a mother, and popular fiction to unwind and have some fun. At one and the same time she is a reader of professional books, health books, books on world affairs, high culture, sports, and homemaking, as well as of best-selling fiction. Most of her interests are shared by millions of other readers, but her tastes in art and music may be quite esoteric and her professional reading, though broad in some areas, may be quite specialized in others.

The small audiences created by the multiplicity of human interests increase in size when a subject is intrinsically popular, or when a title appeals to more than one audience—as a statesman's biography might appeal to historical, political, and biographical preferences—or when an author's superior gifts attract readers to a topic they might not normally pursue. Very few titles appeal to all types of readers. Even mass market and best-seller audiences are limited in number and, as we have observed, normally represent only a modest fraction of the total population.

Only about half that population buys books to begin with. However, the average annual purchases of those who do buy books has increased by 337 percent in dollars and 27 percent in numbers of books purchased during the past fifteen years, from $20.96 for eleven books in 1972, to $91.63 for fourteen books in 1987. By my estimates, in 1987 90 percent of the purchases were made by "core" buyers, who purchased more than one book per month, and who constitute 60 percent of all book buyers. Another 8 percent of the purchases were made by occasional buyers, who purchased between three and four books during the year, and who represent 25 percent of all book buyers. The remaining 2 percent were purchased by occasional buyers, who purchased one or two books in the course of the year, and who represent 15 percent of all buyers.

Most of the popular and nearly all of the specialized books sold to consumers are bought by core buyers. Occasional buyers tend to concentrate on popular books, and rare buyers generally purchase only the most widely discussed best-sellers, or buy books as gifts for others. Core buyers tend to be true addicts, purchasing books through thick and thin, good times and bad. Occasional and rare buyers, on the other hand, apparently can take books or leave them and tend to fall by the wayside in times of economic turndown. As a result, the most popular books, which are favored by occasional and rare buyers, become very vulnerable during recessions, as do the large publishers who usually release them. On the other hand, small presses producing specialized titles for faithful core audiences may hardly feel the impact of an economic decline. On the whole, the book industry is less vulnerable to recessions than many other consumer industries; however, its most popular products may be as much or more affected by bad times than other mass commodities.

The demographics of book buyers are revealing. Overall, the 1983 BISG study found, 60 percent were women, 40 percent were men, 62 percent were under forty years of age, and 66 percent earned less than $40,000 in 1983. (However, in the interim, average age and earnings levels probably rose when the baby boom generation entered the over-forty age bracket and experienced characteristic increases in income as a result.) In 1983, 54 percent had only a high school education or less, 22 percent had some college, and 24 percent had a college education or more. (Given national trends, the better-educated groups have probably gained some ground since.) Less than half were employed (33 percent white collar, 15 percent blue collar), the rest consisted of women at home and retired and non-employed individuals (38 percent) and students (11 percent). The percentage of readers is significantly higher in the West (59 percent) than in other regions of the country (47–49 percent). The study found that book readers purchase about half of the books they read; the rest are borrowed from friends and libraries.

"Heavy" readers, who read twenty-six or more books over a six-month period, represented 34 percent of all readers. Compared to the total reading population, they included a higher proportion of female readers, a considerably larger proportion of readers below forty, more college-educated, more white-collar, and more nonemployed readers.

Purchase sources cited by book buyers included bookstores (64 percent total, 26 percent chain, 16 percent college, 14 percent independent, 5 percent religious, 3 percent secondhand), mass market and other retail outlets (22 percent), book clubs (9 percent), and direct mail (5 percent). Factors cited by buyers as most significant in their decision to purchase were: (1) a book's subject, (2) recommendation of friends, (3) price of book, (4) author's reputation, (5) jacket copy, (6) review in newspaper or magazine, (7) book based on movie/TV show, (8) pages from book sampled, (9) author's TV/radio interview, (10) book sale-priced. Advertising and cover art received surprisingly little mention, and recency of publication or even best-seller status seemed not to carry much weight.

The BISG study also compared the leisure-time habits of book readers with those of the population as a whole and found readers to be generally more active and involved. Proportionately more book readers watch TV, listen to the radio, spend time with their families, listen to music, socialize, bake and cook, exercise, play cards, attend meetings, engage in sports, go to the theater, and attend museums than people in the general population. Heavy readers, particularly, appear to lead very full lives.

Book for book, small presses have been more successful than mainstream houses in marketing to consumers. A number of factors have worked in their favor: their lists are usually specialized rather than broadly popular; they know their audience and are often among its members; they place great emphasis on the importance of marketing and work hard at it; they have been supported only by interested and committed retailers, giving them a more productive bookstore sale while forcing them to explore alternative approaches such as direct mail; and they work closely with authors in generating imaginative and effective publicity. By their successful efforts, small presses have exploded many of the myths the industry has cherished for nearly a century. Yet discredited or not, there is little indication that mainstream houses are ready to abandon the revered tradition.

In the following pages we shall examine the industry's markets in some detail and discover how effectively traditional as well as new approaches are succeeding in bringing books to readers and readers to books.

RETAIL OUTLETS

Bookstores

According to Bowker's *American Tradebook Directory,* there were 21,819 booksellers in the U.S. in 1987. Of these, 6,383 were general book dealers, 5,774 were branches of chains and franchises, 582 were department store book departments, 2,993 were college stores, 12,689 handled new hardcover books, 13,378 carried paperbacks, 8,505 stocked juveniles, 3,900 sold religious books, and 1,297 were antiquarian book dealers. Also, 8,372 carried an inventory of between 1,000 and 5,000 titles, 5,970 carried between 5,000 and 10,000 titles, 4,366 stocked over 10,000 titles, 3,961 had book sales of less than $50,000 a year, 5,781 enjoyed sales of between $50,000 and $100,000, 3,773 had sales between $100,000 and $250,000, 1,898 produced sales between $250,000 and $500,000, 925 recorded sales between $500,000 and $1,000,000, and 416 achieved sales over $1,000,000. No doubt some of the low-volume producers carried books only as a sideline.

Like publishing, bookselling has undergone significant changes in the last forty years. Following World War II, the general field was dominated by department store book departments and mom-and-pop stores. The department store sector included some very sizable installations, notably at Macy's in New York, Marshall Field's in Chicago, Hudson's in Detroit, and the Dayton Company in Minneapolis. There were also large numbers of leased departments and rental libraries operated by national firms, such as Carl K. Wilson and the Walden Book Company. The rest of the field consisted of independents, some large like Brentano's and Scribner's in New York, Kroch's & Brentano's in Chicago, and John G. Kidd in Cincinnati, but most others small and family owned and operated.

No less than in today's struggle between independents and the national bookstore chains, there was often friction between independents and department store people, or more accurately between the "bookish" and the "merchandisers." Many of the independents held the elitist view that books should be the exclusive preserve of intellectuals and the literati, considered popular writing "trash," and were willing to tolerate mass literature only because its sales helped keep their stores open. They looked down upon retailers who to their minds were demeaning books by promoting them like toothpaste or soap. They were particularly enraged at stores that discounted books. Following a celebrated price war between Macy's and other New York department stores, during which Random House's Modern Library was offered for as low as nine cents a copy, independent booksellers successfully supported price-protection legislation, which was only declared unconstitutional many years later.

Expectably, these booksellers also feared and resented book clubs and were greatly disturbed by the emergence of mass market paperbacks, which many stores at first refused to stock. A wave of successful cartoon books during the 1950s so distressed ABA members that it took the full eloquence of the late Frederick G. Melcher, publisher of *Publishers Weekly*, to restrain an annual convention from voting that such titles should be excluded from national best-seller lists.

While many trade publishers and editors, then and now, shared these elitist sentiments, the more populist houses favored the merchandising approach. Simon & Schuster, part owner of Pocket Books, introduced the magazine-style returns concept to books when it offered booksellers a 100 percent returns privilege on the paper-covered edition of Wendell Willkie's *One World*. Despite dire warnings from conservative publishers and booksellers that the returns privilege would prove self-defeating, the practice took hold, became almost universally accepted, and although it undoubtedly played a positive role in the industry's expansion, soon got out of hand.

Through the 1950s, bookstores had been located primarily in the business districts of larger cities. However, as the suburbs grew, branches of downtown stores as well as new bookstores began to open in outlying areas. Soon analysts at Dayton-Hudson Corporation, one of the nation's largest retail conglomerates, concluded that books would be one of the fastest growing retail commodities in the second half of the twentieth century. As a result, Dayton-Hudson launched B. Dalton Bookseller, a chain of bookstores located in major shopping malls throughout the country. At first the venture was not successful. Reeking dignity and prestige, the dimly lit Dalton stores housed only a few fixtures with understated displays of best-sellers, cookbooks, Bibles, and dictionaries—hardly a temptation for book addicts, to say nothing of prospective converts. Discouraged, Dayton-Hudson was ready to give up, when it was approached by Louis Epstein, owner of the celebrated Pickwick Bookshops of Hollywood and Los Angeles, who was retiring and anxious to sell his successful business.

Halfheartedly, Dayton-Hudson executives decided to have a look at the famous Pickwick operation—and were flabbergasted. Pickwick's Hollywood store featured wall-to-wall books! Books everywhere: on tables and shelves, in alcoves and aisles, on the floor—literally everywhere. It was a browser's paradise! Anyone who loved books could not possibly settle for only one visit to Pickwick; they had to come back to explore that enormous treasury further.

Dayton-Hudson's management was astounded even more to learn how slowly, by their standards, Pickwick's inventory was turning. Yet the store was always full of browsers, few customers left without a purchase, and the operation was handsomely profitable. They saw the light: the secret of Pickwick's success was that its wide and varied inventory attracted and satisfied book buyers.

The conglomerate promptly bought Pickwick and hired its merchandise manager, Elliot Leonard, to help convert the entire Dalton chain to the Pickwick image. Other key positions were filled with experienced book people and, expanding rapidly, Dalton's became a solid success. Its flagship stores regularly stocked 30,000 titles.

The proliferation of shopping malls was putting a damper on the volume of downtown department stores, including their book departments. Soon Walden Book Company decided to curtail its department store lease involvement and instead to launch a shopping center–based bookstore chain. Later acquired by Carter Hawley Hale Corporation, another retail conglomerate, the Waldenbooks chain featured a less-varied inventory than Dalton, with greater emphasis on popular titles, mass market paperbacks, and book bargains. In time both chains started book clubs, and Waldenbooks in particular published proprietary titles.

The hospitable climate that had propelled the expansion of the chains, also stimulated the opening of an unprecedented number of independent bookstores. Between 1972 and 1984, the number of booksellers in the U.S. more than doubled. The new crop of independents was very different from the old. Tougher, more businesslike, more pragmatically educated, these were members of a postwar generation that had grown up with cultural pluralism and democratized literature. In their outlook and approach they resembled the small-press entrepreneurs that were shortly to enter the industry in large numbers. Many of the stores they opened, particularly in the West and Southwest, scored outstanding successes and became leaders in the field.

But if the newcomers were more open-minded and better qualified than their older peers to succeed in bookselling, they still faced some formidable odds. Competition from the national chains, for one. Even though many of the independents expanded to become multiple store and even medium-sized chain operations, or joined national franchise organizations such as Little Professor Bookshops, they found it impossible to match the buying power and economies of scale the major chains enjoyed. Still they managed to avoid the fate of many of the older independents who had been driven out of business during the chain expansion because they operated in declining locations, selected their inventories according to their own preferences rather than those of their customers, or operated their stores in unbusinesslike fashion. Furthermore, this was a period of rampant inflation and high interest rates. However, the principal reason why the new booksellers found it difficult to prosper was the same that had haunted bookselling in the past: the surprisingly adversary attitude of trade publishers. Considering the fact that publishers were placing nearly all their marketing eggs in the bookseller basket, it was difficult to understand why they would be so opposed to granting retailers an adequate share of the revenue dollar. If we give booksellers more, they seemed to argue, we'll get less. Accordingly, publishers' discounts and terms to booksellers have traditionally hovered near starvation levels, barely enough to keep the peons alive. Booksellers have argued in vain that publishers would be the first to benefit from a healthier retail industry, gaining far more in increased earnings than they would have to invest in improved discounts and terms. Here as elsewhere, tradition retained its iron grip.

With the 1980s arrived yet another challenge to booksellers: discounting. As it had a half century earlier, the practice by some aggressive retailers to cut prices on best-sellers and other popular titles, threw the industry into a panic. The major discounters, such as Barnes & Noble and a new national chain, Crown Books, combined their price cutting with offering other bargains, notably publishers' overstock (remainders) at greatly reduced costs. The concept was far from new—remainders and cheap reprints had been promoted in various ways since the 1930s—but the advertising and publicity were pointed, the images created were novel, and the public responded enthusiastically to this welcome relief from inflated book prices. Most booksellers countered by discounting best-sellers themselves and by expanding bargain displays they had maintained all along. Independents, particularly, realized that the best way they could compete with this or any other challenge was by carrying the choicest inventory and providing the most satisfying service for their patrons of which they were capable. But the national chains were more vulnerable.

They were largely dependent on volume sales of popular titles for the high-level profits they were required to earn by their corporate managements. They could ill afford the margin losses best-seller discounting entailed.

If you can't beat them, join them. Dalton's decided to start a chain of discount stores of their own under the historic Pickwick label. It was an ill-fated venture, as were a number of other, similar attempts to establish bargain chains. Low margins, insufficient turnover, and high costs combined to rob investors of hoped-for profits. Those who tried discovered too late that bargain bookselling is a speciality with its own expertise, requirements, and pitfalls.

Carter Hawley Hale had earlier been struggling with corporate problems and, forced to sell off assets, had disposed of Walden Books to K-Mart. Now it was Dalton's turn. The Pickwick discount venture had failed, store expansion had slowed as suitable mall and central city locations had become occupied, the bookwise management team had left for greener pastures. The less-experienced executives now in charge once again threw up their hands at Dalton's low stockturn, ordered a drastic inventory reduction and imposed a strict open-to-buy regimen on the chain. Expectably sales plummeted. Before long, Dayton-Hudson sold the Dalton stores to Barnes & Noble.

In the meantime the small-press explosion had occurred. Initially the new publishers encountered great difficulty in trying to penetrate the retail market. Many were unfamiliar with the field, and booksellers were wary of dealing with unknown imprints. But as presses and, particularly, independent booksellers grew to know each other better, and as small publishers proliferated and some scored notable successes, the ice began to break. Soon publishers perceived the advantages of joining forces in approaching retailers, and a number of organizations of various size and shape sprang up representing groups of presses. On their side, independent booksellers perceived that they could gain a competitive edge by carrying titles the national chains tended largely to ignore.

Two principal characteristics distinguished small-press marketing from mainstream practice: (1) small presses, while eager to be represented in stores, also employed other methods, notably direct mail, to reach their readers; and (2) small presses refused to commit economic hara-kiri merely for the privilege of having their titles displayed in bookstores. Many small houses refused to consent to ruinous returns arrangements, and most were careful to deal only with stores seriously committed to selling specialized books.

The wisdom of the small-press approach becomes apparent when we consider the role bookstores play in the total process of distributing books to consumers. Bowker statistics indicate that most bookstores are small, both in sales volume and in the number of titles they carry. For example, 81 percent of the stores take in less than $250,000 a year; only 2.5 percent achieve sales levels of over $1 million; 76 percent carry fewer than 10,000 titles, 44 percent stock only from 1,000 to 5,000 titles. Considering that *Books in Print* lists over 750,000 titles, and that 50,000 new titles and editions are published yearly—about 40 percent of which are aimed at general consumers—it becomes obvious that most booksellers can stock only about 2 percent of the titles in which readers are conceivably interested. Even the few retailers who inventory 30,000 titles are only representing about 10 percent of the total.

Needless to say, this places a great burden of choice on retailers when they select their inventory. Depending on their character, location, and clientele, they will either emphasize mostly popular books, or both popular and specialized. In either case, they will have to choose the titles for which they expect to have the greatest demand. To do otherwise would be fair neither to themselves nor their customers.

Even the most specialized category includes better and poorer selling books. Not only because every specialty has its more broadly appealing as well as its more esoteric facets, but also because some titles are more authoritative, more competently written, or more enjoyable to read than others, or may be better produced, better publicized, or more favorably reviewed. Whatever the reason, booksellers will attempt to represent only titles with the greatest potential.

Furthermore, how successful a bookseller will be in selling specialized books will depend on a number of factors. The population base from which a store draws will be a key. In a large city or suburban area, or in a college town, the population may be sufficiently sizable, diversified, or sophisticated to support a solid selection of specialized books. Not so in a small factory town, where popular books may sell very well, but where the number of individuals interested in specialized titles may be too small to enable a retailer to stock them without incurring a loss.

Another factor will be a store's character and reputation. Book buyers with special interests will not bother to browse in a store that features popular books only, but will regularly frequent one that promotes the sort of titles they wish to buy. In fact, booksellers who develop a reputation for carrying specialized books often find that patrons come from far and wide to visit them, and place mail and telephone orders with them besides.

Nevertheless, it becomes obvious that barring a handful of notable exceptions, even successful and well-stocked booksellers can offer their customers only a small fraction of the popular and specialized titles available, and millions of readers do not have ready access to *any* store that stocks the books in which they are interested.

Figure 8 illustrates these conditions by reproducing a graph from my article "U.S. Retail Book Sales by Subject—A First Estimate," which initially appeared in the Winter 1986–87 issue of *Book Research Quarterly*. In the accompanying text, I stated in part:

The . . . graph shows 1985 unit book sales (number of copies sold) by U.S. General Retailers (i.e. retailers other than College Stores), bookstores, specialty stores, and mass market outlets. Sales have been separated according to subject categories, represented in the graph by cone-shaped triangles. This shape calls attention to the fact that each category is headed by a few well-selling titles, and that, as one descends from the apex of a category to its base, one finds the number of titles that are sold increasing, but the quantities in which they are sold decreasing. The total number of units is shown for each category (in millions) as is the category's percent share of all units sold by General Retailers (1.2 billion in 1985).

While the size of a cone is determined by the number of units in its category, the location of its apex depends on the category's ranking on the demand index shown at the left of the graph. The demand index is based on the percentage of total book readers reported to have read books in each category according to the Book Industry Study Group's *1983 Consumer Research Study on Reading and Book Purchasing*.

The category headings are characteristic of those often used by retailers to identify their section displays. Titles in the "Best-sellers" bracket, which have met the criteria for this classification established in *Publishers Weekly*, may be on any subject and would normally appear in one of the other sections.

The presentation illustrates the virtues as well as the limitations of bookstore distribution. Since most popular titles perform at the peak of their categories, even a small outlet, carrying fewer than 3,000 titles (note the broken horizontal line marked "3,000-title level") is able to stock them. As pictured in the graph, however, sales of most retail books occur below that level, a substantial number even below the "10,000-title level" that most outlets cannot accommodate. Furthermore, most sales of special-interest books, including literary fiction and poetry, occur below the 10,000-title level.

It is physically and economically impossible for any retailer to stock the 300,000 titles in print that might be of some interest to bookstore patrons. Only a handful of booksellers in the U.S. are large enough to accommodate even 50,000 titles, and the audiences for most specialized books, while large enough worldwide to enable the titles to succeed, are too small in most communities to support the bookseller's efforts adequately. Experience has demonstrated that a "horizontal" marketing approach, which utilizes booksellers exclusively, is usually not as effective in the distribution of specialized books, including literary titles, as is a "vertical" approach, aimed

Figure 8. Estimated Book Distribution Through U.S. General Retailers, 1985
(in millions of units and share of total units shown for each category)

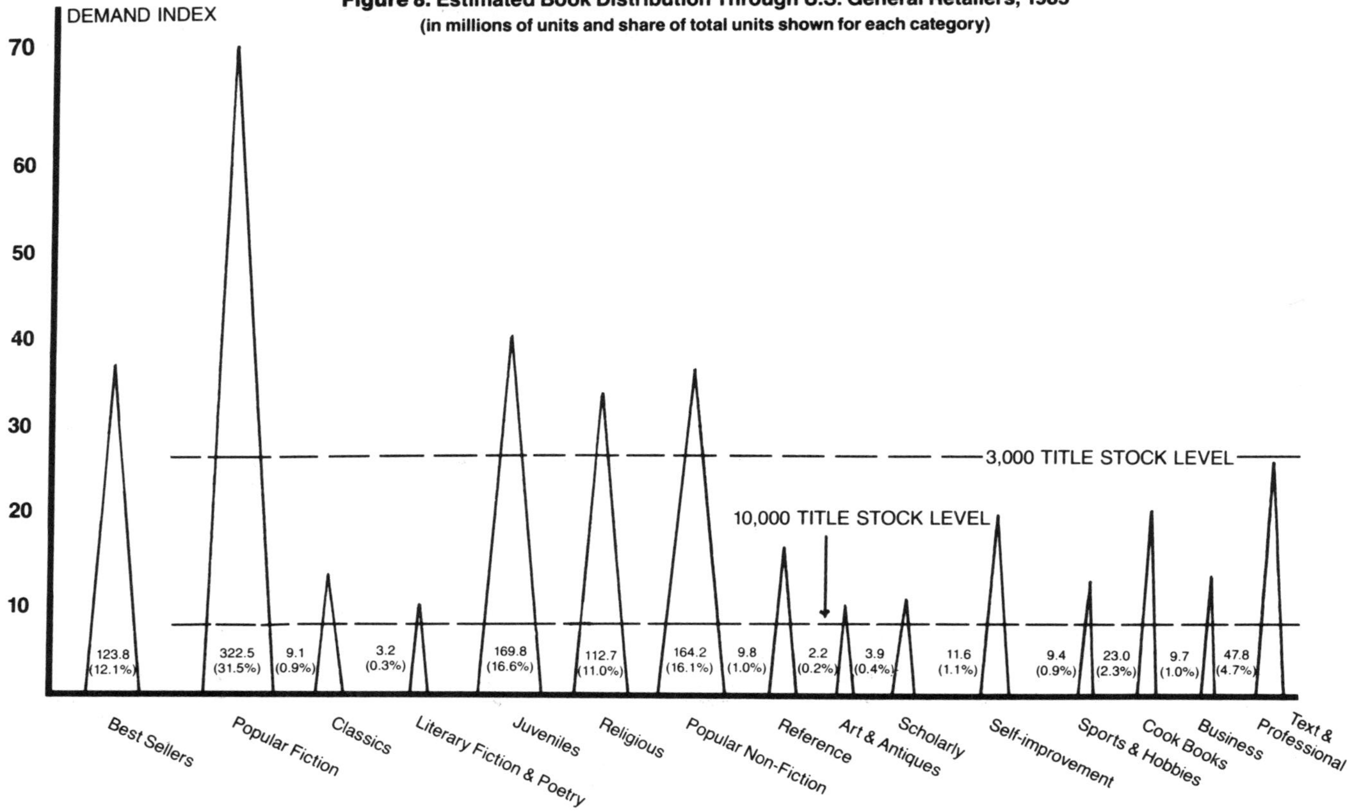

DEMAND INDEX

70
60
50
40
30
20
10

3,000 TITLE STOCK LEVEL

10,000 TITLE STOCK LEVEL

Text & Professional

Business
47.8
(4.7%)

Cook Books
9.7
(1.0%)

Sports & Hobbies
23.0
(2.3%)

Self-improvement
9.4
(0.9%)

Scholarly
11.6
(1.1%)

Art & Antiques
3.9
(0.4%)

Reference
2.2
(0.2%)

Popular Non-Fiction
9.8
(1.0%)

Religious
164.2
(16.1%)

Juveniles
112.7
(11.0%)

Literary Fiction & Poetry
169.8
(16.6%)

Classics
3.2
(0.3%)

Popular Fiction
9.1
(0.9%)

Best Sellers
322.5
(31.5%)

123.8
(12.1%)

directly at the interested audience through book clubs, direct mail, or other means.

Yet retail distribution in all its guises—bookstore as well as mass market— remains the most effective means of disseminating low and moderately priced popular books to consumers. The virtue of direct marketing—the ability to target a particular audience segment economically—is negated when the audience is general rather than fragmented, and therefore the cost of reaching it far outpaces the capacity of a title to return a profit from direct sales. (See the discussion on mail order selling on page 144.) In fact, many of the beliefs mainstream publishers hold about the sale of books through bookstores *do* apply to popular books, including the notion that such titles are doomed unless they succeed in retail outlets. Probably the most difficult consumer title to market—and the one it is least advisable to publish—is the trade book directed to a popular audience which is, however, not popular enough to attract the ready interest of booksellers, publishers' sales representatives, reviewers, and browsers. Unless such a title is supported by exceptionally skillful publicity, it is likely to die a quick, unlamented death.

How Publishers Market to Bookstores

Most books sold by bookstores are published by trade publishers, and with some exceptions the practices established by trade houses are followed by other industry segments—mass market paperback, religious, and scholarly publishers—in attempting to reach this market. Trade publishers cover their major bookstore customers primarily through personal sales calls, supplemented by mailings of catalogs and brochures—particularly to stores which because of their small size and out-of-the-way location cannot economically be covered in person. Publishers also advertise in the trade media, especially *Publishers Weekly*.

Large houses can justify maintaining their own sales force. Smaller houses either arrange to have their books distributed by larger houses or they engage "commission reps," salespeople in business for themselves who may represent as many as sixteen publishers. Sales territories vary in size and scope depending on a publisher's circumstances, but commonly the country is split up into "primary" and "secondary" areas, with the primary territories embracing the important stores in large metropolitan centers such as New York, Los Angeles, Boston, and Chicago, which require more time to cover and demand more experience and skill on the part of the traveler. Secondary territories are usually laid out by regions:

New England, the Middle Atlantic States, the Midwest, the Far West, the Southwest, and the South. A "commission rep" may cover a regional territory, primary as well as secondary accounts, alone or with the help of assistants. A house staff may number as many as a hundred representatives (or "travelers") nationwide, with several working in each region and with primary and secondary accounts assigned to suit the ability and effectiveness of individual representatives.

The frequency with which an account is visited depends on the size of a publisher's list and the importance and volume of the store. As there are two principal publishing seasons, spring and fall, most accounts are visited at least four times yearly: once in advance of each season to solicit orders for forthcoming titles and once during the season to take reorders and check stock. Some publishers have scheduled books for publication also during the summer which has led to some adjustments of sales schedules. In primary territories sales calls will be far more frequent, as often as monthly for major accounts. Chain stores do much of their buying centrally and require special attention.

To prepare the travelers for their task publishers engage in a time-honored ritual: the sales conference. All the representatives meet with the sales manager before seasonal trips and are given information and pep talks on forthcoming books. Editors often make presentations, authors are occasionally invited. The after-hours frolicking associated with these occasions makes them bearable, though not necessarily more effective; some representatives have difficulty staying awake while they are being assured that every book on the list is first-rate and will sell superbly if only the sales rep will apply himself or herself to promoting it. Each rep is given a sales kit consisting of jackets or covers, sample pages, illustrations, etc. (Too often jackets or covers are not ready on time, which can prove to be quite a handicap to the person on the road.) Backlist titles are sometimes discussed though not usually with great intensity or enthusiasm. Some houses assign quotas for total sales or individual new titles to their representatives, but as these quotas are sometimes very unrealistic they are not always taken too seriously. Some houses make proofs of outstanding titles available to their salespeople; it is not certain that they are always read.

The sales tool most reps find indispensable is the seasonal catalog. Even though copywriters sometimes substitute glowing adjectives for solid information, catalog blurbs usually give a summary of the book's content, information about the author, and some indication of the prospective market for the title. Good representatives know the accounts and are aware that they are effective only if they recommend to them titles which they can really sell. If the reps consistently recommend books that prove themselves by their performance, they will gain the confidence of their customers and make their recommendations heard over the years.

Buyers often complain that salespeople understand neither their store nor the books they are selling and often prove naive and untrustworthy in their recommendations. They are also often accused of being long-winded. A rep who insists on making a full presentation on every title in the catalog will soon lose the buyer's attention: the poor individual simply cannot command the required time and energy. So a good salesperson must "highspot," discussing only those books on the list which the store is likely to find successful. Every good sales manager knows this; so does every head of house. Still, most sales conferences insist on tiring, detailed discussions of every title on the schedule, and publishers continue to contract for books their representatives are unable to place in the market.

The terms which publishers extend to booksellers vary a good deal from house to house, so much so that the American Booksellers Association annually publishes the *ABA Book Buyer's Handbook,* a loose-leaf guide designed to keep its members abreast of an unbelievably complicated mass of discount schedules and returns policies. In general, however, trade books in quantities of five or more assorted copies are sold to retailers at a discount of 40 percent off the list price and publishers offer larger discounts on quantity purchases—such as 42 percent on 50 assorted and 43 percent on 100 assorted books.

Once booksellers were required to pay all transportation charges but many publishers now share or foot these costs to varying degrees. The privilege of shipping unsold books back to the publisher for credit was once the almost universal practice; returns are now refused totally by some houses—or limited more strictly than heretofore—in exchange for more favorable discounts designed to enable a retailer to take its own markdowns on leftover stock. Purchasing unsalable stock on the promise of return had trapped many booksellers into loading up their inventory with potentially "big" books rather than tailoring their stock to customers' demands. However, the personnel, transportation, and other costs associated with returning books to publishers can be so staggering that one marvels that the old returns system has managed to survive at all.

Perhaps more booksellers will learn to appreciate what even a slow but steadily selling basic stock inventory can do for them. Fortunately there are still some publishers and booksellers who are convinced of the economic and cultural advantages of a good backlist and the sales people of such publishers carefully check stock when they visit their customers to make certain that missing titles are replenished. Particularly publishers with paperback series are alert to this opportunity. A well-managed store, furthermore, maintains effective inventory control, a requirement that can be met with increasing facility in this computerized age.

Yet the book industry as a whole, which has had as ready access to computers as have the many other industries, which have successfully dealt with their distribution problems, has failed thus far to develop a system that would effectively link retail inventory control with publishers' and wholesalers' order processing and shipping procedures. What could be more logical than to utilize a standard stock control and order form at retailers which would be machine-readable (utilizing the Numbering System already in existence) and which would help make all inventory control, billing, and shipping documents compatible within the industry—a feat that could be accomplished no matter what computer equipment an individual retailer, wholesaler, or publisher might now be using? A number of efforts to achieve this objective at least partially have gone forward and failed in short order. Some programs still functioning are AAP's PUBNET, involving mostly college stores, and the BISAC Committee of BISG staffed by Sandra K. Paul. Despite these efforts, the industry remains largely in the dark ages when it comes to utilizing available technology or updating its creaky distribution machinery.

Nowhere is this failure of the industry to deal effectively with its ordering and fulfillment problems more troublesome than in the processing of special orders. Obviously, a bookseller cannot stock everything published and has to special-order a great many titles in order to keep customers happy. These days it seems that to accept a special order may be the quickest way of making a customer unhappy. Shipments, even status reports, appear to take weeks if not months to process. Customers complain that they have placed special orders, for which they may even have paid in advance, only to learn four or five weeks later that the book is out of print or out of stock at the publisher. Such orders are also usually very costly for bookseller and publisher to deal with—labor, machine time, and materials exceeding the gross profit margins of the transaction. Although ABA sponsors the Single Title Order Plan (STOP) whereby special orders are prepaid by booksellers and in return are given a "trade" discount (40 percent) rather than the usual "short" (20 percent) discount applicable to single books, this plan has not significantly improved publishers' service, promptness of delivery, or the economics of the special-order process. Industrywide cooperation of some sort appears to be the answer. Although a number of plans have been forwarded, the industry has thus far failed to take action.

If publishers are often not very effective in selling or delivering their books to stores they do try to give retailers some support at least on the "big" titles they buy. Publishers' general publicity and advertising efforts, resulting in national review coverage, the appearance of authors on TV, and similar exposure, are mainly designed to benefit booksellers. Publishers also offer dealers cooperative advertising (i.e., the publisher pays for 50 or 75 percent of an ad which is run locally over the bookseller's name) and they arrange for authors' autographing parties in leading stores.

While publishers other than trade houses will follow trade practices to some degree when marketing to bookstores, publishers of professional books are the exception, for they have had to develop policies that reflect the special circumstances of technical, scientific, business, medical, and other professional books. As such books are usually addressed to quite limited and specific audiences and represent very substantial editorial and manufacturing investments by the publishers, they are higher priced than trade titles and are offered to dealers at "short" discounts of 20 to 25 percent. Professional publishers whose lists lend themselves particularly to retail distribution often offer dealers a special "agency" plan whereby the retailer can earn a better (though still short) discount of 30 to 35 percent on the most salable titles provided he agrees to keep a reasonable selection of them in stock at all times.

Discounts are an emotional issue in the book trade. For years booksellers have complained even about trade discounts which they claim are inadequate (as they no doubt are) and have shown themselves reluctant to stock books offered at short discount. As a result, many stores that could enjoy success with professional books do not carry them, depriving themselves of good earnings and their customers of a service that is sorely needed.

The economic argument booksellers use against short-discount books does not hold water. What matters in retailing is the dollar yield of a transaction; discount is only one factor contributing to profit—list price, turnover, and applicable operating cost are at least as significant. If in a week's time I can sell two copies of a ten-dollar trade book on which 40 percent discount allows me a margin of $8.00 before transportation and operating expenses, I am not as well off as I am if during the same period I sell one professional book listing at $50 at a 20 percent discount, which makes my margin before costs $10! If, as is likely, in addition I have heavier handling and higher personnel, storage, and promotional costs on trade than on professional books, and am receiving an agency discount on the professional titles, I may find that I can actually make more money on specialized books at short discount than on trade books at full discount. (See "How to Make a Profit in Bookselling," by John P. Dessauer, *Publishers Weekly,* April 2, 9, 16, 1973.)

Not every bookstore can count on a sufficiently large professional clientele to succeed in this area, of course, just as some dealers cannot command enough patrons to support a diversified inventory. One must have a solid and congenial population base to succeed as a specialty bookseller. Nevertheless many opportunities for such ventures are lost today mainly because dealers lack the knowledge and skill to make them go.

Mass Market Outlets

It is difficult to determine exactly how many mass market outlets exist in the United States. There are the 90,000 outlets served by magazine wholesalers, most of which are newsstands and drugstores but which also include bookstores, department stores, and college and school stores. In addition there are the chain stores, such as Woolworth's, which usually buy directly from publishers. In all, there are probably 110,000 retail locations at which books are sold, and of these some 95,000 are exclusively mass market outlets as distinguished from traditional trade stores.

These mass outlets are cultivated by paperback and certain children's book publishers. Field salespeople are used even in territories where wholesalers affect the actual distribution; publishers feel they must supplement wholesalers' efforts to ensure that their books receive the proper exposure. Such coverage is of a service nature: checking stock, making certain that important titles are effectively displayed, ascertaining that the wholesaler is supplying inventory when needed. Needless to say, field personnel are likely to concentrate on leading best-selling titles; their pinpointed efforts cannot practically be spread to an entire list—even if there were enough room in the stores to display all the books on the list.

In addition to those served by wholesalers, there are mass outlets to which publishers sell directly, such as variety, five-and-dime, drugstore, and supermarket chains. These operations usually buy centrally, are highly selective, and because of their considerable purchasing power receive favorable discounts and terms. It is customary throughout the mass market for the publisher to furnish display racks or rack allowances to house its books, and featured titles are often shipped in prepacked display cartons known as "dump bins." The chains frequently prefer to buy such package arrangements, highspotting titles rather than attempting to offer their customers a wide variety. Given the nature of these stores and the way they must normally operate, this approach makes sense for both chain and publisher.

BOOK CLUBS

Experts on retail merchandising often refer to the present era as the age of direct marketing. Indeed the various techniques of reaching the consumer directly—personal visits, mailings, telephone selling—have been greatly perfected in recent decades. A number of factors are contributing to the advance of direct marketing: increased affluence which is making the indulgence of specialized tastes more feasible and is increasing the consumer's purchasing power; the movement of affluent consumers to the suburbs resulting in more home-centered life-styles; and, finally, the sheer convenience and comfort of shopping from one's armchair.

Not that direct selling, particularly in rural areas, is a new concept. Some of the most successful retailing enterprises in the United States, such as Sears Roebuck and J. C. Penney, have grown to size and eminence by employing, even inventing, some of the direct marketing methods in use today. The direct selling of books enjoys a similar time-honored tradition: companies such as Doubleday pioneered direct mail to the consumer early in this century, and, for decades, encyclopedia publishers have employed sales representatives to call on homes.

When the Book-of-the-Month Club and the Literary Guild were founded in the midtwenties they became instantly successful. Even then many people interested in books did not have ready access to bookstores or were unable to find what they were looking for in their local book outlet. Even then too many books were published, making it difficult for a reader to learn about new titles and to make satisfying choices from the flood. The clubs promised to advise their members about the newest and best and to choose on their behalf. They also offered inducements: free books and substantial savings on selections.

Fundamentally the attractions of book clubs are still the same today, and subscribers still look to clubs for information about significant new books and for the opportunity to buy them conveniently at attractive savings. But the scope and complexity of book clubs have grown. Members are no longer satisfied to accept without question a single monthly selection or even a single alternate: they want a wider variety of titles from which to choose. Also, in response to the steady trend toward specialization, books clubs have become diversified, and many now cater to special classes of readers or to subject interest groups. Furthermore, the book club vehicle has proved to be adaptable to the professional market as well, and a substantial number of clubs now cater to peoples' work interests.

The Book-of-the-Month Club and Doubleday's Literary Guild appeal to the broadest consumer market, as does Doubleday's Bargain Book Club and the Reader's Digest Book Club. Specialized consumer clubs include the Garden Book Club, How-To Book Club, American Artist Book Club, Book Club for Poetry, Catholic Book Club, Classics Club, Conservative Book Club, Cookery Book Club, Detective Book Club, the Ecological Book Club, Evangelical Book Club, the Erotic Art Book Society, History

Book Club (Harcourt Brace Jovanovich), The Limited Editions Club, Military Book Club (Doubleday), The Movie/Entertainment Book Club, Nostalgia Book Club, Outdoor Life Book Club (Popular Science), as well as several clubs for children and students.

In the professional area are a number of clubs operated by McGraw-Hill (Chemical Engineers Book Club, Civil Engineers Book Club, among others), by Macmillan (including Behavioral Science Book Service, Small Computer Book Club, Natural Science Book Club, and the Library of Science), and by Simon & Schuster/Prentice-Hall (Behavioral Book Institute, Technical Book Clubs and Management Clubs).

While the terms of membership and operating methods of clubs vary widely, there are some common features: members are enticed to join by offers of free books or of books at nominal cost, in return for which they commit themselves to the purchase of a minimal number of books for a specified period, although this requirement has been dropped by some clubs. After members have fulfilled their obligation they are encouraged to remain in the club by offers of additional free or nominally priced books every time they make a further purchase. Most clubs work on a shorter cycle rather than on a full calendar month, giving them up to fifteen instead of only twelve selection periods a year. In advance of each cycle members receive a brochure announcing new selections, alternates, and other available books together with a notice that the prime selection will be shipped automatically unless they advise the club by a certain date that another book is wanted instead or no book at all.

This device, which assumes that members agree to select a selection unless they specify otherwise, is known as "negative option" and has occasionally come under fire from consumer groups. So far, however, book clubs seem to have persuaded their critics that the negative option practice, while subject to possible abuses, is fundamentally sound and necessary if book clubs are to survive. The clubs argue that they cannot plan their printings and distribution, and therefore operate efficiently, unless they can establish in advance how many members will accept a selection or alternate. Without the device of negative option many members will not respond on time or will not respond at all to selection announcements. Clubs admit that errors have been made and that members have received unwanted books; that it is a nuisance for members to ship the books back or to have to refuse them; that it is a nightmare for them to be dunned repeatedly or even threatened with legal action for not paying for books they never wanted or had returned. Clubs acknowledge that service personnel are often careless and indifferent even to members' angry or pleading letters, and that controls are necessary to prevent such occurrences.

On the other hand, the economic argument advanced by book clubs appears fundamentally sound, for they can prosper only if their members buy a sufficient number of books. A club must balance the investment in its members—the advertising cost of acquiring them, the cost of books in the introductory offer, and the cost of books purchased, as well as the cost of serving the account—against the income realized through purchases. Members who quit prematurely without buying the agreed-upon number of books may well create a loss for the club. Conversely members who remain active for many years and are faithful in buying titles are a great asset. Experience has shown that professional and specialized consumer clubs enroll members at smaller cost, retain them longer, and sell more books to them than do general consumer clubs. On the other hand, general consumer clubs enroll many more members and benefit from the economic advantages of large size and volume production.

All book clubs enjoy certain cost advantages. When they contract for the rights to a title they usually arrange to print an edition from the publisher's negatives or plates, even joining the publisher's press run in some cases. Thus they avoid all plant and editorial expenses and need only defray the running costs of their edition. Some clubs economize considerably in preparing their printings, furthermore, using cheaper paper, narrower margins, and less costly bindings than the publisher (often to the distress of members who are not enthusiastic about such skimping on the book's design).

Book clubs pay the publisher a royalty on their sales—usually 10 percent of the club price on books sold and 5 percent on copies given away—and the larger clubs offer substantial guarantees, running as high as $500,000 or more on major titles. Smaller or more specialized clubs will usually pay a guarantee coresponding to anticipated royalties from the initial distribution of their edition.

Recruiting of new members is carefully planned, and the results of campaigns are imaginatively analyzed. The major clubs, which advertise regularly in newspapers and magazines and make promotional mailings, have compiled records not only establishing the number of members a certain promotional effort has produced but relating the members' performance and productivity to the medium through which they were obtained. Book clubs are thus able to evaluate the effectiveness of various promotional approaches and to plan their investment in ads and offers with genuine skill.

Important though book clubs are in the general distribution pattern of the industry, they have recently lost ground to bookstores whose expansion and discounting practices have cut significantly into the clubs' appeal to consumers.

MAIL ORDER

Some distinctions must be made again at the outset of this discussion of mail order bookselling. First—some books are designed and published primarily for marketing by mail to the general consumer (and are defined in AAP terminology as "Mail Order Publications"). Many other books, notably specialized consumers, professional and scholarly titles, though widely sold by mail are not specifically and predominantly so planned. Second—quite a few retail bookstores and mail order houses market books by mail just as publishers do. However, because the retailers' method and approach are very similar to those employed by publishers, we shall not discuss their activites separately.

Mail Order Publishing

Mail order publishing has a mystique all its own. Invented by mass magazine publishers, it deals in numbers that leave the traditional publisher breathless: mailings in the millions, sales in the hundreds of thousands, prices that often hover around $50 for single books or a hundred dollars or more for series or sets. Editorial and plant investments are staggering. It is a game for big operators which in its own way has revolutionized the industry as much as the paperbacks have. And we have barely seen its beginnings, with much of the potential of the new technique as yet unrealized.

Like book club selling, mail order publishing is limited to widely popular subjects and requires a big price tag or multiple purchases by consumers for financial success. Its leading practitioners, such as Time, Inc., Reader's Digest, Meredith, and American Heritage, plan and create their own products, usually after careful market research. However, before actually launching the writing of the text and assemblage of illustrations—normally done by an in-house staff supported by outside experts—a beautiful brochure is prepared, featuring sample mock-up pages and color plates from the proposed book. This brochure, with covering sales letter, reply order card, and an occasional gimmick or two, is test-mailed to a representative list of prospective purchasers and the replies are carefully analyzed. The test serves not only to establish the likely acceptance of the product but the effectiveness of various promotional approaches: advance price savings, different types of brochures, order forms, stamps to lick instead of signing cards, etc. The test, or "split test" when more than one promotional approach is being tried, will determine whether or not the book will be published as planned or modified, and how it will be promoted to its full audience.

Publishers rely primarily on the circulation lists of their own magazines and on the buyers' lists of previous products to reach that audience. Promoted are either "continuity programs" (sets or series which the customer agrees to receive a volume at a time with the option of discontinuing any time he or she wishes), or single titles or catalog sales (i.e., titles selected from mailings in which the publisher advertises the entire or partial backlist). Continuity programs differ from book club arrangements in that they do not require a membership commitment.

Mail order publishing as it is now practiced is nearly three decades old, yet it is still subject to many surprises despite careful planning. Conditions in the general consumer market seem to affect its fortunes more than they do other books—which is hardly surprising when we consider that the appeal of mail order products goes far beyond a hardcore book readership to people not accustomed to being sold or buying books often. As they do not have the book buying habit and as the price tags of mail order publications must necessarily be steep, these consumers fall readily by the wayside when the economy turns sour.

But in good times the sales and profits of mail order publishing have been phenomenal. Like the book clubs, mail order ventures have created new readers, new lovers and buyers of books. They have also demonstrated once again that books have an intrinsic aesthetic appeal, an attraction for the eye as well as the mind, and that the desire to build a handsome library can readily be awakened in people when the means and marketing methods are available.

Mail Order Selling

The secret of all good marketing is to bring product and buyer together with a sound understanding both of what one is selling and of the consumer to whom one is trying to sell it. Direct mail is one of the most effective tools in book promotion, but it is costly and demanding and mistakes come quickly home to roost. Unless one has correctly sized up one's product, identified clearly who its customers are, and determined how they can best be reached, one may quickly face disaster in the mail order business.

A look at the economics of direct mail bookselling will demonstrate this fact. On a mailing to a general consumer list promoting a book with a subject of wide interest (an instance characteristic of the mail order publishing operations just described), a return of 1.5 to 2 percent is considered average. This means that for every 1,000 pieces mailed 15 to 20 orders will be received. The cost of such a mailing will depend on the type and number of inserts included in the package and the nature of the mailing list used. The expense of printing the brochures, sales letters, and order cards, of stuffing them into envelopes, of utilizing a mailing list and addressing from it, of bundling, post office delivery, and postage (at third class bulk rates) can run some $750 per 1,000 pieces. If the returns received from a 1,000-piece mailing are 2 percent, and the list price of the books sold is $100, a gross income of $2,000 will be realized. This will leave a margin after mailing expenses of $1,250 to cover the manufacturing cost and royalty on the books (perhaps $600) and general operating expense (possibly $500), allowing the mailer a pretax profit of $150.

Suppose, however, that the return were only 1 percent, or 10 orders per 1,000 pieces mailed. Income would then shrink to $1,000 leaving a margin after mailing expenses of only $250. Although book costs would also go down (to $300) and operating expense would likewise be lower (conceivably $300—some operating expense won't go away simply because not enough books are sold), the mailing would show a whopping loss of $450. The mailer would encounter somewhat the same problem if the book sold were only half as expensive, listing for only $50, even if the return was 2 percent. If, on the other hand, the publisher could increase the return rate to 4 percent it could show a profit even on the lower-priced books while on the hundred-dollar sale it would better than double its profit over the 2 percent return because operating costs would not quite double along with sales. (The publisher might achieve a higher return by promoting several books simultaneously, thereby increasing not only the number of responses but, hopefully, the income per response as well.)

If rate of return and list price are vital factors, costs are no less so. If the mailer were promoting specialized consumer professional or scholarly titles, for example, and did not require expensive color brochures, fancy order cards, or gimmicks, but only a simple, modest announcement letter, mailing expense per 1,000 might be reduced to $350. Assuming the average order to be only $50 in such an instance, with a 2 percent return, the publisher would show a gross income of $1,000, a margin after mailing expense of $650, with book costs possibly of $140, operating expense of $240, and a profit of $270. Should the mailing realize only a 1 percent return or involve orders averaging only $25, the effort would, of course, create a loss.

Some points about direct mail become therefore obvious: books or series must be sufficiently high-priced to support the mailing cost required to promote them. Mailing lists must be carefully chosen so that they will yield a sufficiently high rate of return. Mailing packages (i.e., brochures, covering letters, order cards, other enclosures, even envelopes) must be effectively prepared in order to do the required selling job as economically as possible.

Many direct-mail practitioners place the choice of the proper mailing list at the top of their requirements. There are many sources for such lists: magazines sell address lists of their current or expired subscribers; publishers, like American Heritage, make available buyers' lists of their titles; and in the specialized consumers, scholarly and professional field there are clubs, organizations and learned societies whose membership rosters are obtainable. R. R. Bowker markets mailing lists of booksellers, libraries, and schools. There are many list brokers who represent owners of mailing lists and who are only too anxious to assist the mailer. A directory of such brokers and other mailing list sources appears in *Literary Market Place*.

On highly specialized items, such as some consumer and certain professional works, a good mailing list may be the best if not the only entree to a very precise and very limited market. The mailing itself may be small, but the rate of return can be very high. Also, in specialized mail order one often encounters a phenomenon known as "echo," i.e., orders from bookstores or from libraries in addition to those arriving directly in response to the mailing. Some of the customers to whom the promotion was addressed simply prefer to order through a bookstore, or they recommend the book to the company, laboratory, or academic library with which they are affiliated.

Publishers who regularly promote by mail often find it advantageous to develop mailing lists of their own. This provides them not only with a strong marketing tool but also with a source of income: addressing on good mailing lists can be sold for $50 or more per 1,000. Maintaining a mailing list is a demanding chore, however; address changes in our mobile society are almost constant, and list owners must regularly employ a "list cleaner," i.e., a service reporting address changes provided at nominal cost by the post office. To keep a mailing list effective also requires periodic elimination of nonbuyers; even though a purchaser was placed on a list originally because he or she bought a book may not mean that he or she will continue doing so regularly. Some publishers, particularly those who specialize in consumer mailings, have found the necessary record keeping too costly, however; they prefer to retire the entire list after two or three years and start all over.

What one mails to the customer—the mailing package—is at least as important as the list to which it is mailed. Brochures are basically of two kinds: self-mailers, which require no envelope but can be addressed directly, and enclosures, which must be inserted in envelopes (or occasionally in a self-mailer). Generally, promoters of books have found enclosure mailings to be more effective, albeit more costly than self-mailers, particularly in attempts to reach the general consumer. For trade mailings (to bookstores and libraries) self-mailers are often quite satisfactory. An interesting new wrinkle in direct-mail practice is the card deck in which an assortment of individual business reply cards is enclosed, each card promoting a separate title.

The character of a mailing package changes significantly with the type of person to whom it is addressed and the product being promoted. Mailing on expensive, colorful books to the general consumer will feature elaborate, color-illustrated brochures with strongly "pitched" copy rhapsodizing about the product, accompanied by long, glowing sales letters, order cards with pictures, and reply envelopes. Good direct-mail copy does not rely solely on adjectives or superlatives, however; even the most enthusiastic sales piece should be long on information, description of content, facts about the author, data on illustrations, binding, etc. Facts, not words, sell books. While the words should be lively, clear, and persuasive, they are not likely to succeed if the substance they present is vague and abounds in generalities.

When a technical handbook is promoted to a professional audience the mailing package can be modest, even spartan in appearance and yet be very effective if it features the information the customer will find persuasive: as much specific detail on the book as possible, including, perhaps, sample pages, and solid data on the author. In mailings to scholars and academicians simple, mimeographed announcements have sometimes produced better responses than elaborate brochures; scholars incline to distrust what they regard as "slick" sales approaches, but they will respond solidly to announcements that are factual and resemble in appearance the mailings they receive from colleagues or scholarly associations. Specialized consumer mailings may sometimes require more elaborate approaches, but emphasis should still be on information rather than glitter, and color inserts are rarely necessary.

Some aspects of direct-mail practice, such as the virtue of enclosing sales letters with brochures, are the subject of controversy among practitioners. Tests show that covering letters are very effective in consumer mailings; the evidence is less conclusive where promotion to scholars or professionals is concerned. (The ultimate in sales letters is the computer-addressed and personalized letter in which the name of the recipient may be repeated several times throughout the text—a practice which some recipients of such letters consider intrusive and offensive.) Another subject for never-ending debate is the virtue of promoting a single book as against several in the same mailing. Tests have indicated that mailings devoted to a single title are more effective in promoting that book than mailings diluted with other announcements; other tests show, however, that the total number of responses and the return per response are often greater when several books are offered for sale. The objective of a mailing and its audience require careful analysis, therefore, before a decision is made regarding the use of single or multiple insertions. If a truly important new book is being established in its market, a book which by its substantial list price can make the mailing pay on its own, it is probably wiser to confine the effort to that one title rather than scatter one's shots by including other books. If, however, the title is part of a series, or if its price is too low to ensure a profit on a single insertion mailing, then the better part of wisdom may be to do a mailing featuring the entire series or other books in the same subject area. This is probably true whether one is dealing with a consumer or a professional audience.

In any case, despite recent gains, direct mail is still the most underused marketing technique in the book industry. While some publishers have developed the technique to the level of a fine art, many others, even in the professional and scholarly area, and certainly most mainstream trade-book publishers, have far from exploited the opportunities available to them through direct-mail selling. Many books and series, particularly in the trade-book field, would lend themselves ideally to this promotional approach if their publishers would only utilize it.

LIBRARIES

Like retail outlets, libraries are a heterogeneous lot. There are public libraries, sponsored and supported by cities and towns, some of them organized into large systems with several branches. There are state, county, and regional libraries. There are federally sponsored libraries, notably the queen bee of all, the Library of Congress, but including also libraries attached to government departments and military installations. Educational libraries embrace those of colleges and universities and of public and private elementary and high schools. And then there are "special" libraries: business, industrial, professional, music, art, and historical collections, many in the hands of learned and cultural societies.

Bowker maintains lists of these libraries classified by type and in some cases by the size of their book acquisition budgets. For example, of 8,884 public libraries in the United States, 2,061 have annual funds for purchasing books of $25,000 or more; 1,206 dispose of funds between $10,000 and $25,000; 949 command between $5,000 and $10,000; and 2,380 have resources between $1,000 and $5,000. It is immediately apparent that very few of these libraries were in a position to consider purchasing even the bulk of the more than 50,000 new titles published in 1987; the assurance with which authors and agents sometimes approach publishers, ready to guarantee a big core market for their titles ("every library will buy one, of course"), has precious little foundation.

There are, furthermore, only 1,887 four-year college and university libraries, and of these only 1,261 command book budgets in 1987 of more than $25,000, only 250 can purchase between $10,000 and $25,000, leaving 376 whose annual book acquisition amounts to less than $10,000! Bowker lists give no budget breakdown for 1,179 junior college libraries.

There are 51,000 public elementary, 15,500 public high school, and 12,500 junior high school libraries, most of which came into being during the 1960s under the stimulus of large federal grants. Although the federal largesse in this area has largely ceased, the concept of the library as an integral part of the school and of the pedagogical process has been firmly established and its advantages have been demonstrated. Not only is this a step forward for education, it also is an important advance for the cause of books which children are now accustomed to using and enjoying on their own initiative at an earlier age.

Of special libraries, 3,808 are technical and scientific, 1,959 are business, 1,309 are law, and 3,134 are medical libraries. Some collections house volumes in more than one of these and other categories.

Libraries of all kinds purchased an estimated $1.45 billion in books during 1987, therefore representing some 8.7 percent of the total U.S. consumer market. As John Berry, editor of *Library Journal,* points out, however, libraries absorb a significantly larger percentage of books which are published in quantities under 5,000 copies; in fact, were it not for library consumption, many such books would go unpublished altogether. His point is borne out by the sale of, for example, university press titles, where the library market is nearly 23 percent, of professional books, where it is 21 percent, or even of trade books, where it is 11 percent.

Significantly a very large portion—apparently some 67 percent—of book sales to libraries are channeled through wholesalers and jobbers, which is understandable when one considers the acquisition problems libraries face. To place thousands of orders with individual publishers, process a multitude of small shipments, and pay myriads of small bills, adds significantly to administrative burdens. Since jobbers are able to simplify and consolidate these tasks their services are indeed welcome. Furthermore, there are certain record-keeping and bibliographic steps which jobbers offer to libraries as part of their contract: cataloging, supplying a checkout card in the book, marking a shelf number on the binding. Since jobbers give contract discounts in addition (usually 33⅓ percent on trade books, 20 percent on short-discount titles), discounts which are larger than the 10 to 20 percent library discounts many publishers would allow, it is hardly surprising that libraries generally prefer to deal with wholesalers rather than with publishers directly.

The publishers' efforts in reaching libraries, by mailing catalogs and brochures, by attending library meetings and conventions, and by sending sample books for examination, are often aimed at obtaining orders through jobbers as much as at receiving them directly. In fact, many publishers who relish the task of processing a host of individual orders and shipments no more than the library does, are only too delighted to see the orders they have solicited filled through the wholesaler.

Many librarians are experiencing serious difficulties these days which can be simply summed up in one word: money. Funding in many places is woefully inadequate. In some cases the cost of processing a new book can equal the price of the book itself, according to John Berry, and personnel expense represents more than half of the total budget of most libraries, while journals have absorbed an increasing portion of the shrinking acquisition dollar, at the expense of books. A movement sponsored by authors' organizations hopes to exact royalties from libraries for book use by patrons—a practice current in England, Australia and some Scandinavian countries—which would further add to the already critical budget burden.

The cost problems have been eased in many instances through greater efficiency of operation, including the use of new automated techniques and the sharing of facilities and holdings. Unfortunately vested interests have sometimes opposed such improvements: some people lose their jobs and administrators see their empires reduced when they are implemented. However commercial services, which perform cataloging and other vital tasks at less than internal cost, have made inroads despite resistance from the library establishment.

Many public libraries now offer video cassettes, computer software and other nonprint items for enjoyment by their patrons. Some are operating bookstores. In inner cities new techniques designed to benefit the user have revolutionized traditional approaches. (The Langston Hughes branch of the New York Public Library in Queens is run by nonprofessionals, offers a wide selection of occupationally oriented material, and uses new devices, such as colored tapes instead of numbers, for subject identification.)

National and regional networks, which enable libraries to share information and materials, have sprung up everywhere. Often these facilities link public, academic, school, and special libraries together, effecting cost savings for all and allowing patrons access to the joint resources of the entire network. Networks have facilitated cataloging, interlibrary loan transactions, and joint acquisitions. While it is true that in sharing resources libraries have made their materials holdings more productive, it is generally not true, as some publishers have claimed, that libraries would spend more money on books were it not for their network memberships. On the contrary, because of their specialized nature, some books might not be purchased at all but for the fact that the network member acquiring them can justify their cost by sharing them with other libraries. Book budgets are too tight to enable libraries to keep up with the field as a whole. At least with networking, a library stands a chance of satisfying most of its patrons' needs; without such cooperation, many libraries would have to fall even shorter than they do of patrons' expectations.

WHOLESALERS AND JOBBERS

Wholesalers to Bookstores

Most industries faced with the complexity of product and the delivery problems characteristic of the book field have developed viable wholesaler networks to service their retail outlets. Strangely enough this has not been true in the book industry. While there were once adequate wholesale facilities—prior to World War II the American News Co., with branches in principal cities, as well as a number of independent companies, such as Baker & Taylor and A. C. McClurg, were active in serving retail stores—in postwar decades this facet of the industry declined. Not until the seventies did growth in bookselling once again awaken the interest of firms like Baker & Taylor and Ingram Book Co. in catering to bookstores.

This was good news for publishers and bookstores alike. Rarely can a store manage to buy in advance a sufficiently large inventory of a successful new title to meet the entire demand; even more rarely can a publisher hope to ship all reorders for such a title promptly enough to keep all stores adequately supplied. The situation is aggravated when the bookstore is located at some distance from the publisher: it is not unusual for a bookseller in California to wait up to six weeks for a reorder of a best seller published by a New York house.

If a good wholesaler in the region stocks such a title, however, and is efficient in serving customers, stores can be more readily supplied in cases where the need for rapid service is critical. Wholesalers can also be helpful by stocking the most commonly ordered backlist titles of leading publishers—staples which a store hates to be out of and knows it will lose sales on unless it can obtain them on rapid reorder.

Needless to say, most wholesalers are not able to maintain an inventory of the three quarter of a million titles in print. They may therefore not be able to furnish immediately certain less popular titles on special order but would in turn have to order them from publishers. Still, they might be able to render an important service even here by "funneling" such special orders—consolidating orders to publishers on the one hand and consolidating shipments and invoices to retailers on the other—thereby substantially simplifying the process for both their suppliers and customers and reducing their costs.

Theoretically wholesalers can show a profit as middlemen because publishers give them a favorable discount based on the large overall sales volume they generate (commonly 46-50 percent), while retailers can accept a shorter discount (33⅓ percent) from them because of the more rapid service they give and the lower transportation costs they charge. Because each adds to its sales volume, both retailer and publisher are ahead even if each deals on a less profitable basis with the wholesaler than they would directly with each other; a book sold at a slightly lower gross profit still adds more to the retailer's or publisher's income than a book not sold at all.

Mass Market Wholesalers

Because mass market paperbacks and juveniles are sold not only through mass market outlets but also through bookstores, the wholesalers discussed above who now cater to booksellers are increasingly stocking such mass market titles and making them available to their customers. In doing so these wholesalers are applying their trade book policies, particularly their trade paperback policies, to such distribution.

When it comes to wholesaling mass market titles, however, the lion's share of the business is consummated by nearly 500 "independent" mass market wholesalers (traditionally called "independent" to distinguish them from branch outlets of national wholesale chains), whose primary business is the distribution of magazines. Publishers deal with them directly or through a national magazine distributor. Discounts extended to these wholesalers run from 46 to 55 percent depending on the line or the publisher; sometimes regular discounts are supplemented by incentive arrangements enabling the wholesaler to earn a better profit if he or she promotes and sells books more vigorously and successfully.

Some wholesalers are extraordinarily efficient and enterprising. Their inventory is representative of what is best and most in demand in the field; they serve effectively newsstands, supermarkets, chain stores, drugstores, bookstores, and schools in their territories.

Significantly many of these wholesalers have opened affiliated retail outlets—among them some of the best-stocked and best-managed book-stores in the country—which carry not only magazines and mass market paperbacks but trade paperbacks and hardcover books as well. Over 500 such retail stores were in operation in 1987.

Many wholesalers employ expert field personnel who serve outlets from trucks that carry selective inventories and whose knowledge of books and of their customers leads them to maximize their merchandising opportunities. In other cases experts work within wholesalers' ware-houses, carefully assembling shipments for their outlets on the basis of past sales records and returns. Whether the method employed is "book truck" or "prepack" (to use the industry's nomenclature), what makes a wholesaler effective is the expertise of its staff and its commitment to book distribution. Such a wholesaler can also be counted on to control its inventory with care, to reorder regularly titles that sell well, and to remove from sale promptly those that are not moving.

Not so in far too many other cases. Many wholesale agencies have no book-buying expertise nor any staff available that can serve outlets intel-ligently. Too often books are received at wholesalers' warehouses and shipped to outlets without understanding of their sales potential. Since more books are published than there is room for, this often means that even the best and most salable books are not given a chance; sometimes they are not even unpacked and are returned to the publisher "live" (i.e., in the original cartons, untouched). Publishers try to help matters by sending field representatives to the agencies to help sort out at least the titles with the biggest potential and make certain that they receive ex-posure. Special displays, dump bins (i.e., combination shipping cartons and display units), posters, streamers, special discounts, and other means are employed by publishers to take a title out of the ordinary and give it visibility within the maelstrom. The problem is—for how many titles can this be made to work? A dozen or two a month? In 1987, nearly 4,000 titles were published, or twenty times as many as could reasonably be featured through special promotion.

A wholesaler which does not have a qualified book buyer on its staff has no argument or defense against the indiscriminate flooding of titles to which it is subjected month after month. The efforts of publishers' field staff, concentrated as they must be on a few extraordinary titles, will act as no more than a palliative. In the meantime publishers, authors, and the public suffer.

This is a problem which the industry as a whole will sooner or later have to tackle. Certain wholesalers must be offered opportunities to learn more about book distribution and be given access to book-buying exper-tise. Independent central buying offices that wholesalers could make use of for a fee—somewhat like department store group buying offices—seem one possibility. In addition methods must be found to enable wholesalers to assess the potential of the outlets they serve and match that potential with available books.

Efficiency in buying and distributing mass paperbacks would make the wholesalers more independent of publishers, would give them greater discretion in their book distribution efforts, and would result in the far greater success of good titles in the marketplace. It would also result in the more decisive failure of unsalable titles and even, perhaps, in the elimination of some publishing imprints that are more opportunistic and less responsible than the rest and whose only chance for survival lies in the continuation of the present chaos. Anyone sincerely interested in the future of the book industry, particularly wholesalers who now so often stand no chance at all to make a decent profit on their book operations, would benefit greatly from this development, as would responsible publishers and authors.

Library Jobbers

For the most part, one is likely to encounter the same cast of characters among wholesalers who serve retailers and among those who supply libraries and schools. However, the role of the library jobber is often more extensive than merely to supply books. What libraries require as much as or even more than books is service. So jobbers offer a great many services: cataloging, approval plans, out-of-print search, and above all the ordering and processing of books from publishers with all the correspondence, checking, and follow-up this entails. The library enjoys the simple life: one source, one invoice, only one supplier to complain to. The jobber must deal with hundreds of publishers on thousands of titles; just to identify titles and authors correctly and address orders to the proper publisher in each case can be a herculean job.

To cement their relationship with their library customers jobbers often arrange for exclusive contracts and as part of their terms offer an attractive discount—usually $33\frac{1}{3}$ percent on trade titles, somewhat less on short-discount materials. It has never been clear to me how such a discount can be justified. A library is, after all, a consumer and does not resell books. No doubt the motivation for offering the discount originally, shortly after World War II, was to be competitive with publishers (who then and now offer 10 to 20 percent to libraries), with booksellers, many of whom at one time supplied libraries, and even more with other jobbers. In any case, I believe it was a serious mistake which has hurt the industry because it has curtailed some of its income without justification. Publishers aided and abetted the scheme by continuing to give wholesalers, who were then abandoning their retail customers for the library business, the same large discounts which they had extended to them as middlemen reselling to bookstores. Without this permissiveness by publishers, wholesalers could never have offered the special contract terms to libraries.

Now that many libraries are in bad budget straits seems hardly the time to suggest a change in the discount jobbers should extend to their institutional customers. However, the structure remains a strange anomaly in the American book distribution system. One of its most unfortunate consequences has been that it has put bookstores, which used to be the principal book source for many libraries, out of the business of supplying institutions, thus making it more difficult for many good bookstores to survive.

Among library jobbers are those which work more closely with academic libraries and others which are more extensively involved with public libraries and schools. The increasing demand by schools for paperbacks has swayed some jobbers from their once exclusively hardcover positions. Similarly, certain jobbers have entered the audiovisual materials field, an area in which many of their school and library customers have an avid interest.

Book wholesalers and jobbers serving libraries, schools, and bookstores are listed in *Literary Market Place*. Information regarding independent magazine wholesalers is available from the Council for Periodical Distributors Associations, 488 Madison Avenue, New York, N.Y. 10022.

ELEMENTARY AND SECONDARY SCHOOLS

Since we have already discussed marketing practices relating to school libraries, the present observations on the schools as publishers' markets will be confined to their acquisition of materials for classroom use. Here we will remember that 22 states currently engage in some form of state adoption whereby districts are limited in their choice of titles to those approved by a state board. Such adoptions are usually made for a period of five years after which new and formerly adopted materials are again submitted and a new adoption list is prepared.

Because state adoptions mean a great deal to school publishers—even though the system is generally on the wane and the trend is toward increasing autonomy by local districts—much title and series planning revolves around the five-year adoption cycle. Often when a major state adoption is up for consideration publishers will schedule the development of a new title or series to coincide with it. This means that they must have the materials ready for demonstration purposes the preceding fall. States usually make available a list of official evaluators, and publishers then arrange for presentations of their product which may include appearances by authors and by "consultants" (i.e., teachers retained by the publisher to demonstrate the materials).

A publisher whose title is selected for adoption is thereby granted a hunting license to seek out local districts and persuade them that of the four or five competitive titles chosen by the state the publisher's is the most meritorious. As adoption lists are usually released by the first of the year, this gives the publisher some three months (January to March) to make local presentations. Representatives contact superintendents and advisory committees in the districts, leave samples of books behind them, and make appointments for formal presentations to be made before school authorities and/or their advisors. The distribution of free sample copies is one of the publisher's most important promotional devices; it is not unusual for a publisher to give away 20,000 copies of an important title during a single year.

The sales presentations themselves, in which consultants usually participate if the materials are on the elementary level, while normally the salespeople alone will conduct them if secondary level items are under consideration, will emphasize the pedagogical features of the titles submitted and may offer data on field test results. In addressing teachers, emphasis is usually placed on the ease with which the materials may be used in the classroom; when approaching superintendents and school boards, validation is made much of and accountability is stressed.

Since both sales reps and consultants are for the most part former teachers who speak the language of the schools and are thoroughly familiar with the problems and attitudes in vogue, the presentations usually assume an insider's, colleague-to-colleague air.

The role of salespeople, and even more that of consultants, does not stop with this presentation. If the district decides to select the product, particularly if it is on the elementary level, consultants will return to demonstrate to teachers how the product should be used. In fact in many districts such demonstrations are required and without them a purchase contract would not be awarded to the publisher.

In nonadoption states the technique of selling to local districts is much the same except that publishers do not have the advantage (or suffer from the impediment) of a special state adoption list. The field is totally open and publishers must make their way with sample copies and persuasive demonstrations. The way may have been paved by favorable advance comment on a title within the profession, by reviews in pedagogical journals, or by evaluation services. The reputation of authors will have an impact, as will friendships with superintendents and evaluators cultivated over many years by sales staff and consultants.

Publishers do some advertising in magazines for educators but this does not produce massive results; rather it serves to alert prospective buyers to the existence of a product, thus preparing the way for other sales efforts. The same is true of mailings to teachers and exhibits at teachers' meetings.

From the publisher's standpoint district-level selling and selection is the most advantageous. State adoptions, despite the bonanza they create for a few winners, leave nothing for the losers; the hit-or-miss character of the adoption system tends to concentrate success or failure too much and offers too little opportunity to the average title or publisher. On the other hand, the tendency in some areas to localize the selection process even below the district level and to allow every teacher to select materials for his or her classroom, is equally hazardous for the publisher because it makes the cost of marketing the product prohibitive. Who can afford to furnish a sample book to every teacher or to invest in a personal sales call on every classroom?

According to estimates by the National Center for Education Statistics, there were 3,263,000 elementary and secondary classroom teachers in the United States in 1987. The number of schools, last reported for 1983–1984, was 57,471 public elementary, 22,336 public high, and 1,611 combined public elementary and secondary schools, as well as 2,760 unclassified schools, organized into 15,747 school districts in the fifty states and the District of Columbia. In addition there were 13,333 private elementary, 3,219 private secondary, 3,459 combined, and 1,753 unclassified private schools. It takes little imagination to conclude that selling to every teacher would be beyond the realm of possibility even if publishers were much larger and much wealthier than they really are. Even to cover all schools individually would be a staggering task. Ultimately the district-marketing approach is the most economical and most efficient because it is the one in which the taxpayer is least likely to have to pay excessive prices for materials just to cover their abnormally high cost of selection.

Whether they quote on a state or district level, publishers must guarantee firm prices on their products for all or part of the life of the purchase contract. Nominal discounts are given, but everyone realizes that for practical purposes the price of the product is the price at which it is billed to the purchasing school. Transportation is usually paid by the purchaser, although publishers have sometimes agreed to prepay shipping costs in exchange for reduced discounts.

In some states publishers are required to ship books to designated official depositories, usually private firms operating under state contract charged with housing adopted materials so that schools can readily draw on them as they are needed. Arrangements by publishers with such depositories usually involve a consignment of inventory (i.e., placing the stock in the depository, with books paid for only when actually sold) and a charge by the depository for the warehousing and shipping services provided.

COLLEGES AND UNIVERSITIES

The adoption process in higher education shares some characteristics of the elhi-level procedures but there are substantial differences as well. On the college level, marketing efforts are also directed at the faculty: salespersons call on department heads, professors, and instructors. In some cases, particularly those involving basic freshman and sophomore courses, books may be selected by a departmental committee. In most other instances, however, the instructor teaching the course decides what materials he or she will use. In fact, the general trend is toward increasing autonomy by individual teachers with diminishing interference from the departmental administration.

Instructors or departments very rarely do the purchasing, but leave the chore to the institutionally or privately owned bookstores serving the campus. Ideally professors should make their choices of books several months in advance, for example, by April for the following fall term. Local bookstores are then notified of the titles that will be required or recommended, along with estimates of the number of students expected to enroll in the course. It is then up to the stores to acquire sufficient stock by ordering from publishers or buying back used books from students.

It is a good system in theory. Unfortunately too many things can go wrong with it in practice. To begin with, instructors and departmental committees often make up their minds late. Despite constant urgings by bookstores to advise them of their choices early, professors have been known to delay determining their requirements even until after their courses have begun. If the store does not then produce the needed books almost overnight, the professors are often peeved. Frequently books are adopted that are out-of-print, that are published abroad and it takes months to import, or that are published by publishers which are difficult to locate and deal with.

Additional problems are created because professors are often very inaccurate in estimating enrollment in their classes. Predictions that scores of students may take a course may turn out to be only 60 to 40 percent correct. If the store has ordered stock to fill the initial prediction, it will be forced to return a large quantity of books to the publisher at considerable cost and inconvenience.

Despite all, the stores attempt to deal effectively with these problems, and many have developed good techniques for acquiring and marketing course materials. Their trade association, the National Association of College Stores (NACS), has played a significant role in making its members more efficient. For example, when it became apparent some years ago that paperbacks would be used increasingly in course work, NACS founded a wholesale enterprise that makes available to its members most of the steadily demanded trade and college paperbacks. NACSCORP, as this operation is known, stocks its inventory in a warehouse adjoining the association's headquarters building in Oberlin, Ohio.

College stores have learned to capitalize on the demand for used books. Why let students themselves do all the profitable trading? Through NACS, lists of available used books are circulated among the stores, enabling them to buy surplus stock from each other. There are also a number of wholesalers in the field who purchase surplus used books from stores or, through the stores' facilities, directly from students, and who conduct a brisk and profitable trade with retailers. The frequent changes in text adoptions, whereby even some of the big basic course textbooks may be dropped after a year or a semester (or trimester or quarter where schools are on shorter cycles), have made the wholesale and intraretailer exchanges of used books a sizable business.

The college store field consists largely of three types of operations: the institutionally owned store, sometimes functioning at a loss and subsidized by its owner; the privately owned and usually profitable store; and the leased store operated by a private entrepreneur for the college, involving financial arrangements satisfactory to the institution and designed to be profitable for the operator. Many of the leased operations are parts of chains which also conduct a lively used book business; some of them, in fact, are affiliated with the wholesalers of used books mentioned above.

Publishers, always wary of a strong used book market, are concerned about leased operations. They are apprehensive about the economic power which is being concentrated in the chains and which they fear will become dominant in the field. Used books have, however, always been part of the college textbook scene. By the very nature of things demand for them always exceeds supply (many students do not sell their books, and some books simply wear out after passing through two or more owners). Used books are apparently a necessary evil, an irradicable nuisance, from the publisher's point of view. The growth and prosperity of the leasing chains, furthermore, may actually turn out to be a boon for the industry. By bringing effective merchandising and management techniques into the picture in many places (where such expertise may previously have been lacking), they may be contributing to the long-term health of the college book field.

Traditionally textbook publishers have extended a 20 percent discount to college stores. The stores complain that they are unable to survive on this discount. They emphasize that their interest in handling used books is stimulated by their ability to show a much better profit on them. Stores usually buy books from students at 50 percent of list price and sell them at 75 percent, thus giving them a substantially larger dollar yield on the transaction and on their investment than can be obtained from the sale of new books. A few publishers have increased their textbook discount to 25 percent, some in exchange for a more limited return privilege.

A study by DeWitt C. Baker and James Hileman issued in 1987 takes publishers to task for allowing the used-book business to flourish, thereby depriving publishers and authors of income they would be receiving if only new books were sold. The study argues that publishers' failure to devise effective countermeasures, coupled with their long-standing indifference to the concerns of college stores, have created the opportunities used-book wholesalers are now enjoying. Baker and Hileman propose that publishers reduce the prices of their textbooks substantially after one year of publication to take the attraction and profit out of the used-book trade. As mainstream publishers often do in the face of criticism, the established industry appears to have ignored the report. On the other hand, major publishers have discussed attempts to capture a share of the used-book market themselves, and a cooperative plan was recently launched to achieve this objective.

The return privilege has been another area of controversy between store and publisher. Many publishers limit the portion of the store's purchase that may be returned, whereupon bookstores complain that this places the full burden on them when professors guess wrong and students fail to buy adopted materials. Publishers reply that they do not want to carry the full burden either, that accepting already large portions of unsold goods is punishment enough. Certainly neither store nor publisher can afford to absorb the kind of punishment that has been meted out to them in recent years. There really should be ways that require the responsible institution or its faculty to absorb at least the excess burden that results from their actions and decisions.

Traditionally publishers have supplied free copies to professors for their examination in order to facilitate their decision making. When a book is adopted the publisher is prepared to furnish a free "desk copy," i.e., a copy to the teacher of the course (unless a free examination copy has already been sent), or even several such copies if the course is large enough and is taught in several sections. Publishers usually stipulate that an adoption must result in an order for at least ten copies before they can justify supplying a desk copy. Unfortunately some college instructors apparently feel that the publisher should accommodate them with an almost unlimited number of free books, and they are decidedly unsympathetic when the publisher maintains that free books are a promotional expenditure that must be kept within bounds. Some faculty even show no compunction about selling the free books supplied to them to used-book dealers despite publishers' protests that this represents a grave abuse and, when the books are resold to students, a loss of income to publisher and author.

Another area where the publisher appears to be regarded as fair game by some faculty is unauthorized copying. Although the copyright law is clear and publishers have gone on record often that they regard the indiscriminate photocopying of their materials to be illegal, many college instructors continue to duplicate whole chapters and sections from books, distributing copies to students, sometimes even selling them through bookstores or in the classroom.

Sometimes, however, faculty compete with publishers quite legally by issuing proprietary textbooks, i.e., volumes specially prepared for use in their own classrooms. This interesting phenomenon permits the teacher to construct course materials entirely to his or her liking without having to depend on the approach of another textbook. A number of firms now exist who will publish such textbooks for instructors cheaply enough so that the price remains within the reach of students yet allows a modest income to the author. Such tailor-made texts are usually sold through the local bookstore. They add another challenge to the many problems currently facing college publishers.

Yet all participants in the process—the faculty, bookstore, publisher, and student—share common interests. Most professors and students realize that bookstores and publishers basically want to serve them well and, granting a few unscrupulous exceptions, honorably. Bookstores and publishers themselves continue to engage in fruitful dialogue and cooperative efforts, such as the electronic ordering system "PUBNET," a vital innovation that has expedited the delivery of textbooks to stores.

REVIEWS AND PUBLICITY

One way to define the term "publicity" as commonly used in book publishing is as free advertising. Of course it is not entirely free. To obtain review coverage one must distribute review copies to the media, and to expose an author on television may involve a good deal of expensive time and effort on the part of a staff or a free-lance public relations expert. But the exposure in newspapers, magazines, or on the air is not itself paid for.

Although publishers of all descriptions seek to obtain review coverage of their titles, the more glamorous public relations efforts that send authors on tour or get them on a "Today" or "Tonight" show are undertaken by consumer-oriented trade and mass market paperback houses. In such houses there is usually a publicity manager who assumes responsibility for the whole free advertising area, sends out press releases, visits reviewers, arranges for the distribution of review copies, and attempts to gain public exposure for personable, photogenic, pleasantly articulate, and newsworthy authors.

It's an uphill fight. Once again the sheer volume of titles and authors and the limited available news, review, and air space make for a fiercely competitive situation, one that is a source of constant frustration to publishers and authors. To begin with, there is only a very small number of regular consumer book review media. The *New York Times Book Review,* the *New York Review of Books,* are now the only significant national publications in the field. While some magazines like *Time, Newsweek, Harpers,* the *Atlantic Monthly,* and *The New Yorker,* as well as the so-called journals of opinion (such as the *Nation, New Republic, Commentary, Commonweal,* and *National Review*), carry book reviews, all such media in combination cannot begin to treat even a fraction of newly published titles. The Sunday supplement *New York Times Book Review,* without question the leading medium in the field, can give prime attention to, perhaps, thirty titles a week and brief reviews to, possibly, another twenty. With fifty-two issues a year this means that at the very most some 2,600 titles can be noticed. This is not an unimpressive record but it appears slight considering that nearly twenty times that many original new titles are published each year. Although these releases include text and technical titles inappropriate for review in such a medium, it is probably fair to state that at best some 10 percent of all genuinely eligible items find their way into the *Book Review*'s pages.

There is, of course, some daily review coverage of books in the *New York Times,* just as there is in a number of other important newspapers. (A list of these media appears in *Literary Market Place.*) The *Times* sometimes carries two reviews a day, so that in a year's time perhaps 500 titles are covered. For the most part these duplicate the attention given to these titles elsewhere, in the Sunday *Review* section and in other media, so they fail to increase the number of books that receive attention, though they reinforce awareness of those reviewed.

Although there is every indication that American consumers read and buy more books each year, the news media, with notable exceptions, have shown little awareness of this growing interest by their readers. In a column in the *New York Times Book Review* of November 18, 1973, Richard Kluger, who at one time had edited *Book Week,* wrote:

> One wonders, finally, why the press persists in regarding books as the limpest of watercress on its daily menu. Books are news, often decidedly more so than the toxic gruel dished out by flacks and advance men. Books are bearers of ideas, sometimes profound ones, if anybody would take the time and trouble to digest them, and the space to report them. Thus the ideas in John Kenneth Galbraith's latest book on the future imperatives of our economy were almost nowhere treated as the mainstream news they were. Perhaps a dozen such books a month are published, moreover, that scrutinize a major social problem with far more care and insight than the press itself, forever jostled by the deadline, can manage. When will newsmen recognize that books are not only good copy but also, at their best, the ultimate embodiment of their own craft?

The major review media also appear to harbor a decided bias against popular writing and to stress literary and high-culture titles at the expense of those appealing to wider audiences. While one naturally applauds the attention given to serious, artistic writing, one cannot help deplore the elitist onesidedness of the media's coverage. If popular writing is often poor and substandard, it is in no small measure due to the neglect it is receiving from the critical community that largely ignores it, or lambastes it unempathetically on the rare occasions it pays attention. Yet popular writing is what a vast majority of Americans—including the highly educated as well as the political and economic leadership—are reading. By indulging the literary snobbishness of their critics, the media fail seriously in their responsibility to an overwhelming majority of their readers.

In a similar vein, most review media still display a reluctance to review paperbound books. Considering the importance of many titles published exclusively in paperbound form and the fact that the buying public has taken to the paperback format, this large-scale indifference to the merits of paperbacks has been, to say the least, astounding. The coverage given to some outstanding paperback reprints and a few originals may be progress—but it is still a long way from the ideal when each book will be selected for review on the merits of its content rather than on the incidental features of its manufacture.

The situation is slightly better in the many specialized media which review books in specific consumer and professional interest fields. Here at least there is more extensive, though far from complete, coverage. Unfortunately another, serious difficulty afflicts reviews in many professional and scholarly journals: delays of sometimes a year or more. Again one suspects that the sheer volume of new material is one cause of such delays: journals naturally attempt to choose the best people in their fields to write reviews, people usually spoken for for months on end because of the flood of reviewable titles—totally aside from the many other commitments such prominent authorities usually have. Other factors creating delays result from the specialized publications' budget limitations and the fact that their editors are usually volunteers who take on such chores in addition to too many other duties.

Even when books are reviewed, however, publishers and authors are often frustrated by the nature of the reviews themselves. Criticism is an extremely difficult and challenging art—and in an age in which mediocrity is often widespread one has every sympathy for reviewers who, while meaning to be constructive, find themselves put off by the inadequacies of the work itself. But as my father, the art critic Wilhelm Dessauer was wont to point out, the ultimate objective of criticism must be to enhance appreciation. This means that critics should be motivated by a desire to serve the interests of both the work and its audience. They will therefore shy away from exploiting the occasion for narrow personal advantage: to demonstrate, for example, how they would have written the book or to air their own views of the subject which the author has treated. In its extreme form the egocentric review becomes a long essay in which the reviewer does his or her "own thing," using the author's work at best as a jumping off point, at worst as a foil. This certainly does little to enhance appreciation or to serve the cause of books.

Some of the large consumer review media use academic critics on an extensive scale. Academic critics, of course, vary greatly one to the next; some are extremely lively, dedicated to doing justice to the work under review, fair, generous, and determined to keep self-interest out of their assessment. Too often, however, academic reviewers become entangled in scholarly controversies and personal disagreements, and some seem unable to resist the temptation to grind their own axes. Too often, therefore, the book suffers and the cause of books generally is let down. In professional and scholarly media some controversy, one supposes, is essential to the critical process; after all, such reviews attempt not only to enhance appreciation but also to evaluate books as contributions to their scholarly or professional disciplines. Even here, however, emphasis should be on the book and on what its author has to say rather than on the critic's viewpoint.

When it comes to literary fiction—one prays for the day when authors will be discussed not by comparing them with every other writer since Dostoyevsky but in the light of their own individuality, unique talent, and ability. There is a recognizable mannerism in much of the reviewing of such fiction: an eager search for symbolism, much psychoanalytic interpretation of characters, and the discovery of a thousand similarities to other books and writers. The critic's language appears to make up in exotic coinage and tortured construction what it lacks in clarity and depth. So readers do not receive what the price of admission entitles them to: a straightforward, to-the-point evaluation of the novel. Instead what they often get is a display of verbal and intellectual pyrotechnics, a sort of doctoral dissertation exhibition of critical technique quite derivative and lacking substance.

For most mainstream trade publishers, the publicity effort ends with the distribution of review copies and the exposure of big-book authors on TV. Not so for many midlist authors, small presses, and their consultants, who have devised a host of ingenious ways to call attention to their books. One need only listen, for example, to the six hours of ideas and suggestions offered by Marilyn and Tom Ross in their audiocassette program *Book Promotion and Marketing* (published by Communication Creativity of Saguache, CO) to discover how clever and effective some of these approaches can be.

Whether the author or a publisher sponsors the publicity, the author is destined to play a large role in it. Often the sponsor will seek the aid of a consulting firm in planning a campaign. Florence Janovic, who with Judith Appelbaum operates the promotional consulting agency Sensible Solutions, described the basic approach of most programs in "Marketing Strategies: Notes on Theory and Practice," which appeared in the Spring 1986 issue of *Book Research Quarterly:*

> Authors already have most of the data marketers need. They know the fields their books relate to; they're familiar with key opinion makers, the important publications and organizations, the places where people interested in particular fields gather and shop. With help from someone who understands publishing, they can quickly put their knowledge to work for their books. Furthermore they are generally eager to put themselves to work as well. Most authors are happy to make speeches, write articles, come up with mailing lists, and otherwise expend time and energy both behind the scenes and up front—especially if they've been published before and have learned the hard way that standard operating procedures won't let them reach their readers.
>
> Time and again, authors declare that they're willing to do whatever is necessary to make their books succeed. And, realistically, they don't equate success with being on best-seller lists. What they want is the right readers, whether their natural audiences are in four figures, or five or six.
>
> What's necessary varies, of course, from book to book, but tactics for hitting gatekeepers of information, opinion leaders, and adopters include

sending advance copies of the book along with carefully crafted personal letters to influential people in the field, generating articles about the book in specialized publications whose readers may recommend it to their clients/ customers, having the author speak before members of the target audience(s), creating mail-order flyers for potential buyers, getting professional or trade journalists to interview the author, adapting sections of the book for publication and sending them to editors of specialized periodicals with strong covering letters, and arranging for the book to be promoted and/or sold in places its audience regularly frequents.

ADVERTISING AND PROMOTION

When authors of trade books air their grievances against mainstream publishers they usually complain about insufficient advertising. That large trade publishers often fail to support a publication with a sufficient promotion cannot be denied. But in most cases the lack of promotion is a symptom rather than a cause among complex factors that result in a title's failure in the market.

Mainstream trade publishers almost invariably engage in certain standard efforts on behalf of a book: they include it in their seasonal catalogs and in their "trade list" (i.e., a complete catalog of their publications in print which is distributed separately as well as bound into a massive compendium of such catalogs, the *Publishers Trade List Annual,* published by Bowker); they distribute some 200 to 500 review copies to general and specialized media; and they include the title in their announcement ads to libraries and booksellers appearing in special seasonal issues of *Publishers Weekly, Library Journal,* and other trade publications.

Books with major potential receive, in addition, advertising exposure in the national review media (notably the *New York Times Book Review* and the *New York Review of Books*) and in some major newspapers, magazines, and journals of opinion. When they are not merely a perfunctory gesture to please the authors, these advertising efforts are intended to support the retail market, to alert the public to the existence and merits of a book, and to send interested customers to their bookstores inquiring for it. This approach works well if the book is available in the stores. If it is not, the effort is largely wasted. In rare cases the customer inquiries will result in enough special orders from bookstores to offset the cost of advertising, and in even rarer cases the demand may become sufficiently great to convince some stores that they should stock the book in question. In general, however, national advertising is productive only in the case of those few hundred titles each year which are bought in substantial quantities and featured and promoted by retailers.

Somewhat the same situation pertains with regard to the cooperative advertising publishers arrange with booksellers. Here the publisher contributes a major portion of the advertising cost (usually 75 percent) in return for which the title is promoted in local newspapers (taking advantage of the contract rate the bookseller usually enjoys because of the volume of advertising in the local paper). To justify such an insertion, however, both publisher and bookseller must be able to anticipate fairly wide sales of the title in question; in other words such advertising is again likely to be limited to major books which the bookseller has stocked in quantity.

Even then advertising cannot guarantee that a book will sell. Nor can a book's success be ensured by a favorable review or a personal appearance by the author on a national TV show. The book must have that mysterious appeal, that intrinsic fascination which makes readers respond; all the enthusiasm of publishers, booksellers, reviewers, and talk-show hosts will not necessarily make it go. There are many cases on record where such enthusiasm turned out to be largely fruitless. Of course enthusiastic reviews, TV appearances, and promotion by publishers and booksellers will help sell a title if it has the ingredients to which the public is ready to respond. As advertising experts have been saying for decades: advertising will make a good product sell better; it cannot turn an unsalable product into a success.

Given the fact that most books are not adequately represented in bookstores and cannot be expected to sell in sufficient quantity to warrant the expense of national or cooperative advertising, it is hardly surprising that most books are simply not advertised to any great extent. Advertising is to total distribution what grease and oil are to an engine: necessary lubricants which will make the engine function more smoothly and successfully. If the engine lacks power, is antiquated, and in bad need of overhauling, pumping more oil into it or greasing it more will do little to improve its performance.

Of course advertising is a key tool of publishers who resort to direct selling; direct mail or coupon ads in popular or specialized media are ways of obtaining a consumer's order without relying on retailers. Sometimes such advertising can benefit even retailers, however, by sending them customers who prefer to obtain the book locally rather than order it from the publisher. At times publishers even imprint circulars for retailers who have good mailing lists or who specialize in mail order, thereby enlisting their partnership in the direct marketing effort. And, of course, there are many consumers who are far removed from any significant book outlet or whose local bookstore is a best-seller and cookbook outlet where most books are simply unavailable. Direct marketing by the publisher or by an enterprising book club or mail order house may then be the only means of bringing books to that consumer.

Direct advertising to specialized audiences is particularly easy to justify, and specialized consumer books and professional and scholarly titles are usually promoted by mail or through ads in disciplinary publications. Costs of such efforts are proportionately lower and response higher, thereby creating a more favorable environment for the effort than exists in the general consumer field. Also, the retail exposure of specialized books is so limited that direct marketing by the publisher becomes a necessity.

In addition to space advertising and direct mail, publishers' promotional efforts include furnishing posters, display materials, and special racks (favored especially by large trade and mass market paperback publishers); exhibits at meetings of booksellers, librarians, and professional and scholarly associations; and consumer book fairs (managed by booksellers and/or publishers). The industry as a whole, through such programs as National Literary Week, Children's Book Week, and the American Book Awards, engages in some promotional efforts on behalf of books and reading, as do the various trade associations, the AAP, ABA, NACS, and Children's Book Council, individually. Perhaps such general efforts, particularly those directed to the young, are the most productive of all.

INTERNATIONAL MARKETS

There are a number of ways in which American publishers place their books on foreign markets: they export copies of American editions to booksellers and libraries abroad; they arrange for the sale of entire editions to foreign publishers; they distribute their books in foreign countries through their own subsidiary companies; and they sell translation and/or publication rights of their titles to publishers in other lands. Since the marketing of rights, including those placed abroad, is discussed in the next section, we shall confine ourselves here to reviewing the sale of American *books* in foreign countries.

By far the most common arrangement involves the export of copies of American titles to foreign customers, be they individuals, booksellers, or libraries. Most publishers employ foreign sales representatives, usually American firms such as Feffer & Simons, or Kaiman & Polon. These firms engage sales travelers who call on bookstores, wholesalers, and libraries abroad, soliciting orders for the most salable titles. They also act as clearinghouses for special orders placed by dealers and institutions. Among the services export agents provide are credit checks on foreign customers, or even the assumption of all credit risks for an extra commission, a most important consideration since debts from foreign sources are sometimes difficult to collect. They also keep their publisher clients advised on currency problems, another important consideration since certain Asian and African countries are periodically short of dollars, and export to them must at times be severely restricted or credit extended for unusually long periods.

For the most part the orders thus obtained are shipped by the American publisher from its domestic warehouse. However, the foreign representative usually has warehousing facilities in key locations abroad, and some publishers will stock some of their titles for immediate delivery at the foreign locations.

There are some striking differences in the level of export sales for different types of books. According to estimates for 1987, only 4.6 percent of adult trade hardbound and 4.3 percent of adult trade paperbound total sales were exported, while 12.5 percent of professional and 28.0 percent of university press sales were shipped aboard. College text exports represented 8.4 percent of total sales, elhi text exports 4.8 percent, and mass market paperback exports 10.4 percent. It is not surprising therefore that among publishers operating their own facilities abroad are principally college textbook, professional, and scholarly imprints. These facilities are usually incorporated in the foreign countries, staffed by indigenous personnel, and operate as local publishers. While some import copies from the parent company in the United States, others manufacture editions locally, often translated into the language of that country, or with text adaptations that make them more marketable in their own area.

American publishers are well advised to institute such subsidiaries abroad—although, as Kenneth T. Hurst, former President of Prentice-Hall International, has pointed out, only substantial sales and a sizable program can justify such a move—for the nature of overseas interest in American text and professional publications has changed. At one time the unique quality of books originating in America made them superior to most others emanating from other countries and therefore gave American publishers a significant dominance in the field. However, Japanese, Scandinavian, and other European publishers have developed publishing programs in the sciences, technology, and business which not only rival U.S. books successfully, but which are sometimes more appealing to local audiences because of their indigenous orientation and focus. By developing similar publishing programs locally, American publishers can maintain positions, if not of leadership at least of competitiveness, in the world market.

Even publishers who do not operate their own foreign companies, however, often find that titles they originate will have a sufficiently strong appeal abroad to justify indigenous publication. They may then make arrangements with a foreign publisher for the exportation of an entire edition, either in sheets to be bound abroad or of fully bound and jacketed copies. Not infrequently, in particular where expensive art books are involved, publishers from several countries will collaborate, each planning an edition for its own market with a text in the market's language. Joint editions will then be manufactured, in whole or in part, in an area of the world where quality and price prove to be most advantageous for the entire venture.

International publishing is not without its hazards. In addition to credit risks and currency problems, publishers have had to deal with piracy and with demands by underdeveloped countries for total freedom in reproducing copyrighted books. As the United States is a signatory to the Universal Copyright and Berne Conventions, and as American books with foreign sales potential are usually copyrighted simultaneously in Canada or another signatory to the Berne convention (which offers somewhat greater protection than does the Universal Copyright Convention), American books are protected by international agreement in most countries of the world including the Soviet Union. Furthermore, an agreement concluded in Paris in 1971 is designed to offer maximum opportunity to developing countries for acquiring rights to books published in developed nations without, however, destroying the protection of international copyright.

Developed nations, including the United States, are aware that in the long run any contribution to the educational development of underdeveloped countries is bound to create new readers and therefore benefit publishers wherever they may be. In consequence the Paris agreement has the support of U.S. publishers. What is more difficult to deal with is outright piracy: the unlicensed reproduction of American books by foreign publishers. Generally, the governments of the countries where such piracy has occurred have cooperated with the U.S. State Department, acting on behalf of American publishers, in bringing such offenders into line.

In addition to publishers, there are a number of wholesalers engaged in significant book export from the United States. Among the most active in this area are firms which ship books to military installations, government operated schools, and Information Libraries abroad, under government contracts.

MARKETING RIGHTS

Large trade publishers in particular have such a great stake in the sale of subsidiary rights that the responsibility for handling such sales is usually placed in the hands of a skilled and experienced person or staff. Book clubs, reprint publishers, magazines, and other media that might use an entire work or part of it are approached, usually at very early stages of a book's production, to explore the extent of their interest. Advance proofs are a common means of exposing a project to a prospect.

Where book clubs are concerned, arrangements on major titles are usually made with the larger clubs on an exclusive basis: only one club may distribute the book to its members. Where smaller clubs and books of lesser drawing power are involved, the title may well be sold to more than one club. This is particularly true of titles that clubs acquire for use in introductory offers or as premium or bonus books to reward faithful members. Clubs have been known to use classics and reference works for such purposes which have been in print for years and where exclusivity would be meaningless.

When negotiating with reprint publishers, of both trade and mass market paperbacks, discussions are often initiated when a manuscript is first accepted or when a project is placed under contract. Like authors' agents, publishers may hold auctions on major titles inviting several paperback houses to submit simultaneous bids. Or joint publication may be arranged, under which originating and reprint publisher assume part of the responsibility for author's advance, promotional, printing, and other publishing expenses, and also share income in proportion.

Foreign and translation rights are sometimes handled by special agents retained by the publisher to represent it in a foreign country (assuming, of course, that such rights have not been reserved to the author, as TV and film rights now usually are, and will therefore be disposed of by the author or his or her agent). There is also a great deal of visiting going on, with foreign publishers coming to this country and American publishers going abroad to discuss and conclude arrangements. Here, too, advance copies of manuscripts or proofs may serve as vehicles for examination, with foreign publishers requesting exclusive option for a limited time. Top items may well be subject to auction just as they are for domestic reprint. There is also a great international publishing meeting, the Frankfurt Book Fair, held each October in Frankfurt am Main, West Germany, where publishers do a great deal of buying and selling of international rights as is the case at several other fairs of lesser scope, and at the ABA convention.

Serialization and excerpts by newspapers and magazines may involve use of the material before publication (first serialization) or after publication (second serialization). Both are encouraged not only because of the income they may yield but because of the valuable publicity for the book such use by mass media usually represents.

Finally, publishers derive a small but steady income on their own behalf and that of their authors through the granting of permission for the use of incidental passages or sections from their books, usually in other books. Collections of readings for college and secondary text use, anthologies for popular consumption, works of scholarship or literature utilizing extensive quotations, are typical of the projects to which such permissions are granted for a fee. Short quotations, exempted from copyright protection under the doctrine of fair use, are not usually charged for.

SPECIAL SALES AND REMAINDERS

The term "special sales" covers transactions outside the publisher's usual channels, such as premium sales to industry. Enterprising publishers have found that handsome income awaits the house that has the imagination to promote its books off the beaten path. One need think only of road atlases imprinted for motel chains, for example, or various books on sports which are offered as giveaways on TV, to recognize the popularity and volume of distribution that is often enjoyed by such arrangements.

Remainders are overstock that has ceased to sell at full price and is therefore disposed of far below its usual cost. Some publishers run their own remainder sales by making special offers to dealers or to consumers by mail. There are also wholesalers of remainders who buy overstock in bulk, disposing of it in a variety of ways, such as through one-priced assortments marketed by department and discount stores, through mail order catalogs imprinted for dealers, and through promotional sale ads run by department stores and bookstores. Some books do so well as remainders that the wholesaler will reprint them after the remainder stock is exhausted, and entire hardcover reprint series have been developed to take advantage of this phenomenon. What makes such books especially attractive is the comparative price ("published at $25—now only $4.95"), while the sales volume created by the special promotion makes it economically possible and profitable to reprint the books at the lower price. The original publisher normally furnishes negatives for the reprint and earns a small royalty per copy on the deal.

What contributes to the success of remainders—and the reprints they spawn—is the fact that the titles thus promoted are often coming to the attention of a broad public for the first time. They are titles which on their original publication became lost in the shuffle, inundated and submerged by too many other books which were getting the lion's share of attention. Often, too, they were overpriced for their market and became successful only after they were sacrificed at the remainder or reprint price. Some dealers specializing in remainders even bring in such items from abroad as they have discovered that a reduced-price market will make an item popular and profitable which would have died on the vine had it been imported under normal circumstances.

The experience of remainders, and reprinted remainders, offers one more proof that consumer interest in books—including serious and important books—is widespread and that often all that is required to exploit it is an aggressive and attractive way to market such books.

VI

How Books Are Stored and Delivered

The "fulfillment" function discussed in this brief chapter embraces two principal areas: the processing of customers' orders, including billing, maintenance of accounts receivable, and related preparation of sales and inventory reports; and the warehousing and shipping of books. These appear at first glance to be humble and relatively insignificant tasks—housekeeping chores which have little or no bearing on the creative aspects of the publishing process. How fatal a conclusion that would be! Many a battle in publishing has been lost for want of a horseshoe nail—in fact, the inefficacies of the present system of book delivery are among the principal reasons why the industry is failing to fulfill its promise and potential.

ORDER PROCESSING

Under AAP survey definitions, "order processing" includes the following activities: "order editing, invoicing, preparation of credit memoranda, inventory control, maintenance of accounts receivable, credit control, and production of periodic sales and inventory reports. Also included is the so-called 'customer service' function—an activity devoted to handling order inquiries and complaints."

Since these tasks, as well as those of shipping and warehousing, are closely related to the other business and financial concerns, such as accounting, to which a publisher must attend, in large firms they are usually performed under the supervision of the business or financial manager of a house. And since they are commonly computerized (electronic data processing or EDP), the work may be farmed out to service organizations. Invariably, however, the publisher must exercise strict watch over the process whether it is conducted in house or delegated to an outside firm. So complex are the tasks of fulfillment, so easily disrupted, and so costly to restore once they have malfunctioned, that a publisher can simply not afford, financially or because of customer dissatisfaction, to neglect this vital area.

Order Editing

It would be easy to assume that an order received from a bookseller, library, wholesaler, school, or individual would need simply to be invoiced and shipped—and there would be an end of it. Unfortunately it's not that simple. To begin with, many orders are incorrectly or incompletely prepared. Many fail to identify author or title properly; names are misspelled, words confused or badly remembered (too many orders are obviously prepared from memory, without consulting catalogs), prices are wrong or outdated, International Standard Book Numbers (ISBN)—when not neglected—are often misstated. Many orders fail to identify the edition wanted when more than one is available, such as in cases of hardback and paperback versions. Many orders include requests for books that have been out of print for years or for books published by other publishers.

The publisher's first task, therefore, on receiving an order is to clean it up so that it can be billed and shipped. Authors and titles must be properly identified, and since most publishers now maintain their title file by the ISBN the correct number must be noted. Where such identification is not possible, where the customer must supply additional data or be advised that the order cannot be filled as placed, the customer must be notified either separately or on the invoice which covers the shipment.

To simplify the chore of notification, most publishers use a common code of abbreviations to cover the most frequently encountered problems. Notable among these are OP (out-of-print), for books whose stock is permanently exhausted; TOP (temporarily out-of-print), where plans for reprinting the book are somewhat indefinite; OS (out of stock), where a title is temporarily unavailable but expected in the near future, with the estimated arrival date usually noted; NYP (not yet published), in cases where books are ordered in advance of the publication date; and NO (not ours), for titles not published by the house.

There are other reasons why an order must be examined before it can be billed. Since discounts in many cases are contingent not only on the type of book or the quantity ordered but also on the type of account placing the order (wholesalers and agency accounts are examples of customers who would be entitled to preferential discounts), instructions are often needed so that billing clerks will extend appropriate discounts in each case. Such discounts can vary considerably from title to title, even on the same order. To take an example, a retailer ordering books from a publisher of both trade and professional books may be entitled to the regular quantity-related discount on trade titles ordered, to an agency discount on certain of the professional titles, and to a standard short discount on other professional books not covered by the publisher's agency plan.

Many customers, notably those affiliated with governments and municipalities, have highly complicated procedures for purchasing materials which necessitate a good deal of extra paperwork on the publisher's part. Some require the submission of advance quotations or competitive bids—even for a single copy of a book—before they can award a purchase contract. Others must be invoiced in sextuplicate or septuplicate, with notarized affidavits of compliance with numerous regulations attached. Similar demands accompany many shipments to foreign destinations. All such orders require careful inspection and instructions in advance to make certain that requirements are conscientiously followed.

Needless to say, the task of order editing is a demanding one and can only be assigned to a highly competent individual thoroughly familiar with the publisher's list, prices, policies, and customers. The developments which have automated—and necessarily so—much of the routine of order processing have placed even greater weight on the importance of the initial review, because orders can be handled effectively and correctly by automation only if they have first been subjected to the most rigorous and intelligent editing. Machines don't think—they only carry out orders, hopefully issued by people who think!

Credit Control

Any business can make a great many shipments and issue a great many invoices, yet little is accomplished unless customers pay their bills. Since in the field of bookselling as in many other mercantile fields, some customers pay slowly or not at all, publishers cannot indiscriminately process every order received without ascertaining that the account in question has a good credit standing.

In the case of existing accounts this requires an examination of their indebtedness and past payment history. A customer who owes for excessively long periods and whose indebtedness has built up to a dangerously high level, may have to be told that shipment cannot be made until payment is received. The terms publishers normally extend to their customers are 30 days net, requiring payment within a month. When payment is not received within the specified period, statements are forwarded to the delinquent account and, after 90 days or so, the customer may well be "cut off," i.e., be refused further shipments on open account.

Exceptions are of course made for institutions whose cumbersome payment procedures often make it impossible for them to pay even within 90 days. Also certain accounts—like college stores during the summer months—may be given "advance dating" on their invoices, i.e., payment does not become due until a later specified date, normally to give the customer an opportunity to see some of the merchandise before having to pay for it. Similarly, longer terms are extended to foreign accounts to allow for the additional time consumed in transporting goods to overseas destinations.

Should a customer fail to pay even after repeated warnings, the bill is usually turned over to a collection agency, i.e., a commercial service that collects past due accounts for a percentage (usually 50 percent) of the overdue amount. Only in the case of a very sizable debt would the publisher find it worthwhile to go to court after the collection agent has failed; instead it would be better simply to "write off" the uncollectable amount (i.e., treat it as an expense of doing business).

Accounts that establish a reputation for nonpayment of bills are simply refused credit and are asked to pay for their books in advance of shipment. Since the known offenders are usually impartial in owing all publishers with whom they deal, a regular warning system, exchanging information among publishers, helps to identify them and prevent too many publishers from running into difficulty. Among the sources of such information are the collection agencies, such as Stanley K. Oldden Inc., which issue confidential bulletins about bad accounts to their clients.

When a new trade account requests credit, it is usually asked for references, notably from other publishers with whom it deals or for evidence at any rate that it has the resources and the integrity to honor its debts. Sometimes the publisher will extend credit only up to a certain limit because the data provided by the customer indicate that its resources are too limited to argue for unrestricted credit. Institutions and governments are not subject to such controls, of course. Nor are individual consumers in most cases. The publisher who deals with individuals as a matter of policy recognizes that the cost of checking the credit of each one would exceed the collective bad debt that would result from extending ready credit to all applicants.

In theory, then, a customer who fails to pay bills with reasonable promptness will not be shipped on open account, and the business management of a publisher is usually ready to stick by this sound policy. Unfortunately, such a policy has a tendency to keep down sales, and so the sales management of the same publishing house will often argue for more liberal terms. Not infrequently this leads to rather unfriendly discussions between sales and business managers, and top management must step in to arbitrate. Characteristically it arbitrates on the side of sales, harkening to such arguments as "books in the warehouse do no one any good," or "how can we increase sales when you tie our hands this way?" In vain will banks that lend money to publishers hold seminars urging them to be less liberal in extending credit to doubtful accounts. In vain will collection agents warn that such liberality may only have the result of encouraging booksellers or wholesalers to overextend themselves and hasten bankruptcy, a bankruptcy that might have been prevented had sound business restraint been used. "Good" sales figures—whether they turn out ultimately to be really sales or not—are apparently too much of an enticement to keep some publishers from taking the long view.

Invoicing, Payments, Credit Memoranda, and Reports

Most invoicing is done through automated systems, and EDP can even perform some functions involved in credit control, such as checking an account's indebtedness and automatically rejecting an order if the account has exceeded its limits. Most systems, too, are able to assign appropriate discounts automatically—particularly if exceptions have been noted in editing.

In the course of billing, important information is gathered or updated: inventories of titles on hand, advance orders for unpublished titles, and sales information, usually broken down by title, type of customer, and customer's geographic location. The inventory data include warning of titles running low so that reprint orders can be placed early enough to keep most active titles in stock, at least most of the time.

The system is designed, further, to post payments and to prepare periodic statements (i.e., summaries of accounts) for customers who owe money. When books are returned or errors are made in billing, credit memoranda are issued, in effect reversing the billing, with resulting additions to inventory and deductions from sales records.

Very often systems fail and chaos sets in. This has been particularly true when a system has first been installed by a publisher; customers have learned to expect malfunctions and disruptions in service whenever a publisher announces conversion to a new system. Both publishers and booksellers are then tempted to blame computers for their troubles—as though computers had minds of their own or were faultily constructed. The truth is, of course, that computers follow human instructions and commands. Many of the installations made in the publishing field are programmed by people who are not familiar with the book industry, who assume that because the book world bears a superficial resemblance to other mercantile industries, the same procedures as would work in processing hardware or canned goods might safely apply to books. Screws and bolts don't have authors or titles, however; they are not sold under significantly different circumstances to a variety of markets and different types of customers; they don't come in different editions on which different discount schedules might apply. Nor is their inventory control and stock replenishment as frought with complexities, nor must cumbersome records be kept so that royalties can be paid correctly in accordance with intricate contractual arrangements.

Most of the difficulties computer installations have caused in the book field have been due to a profound lack of communication between the people who furnished the computers, did the programming, and made the installations and the staff of the publishing houses who were subsequently asked to work with the new systems. Unbelievable though it may sound, case after case is on record involving computer installations where the installers did not acquaint themselves with the business they were about to serve, where the first conversation they held with the publisher's fulfillment crew occurred *after* the computer was on the premises and all the programs were already written. Subsequent failures were then often blamed on the hapless staff that had not been prepared for their new assignments; they were accused of hostility toward the new system, uncooperativeness, or even lack of intelligence.

The grief that has come to publishers and their customers as a result of such ill-conceived and badly executed systems installations, has exacerbated an almost mystical distrust of computers that has been bred into the souls of many publishers and booksellers. They see automation as the wicked world of technology taking over and destroying the vital, humane, and urbane world of literature. That their vital and urbane world is riddled with near fatal inefficiencies that could be effectively resolved by the computer when properly programmed and that, in fact, nothing may save that world but such effective application of the new technology does not apparently persuade them. Yet their antipathy represents a formidable obstacle to attempts to put the industry's fulfillment house in order.

WAREHOUSING AND SHIPPING

Just as there is a variety of order processing arrangements, involving internal installations as well as the use of outside services, so there is a variety of warehousing and shipping arrangements in use within the industry. Large publishers usually operate several warehouses located in different parts of the country; others utilize only one warehouse. Some middle-sized and smaller houses share joint facilities; still others make use of commercial shipping services. Nearly all publishers stock inventories at binderies and may occasionally make very large shipments of single titles directly from binderies.

The major problem is that for the most part they "go it alone." Every day a vast tonnage of books is shipped from eastern locations to other parts of the country, for example, without any attempt to consolidate these shipments. Conceivably several trailer trucks or railway freight cars could be filled daily, yet a major effort to organize such an operation recently failed due to lack of cooperation from mainstream publishers and only limited participation by booksellers. Still, nothing would have been more logical. The book industry, though sizable and complex, is concentrated to a significant extent in larger metropolitan areas. Considerable time and money could have been saved just by consolidating a vast number of small shipments many of which now travel by book post, and most of which are directed to a relatively small number of wholesalers, booksellers, libraries, and institutions in a few urban centers.

In past decades the idea of regional warehouses operated by the industry has often been mentioned. This was a sound concept when fewer books were published and before many of the larger publishers invested large sums in constructing warehouses of their own. But while regional warehouses might no longer be practical, regional processing centers might be. Such processing centers need not stock inventories but could consolidate orders from wholesalers, booksellers, and institutions, receiving consolidated shipments in return, which they could then distribute, in reconsolidated form, to customers. The processing centers, located perhaps in some twelve key locations throughout the country, could function with the use of a central computer, and could use standard order forms, standard book and customer numbers, standard billing and reporting procedures (though still, of course, implementing faithfully each publisher's specific discount schedule and operating polices). The centers could also employ consolidated shipping services, operating, conceivably, their own fleet of trucks. They would be industry-owned and operated not-for-profit.

It is possible, of course, that the increasing role played by wholesalers might sooner or later lead them to assume a greater part in the process and help make the industry's delivery system more efficient. Yet there are serious questions whether wholesalers will ever find it sufficiently profitable to process the many special orders at short discount that now constitute a significant portion of the shipping volume that requires consolidation.

Assuming that wholesalers, although likely to perform increasingly valuable services—by making books that sell well more promptly available to bookstores, for example—may indeed find it impractical to take on the industry's entire delivery burden, a system of nonprofit, regional processing centers may well prove to be the solution to the industry's very critical fulfillment impasse.

VII

How Publishers Finance, Plan, and Manage

The organization, structure, and business and financial management of publishing houses are the final subjects in this survey of the industry. Like other aspects of the field, business and financial characteristics vary from house to house and depend on the type of publishing in which it is engaged. These aspects are also heavily dependent on size and management philosophy.

STRUCTURE AND ORGANIZATION

In Figure 9, the organization of a publishing house is shown. What is envisioned here is a medium-sized enterprise engaged in, basically, only one kind of publishing (such as trade or college). In a small press, the entrepreneur will combine all functions, or share them with family or a handful of employees. In a smaller mainstream house, some of the man-

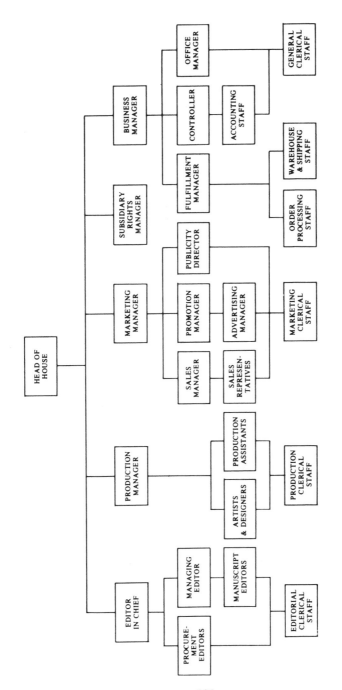

FIGURE 9. Organization chart of a publishing house.

agement positions charted would probably be combined and managers would be involved substantially in the everyday activities of their departments. Thus an editor in chief would probably do a great deal of procurement and serve also as managing editor (i.e., control the flow of work in the department and supervise the copy-editing staff directly). The head of the house may function also as an editor, or as the marketing manager, and the roles of sales, promotion, and advertising manager may be combined. Small houses, furthermore, rely more on outside or free-lance assistance; they might farm out all copy editing, possibly all production work, and, very likely, all fulfillment.

In larger houses, on the other hand, specific functions additional to those shown in Figure 9 would probably have to be charted. The editorial department, for example, would probably include manuscript readers. The marketing department may well have a separate international sales manager, a direct mail manager, a market research director and staff, and regional sales managers. Reporting to the business manager may be a legal counsel, a financial planning and/or corporate research department, and a manager of electronic data processing (EDP) with a staff of programmers.

A subsidiary rights manager is shown on the chart, a position that would probably function on such a high level only in a trade house. The organization of an elhi publisher, on the other hand, would have to include consultants in the marketing area. Furthermore, the terms used to designate certain responsibilities vary greatly from house to house as does the distribution of these responsibilities themselves. As in other contexts, we have employed the concepts and definitions utilized in AAP surveys, thus representing what is majority practice in the mainstream industry.

Relatively few major publishing houses are today engaged in only one type of publishing, and their organization charts would therefore show several divisions (such as professional, elhi, and college). Such divisions may operate almost autonomously so that their individual charts may well look much like the one we have illustrated. More commonly, however, each division will control only its own editorial and marketing departments and will share joint production and business services with the other divisions.

Behind the method by which a multidivisional publisher is organized lie important concepts of management philosophy. Some managements believe in strong centralization, arguing that the more services that can be performed under a single supervisor, the more efficient and economical the entire operation will become. Others are convinced that the more autonomy is granted to a division and the more of its services it can render under its own auspices, the more productive and excellent its performance is likely to become. There are strong and persuasive arguments for either point of view, and there are many examples of good and efficient management under either alternative, just as there are examples of failure under both. In the end what seems to make the difference between such success or failure is not so much the theoretical structure employed or the philosophy espoused as the ability and commitment of the people, both in top management and on the operating level, who must carry out their responsibilities within the structure. A well-managed, productive organization appears to be one in which senior management is able to inspire its staff to do their best and where operating executives and personnel are both capable of and committed to performing their tasks well.

It matters a good deal who the people performing the various functions are and under what conditions they will perform them best. Good people are not always available for every opening, however, and sometimes a particular post is extremely difficult to fill. Even though, in theory, decentralization may be the more desirable arrangement, it will not always be possible to realize it in practice unless the resources of the house and favorable circumstances permit it to attract first-rate talent. To a large extent intelligent organization will be less inspired by theory than by the pragmatic consideration: what type of structure will work best for the people on our staff?

Multidivisional houses are faced with an additional organizational challenge: overlapping markets. At one time, notably before World War II, a house that organized itself by product or editorial divisions found that its marketing structure naturally followed suit: trade books were marketed to trade outlets, college books to college outlets, elhi books to schools, etc. Today, of course, this identity of product and market sphere no longer holds, as many trade books are marketed to schools and colleges, college books to secondary schools, and so on.

Most multidivisional publishing houses are still organized according to product-editorial criteria even today, however, with the result that a division's marketing department is usually unable to dispose of all of its own products in its own market and is engaged in selling a good deal of another division's materials in addition to its own. Since divisions are conceived to be profit centers (i.e., their profit and loss performance is carefully analyzed by management, and division heads are held responsible for that performance), financial adjustments must be made within multidivisional companies to allow for the interdivisional selling of products. A variety of methods is used to achieve these adjustments, such as one division actually selling its books to the other, or paying its sister division sales commissions for marketing services performed.

PERSONNEL POLICIES AND MANAGEMENT

Management Attitudes

The key to good publishing, we have suggested, is primarily good people: good people at the top who will in turn attract good people to the middle and to the bottom and create such an environment and atmosphere for their work as to enable them to do their best. No doubt it is possible to violate these rules for a time, to enjoy brief periods of success even while ignoring every good and responsible personnel practice, but it is very doubtful that a publisher can hope to survive and prosper for a long while disregarding the essential fact that the quality and effectiveness of a program must ultimately depend on the quality and effectiveness of the staff.

Publishing is a people business. From the editor who must gain an author's confidence and nurture him or her along to turn out the best manuscript possible, to the shipping clerk in the warehouse who must care enough so that an order is picked and packed correctly, the entire industry rises and falls with the capacity and commitment of its people.

It is astonishing that some publishers seem to disregard, or pay inade-quate attention to, this vital fact. Although for years—in book published by publishers—industrial psychologists have attempted to encourage sound personnel policies, certain publishing executives appear to be un-aware of them. Apparently they don't read their own books!

The insights industrial psychologists have emphasized are that people look upon work as a source of self-fulfillment, that they want to be able to believe in and take pride in what they do, that they want to feel that they are making a contribution, and that they are motivated as much or more by these considerations as by the money they are paid or by the fear of losing their jobs. If this is true of people in general, how much more so of the creative people who are likely to be attracted to and be engaged in most publishing jobs! More sensitive, more highly motivated, more committed to their self-development than the average, creative people are likely to respond more readily to good personnel management and far more ad-versely to poor personnel practices than most.

How does some publishing management, however, hope to gain the commitment of its people when it shows slight regard for their efforts, firing editors and marketing people because a product does not live up to expectations? Publishing is after all a business of risks; even people with excellent judgment are bound to make mistakes sometimes, particularly since overproduction has glutted distribution channels and even worthy titles often suffocate for sheer lack of breathing space.

Or will certain publishing management motivate its staff when it fails to utilize their talent and judgment, refusing to delegate authority to people well able to handle it? Why hire editors, production chiefs, designers, or salespersons—ostensibly because of their creative capability and sound judgment—then make them toe a narrow line, have no creative leeway, and be no more than rubber stamps for their superiors?

Will some publishing management inspire its employees when it appears unclear in defining its policies and objectives, changes them suddenly without warning, and acts indecisively, capriciously, and arbitrarily? Or will some management enlist the warm commitment of its staff if it is devious and dishonest and asks the staff to act dishonestly toward authors, suppliers, and customers?

Should not management in a communications industry communicate with its employees, or in a cultual industry show respect for their dignity as persons and for their sensitivity as human beings? Publishers who treat their staff as partners in their creative enterprise, who fully utilize the talents of their employees and extend to them the simple courtesy to which they should be entitled reap great benefits from such seemingly obvious and basic attitudes. Their people work with enthusiasm and concern. They make the publisher's objective their own and identify readily with the publisher's interests.

Let me not be misunderstood. Not all employees, particularly the talented, are reasonable or capable of responding to courteous, responsible management. We live in emotional times in which personalities often tend to extremes, the creative unfortunately more than the average. Hostility to all authority, to all business enterprise, even a culturally oriented one, afflicts some, not only among the young. Nothing that management can do is likely to enable such people to come to terms with a world with which they are fundamentally at odds, or with a social structure they despise. Unfortunate though it may be, such people cannot be humored; if they cannot adjust to the necessary routine of a publishing house, no alternative is available but to dismiss them. Such instances are tragic because, were it not for their personality difficulties, such people could be highly useful to the industry and happy in their work.

But a manager who decides that he or she is dealing with a hopelessly rebellious personality should consider first whether the hostility is really incurable or whether it is simply a response to the manager's own ineptness and heavy-handedness. From what I have observed in the industry, far more discontent is engendered by poor management than by cultural disorientation or personal alienation.

Education and Training

Although a number of academic programs throughout the country offer courses on book publishing, most of the education and training given to employees in the industry is imparted on the job. While much may be said in favor of one-the-job training—it is often more realistic in its approach than academic career training—when it becomes the only method of preparing people for a career it turns out to be very costly for the industry, as well as both employer and employee. The industry suffers because past errors tend to be perpetuated and outdated practices fail to receive the critical scrutiny they should from an independent educational establishment. Employers must invest staggering amounts of supervisory time in the training process, and employees often do not discover until long after that they are in the wrong spot or even in the wrong industry. High dropout rates and excessive turnover result which are inherently costly for all concerned. Furthermore, some people do not learn well under the kind of pressure characteristic of on-the-job training, and some supervisors are poor teachers.

On-the-job training inclines, furthermore, to be rather narrow in its approach, concentrating on the job at hand and on little more. It is amazing how many capable editors, production people, marketing people, and accountants in the mainstream industry know little more than the editing, production, sales, or financial tasks they must perform daily; they are literally insulated from other people in the field, even from others within the same house. Few individuals in this "knowledge" industry appear to acquire a broad, comprehensive knowledge of the field in which they earn their livelihood, to place their own role into industry context, or to place the industry itself within the context of the world at large.

Some publishing houses offer formal and broadly oriented training courses within their own walls—and these have been of some help to their staffs. But such "cram" courses—and they can afford to be little else— still cannot solve the problem of an antiquated industry tradition that is being passed on intact. Nor can they deal with the difficulties of the person who entered book publishing having dreamed of working closely with authors and of influencing the course of American literature, only to discover that mainstream trade editorial positions are very few and far between and are usually not awarded to people until after they have spent many years learning their craft. Just a little advance information about the industry, how it works and what opportunities are available in it, might have saved such an individual a good deal of frustration and disappointment.

Recruiting Talent

As it turns out, many persons with noble editorial ambitions now accept what they consider to be second best—such as a production, sales, or clerical job—just to be in the publishing world, or in the hope of eventually realizing that first dream. Others drift into professional or educational publishing as a second choice when they discover that the trade publishing job they sought is just not available. Since man's accidents are often God's purposes, such persons sometimes become sublimely happy in the positions in which they eventually find themselves. Very frequently, however, this happens only after much painful trial and error, and all too often things don't work out at all.

Although the industry has no formal recruiting program, and few general publishing houses engage in recruiting on their own, in professional and educational publishing conditions are somewhat better because these publishers are in closer contact with their readership and draw much of their talent from it. Many a professor, schoolteacher, or professional person with literary flair and an interest in publishing has gone to work in a publishing house as an editor, sales representative, or consultant. College publishers actually engage in intensive recruiting of students about to graduate from college, who usually begin their careers as field representatives, many eventually rising to editors and managers.

Like other industries in recent years, book publishing has struggled with the problems of minority employment—with moderate success. It is probably fair to say that the atmosphere for ethnic minorities is more hospitable in cultural industries than in other segments of the economy; the artistic and intellectual strata of society—whatever their other failings—have always been less riddled with raw prejudice than most. At the same time, members of minority groups have been quite diffident about seeking employment in cultural industries, an understandable attitude in view of the cultural and educational deprivation to which they have been subjected. Outreach programs, in which active recruitment of minority employees is coupled with intensive efforts to make up for educational and cultural disadvantage, have met with only marginal response from both publishers and minority candidates.

The position of women in the industry is actually fairly good—compared to most other industries. Women have headed publishing houses in the past and they do so now and women often hold chief editorial, production, business, and sales positions. There has certainly been more opportunity for women in this and other cultural industries than in the general manufacturing and mercantile fields that constitute the bulk of American commerce. This does not rule out the fact, however, that women are often paid less than men for identical responsibilities; in fact some of the advanced positions women have earned in the field have at least in part been awarded to them because publishers know that they could pay them less than men. And undoubtedly in some of the larger houses, particularly some educational and professional imprints owned by conglomerates, formidable obstacles exist for women who hope to rise to the top. One surmises, however, that the innately more hopsitable attitudes prevailing in the field will continue to result in more rapid gains for qualified women here than perhaps in other industries.

Promotion, Advancement, and Compensation

The matter of promotion and advancement in the mainstream industry is itself a delicate issue because here as in so many other fields where special skills earn the recognition of management, people are often promoted to managerial positions even though they may lack the qualifications for holding them. It is simply not true that a superb editor, excellent designer, highly effective salesperson, or first-rate financial planner will necessarily make a good editor in chief, production manager, or sales or business manager. On the contrary—the very fact that his or her talents are concentrated in a special field may make that person less qualified than others to be a manager.

To be a good manager in a people industry calls primarily for the ability to work well with people and to inspire them. It is not likely that an individual will succeed as a manager unless he or she fundamentally likes people, can relate to them easily, empathize with them, take a genuine interest in them, and develop honest regard for them. Obviously people with hang-ups, with strong neurotic tendencies, make very poor managers; their excessive preoccupation with self and their insecurity will constantly get in the way of their developing constructive relationships with others. Similarly professionals whose first love and major interest lies in the pursuit of their craft may simply not be able to muster the psychic energy a manager must be able to invest in relationships with employees.

Promotion to managerial responsibility should never be regarded as a reward for good professional performance. Professional excellence deserves professional rewards, both financial and in public recognition; however, as in the academic and other professional fields, honors can surely be bestowed on people without inflicting them on others as managers. The true facts regarding qualifications for management call for a major reorientation on the part of some ownership and top-level administrators in publishing who must begin to appoint people to such vital roles only on the basis of the belief that they will really make capable managers.

One suspects that once the quality of management improves, some of the disastrous and debilitating interdivisional and interdepartmental conflicts one witnesses so often in mainstream publishing houses will also begin to subside. Now frequently tugs of war between editors and production people, between editors and salespeople, between businesspeople and all the rest, disrupt the orderly and productive process of work and victimize authors and customers. Good managers could keep professional jealousies in check and put dampers on unruly egos, at least sufficiently to prevent the publisher's work from suffering.

As for compensation, salary levels vary widely depending on the type of publishing involved, the size of a firm and its location. In general, mainstream professional and textbook publishing personnel are competitively compensated, as are senior professionals in trade operations. However, salaries of entry-level jobs in large trade houses have long been scandalously low, particularly in New York City. The trade giants take advantage of the fact that there are multiple applications for every such opening and that they perennially enjoy a wide choice, often of overqualified candidates. The traditional parsimony, which has worsened in recent years, exacts a high price, however. Twenty-three students of the Radcliffe Publishing Procedures course, the most prestigious of the academic institutes offered every summer, called attention to the adverse consequences of the practice in *Publishers Weekly* on August 29, 1986.

> Publishers insist that low starting salaries are all they can afford; and, after all they suffered from them, why shouldn't we? There is some logic to this. But entry-level salaries seem to have increased only about 2%–3% a year in the past ten years, despite inflation that has ranged from 4%–15% a year. Publishers also say that they pay poorly because they cannot afford to train and then lose people to other companies. But everyone in publishing trains neophytes for everyone else. The costs and the benefits are spread around. The neophytes are the losers.
>
> The publishing industry loses too. The Radcliffe Course graduates about 85 bright-eyed enthusiasts every summer, but on an average only half are still in publishing five years later. Thus, when the viability of the book industry and the future of the printed word are constantly questioned, the most committed and energetic new blood is being driven out toward banking, law and even teaching. Of course, publishers can always find another hopelessly idealistic prospect to occupy the next typewriter or phone bank. But in the long run, few but the independently wealthy survive—not necessarily the most capable, most imaginative or original. This is a recipe for an even more elitist, weak-blooded and inbred industry than, according to many speakers

at the course this summer, already exists. The time has come for Hell Week to end.

Reacting to the above, Cindy Adelman, then a publicist for Times Books, added the following in *Publishers Weekly* on September 19, 1986:

> A favorite irony: Radcliffe grads *do* have an extremely high placement rate in publishing (82% of last year's class had found jobs two months following graduation). But they've just paid $3,150 for a six-week crash course in the business to land a job that will pay them around $12,000.
>
> After five years in publishing, no wonder 50% of the people have left permanently, in many cases escaping to law school or business school. Money is one reason for leaving, but they also leave because they have not been given an opportunity to develop their talents fully.
>
> Everyone knows that editorial assistants are hired to perform secretarial duties as typing, filing, answering phones, photocopying, *as well as* editorial duties such as evaluating proposals, writing flap copy, tracking manuscripts through production phases and maintaining contact with authors. Interestingly, a person hired as an actual secretary will be making more than an editorial assistant—about $378 per week compared to $230 per week.
>
> The job turnover in many of these assistant spots is incredible: most people remain in their first job for about six months to a year. Assistants jump from job to job and house to house hoping to increase their paltry salaries. People in executive-level positions in publishing recall that they were not paid particularly well when they began and feel that their assistants, too, should struggle along; they prefer to ignore cost-of-living increases and competition from other areas of work that are far better paying.
>
> It is both high-handed and shortsighted to imagine that one can always fill these assistant spots with this year's crop of eager graduates. Publishing should have a vested interest in hiring the best people for entry-level positions and make a real effort to keep them on staff to develop their talents, listening to what they have to say and contribute.
>
> Constant turnover in the lower ranks of most publishing houses results in a lack of continuity that can be seen in unnecessary production delays, loss of potential publishing ideas and low company morale. Make an investment in these people—don't look at them as a disposable commodity.

Significantly, increasing numbers of students graduating from publishing institutes, as well as young fugitives from mainstream houses, are turning to small presses where they find their work both monetarily and psychically more rewarding. In 1988 there were some indications that the availability of entry-level talent willing to submit to mainstream abuses were drying up and that a growing scarcity of new recruits would begin to force changes in the traditional system.

It is important to note, finally, that in addition to full-time staffs a major labor resource in the industry consists of the many free-lance editors, production people, and commission salespeople, along with a variety of fulfillment and other service organizations. These are utilized particularly by smaller publishers, although even larger houses often call on them for special projects or to supplement their own staffs. Because the free-lancers make highly skilled and experienced labor available on an ad-hoc basis they give even the smallest house an opportunity to avail itself of competent professional services and enable larger organizations to overcome problems caused by seasonal or temporary fluctuations in their work load. (A list of such individuals and service organizations, though necessarily incomplete, appears in *Literary Market Place*.)

FINANCIAL MANAGEMENT

Accounting and Its Role

A convenient way of approaching the economics and financial dynamics of book publishing is to examine some characteristic financial statements. For accounting is really nothing more than an attempt to portray the circumstances of a business in quantitative, i.e., numerical terms, and financial statements are the means accountants use to illustrate their findings. I have therefore developed a fictitious cash flow projection, operating statements, and balance sheets, for a small press, as well as statement formats for a trade publishing house and elhi imprint. While these statements are wholly imaginary—and any resemblance to actual operation would be entirely accidental—they do incorporate the experiences a publishing house might encounter in today's economy and could therefore be termed fairly typical.

I hasten to add that "typical" allows for a wide range of circumstances. Because publishers deal in products of highly individualized nature, each with its unique character and performance in the marketplace, and because publishers themselves act and think very individualistically, there are no two publishing houses wholly alike or even very nearly alike in their income, cost, cash flow, and other fiscal experiences. Thus while the data we shall discuss may be instructive in revealing the type of economic activity or performance factors one is likely to encounter in analyzing the finances of a publisher, there will be wide departures from the specific amounts and ratios cited in the actual experiences of houses.

The very methods of accounting and preparing financial statements reflect diversity. Contrary to popular notion—and contrary to the impression accountants sometimes manage to create—accounting is not an exact science. Any capable and conscientious member of the profession will adhere to "generally accepted" standards of practice, but still has a great deal of leeway in selecting alternatives from a wealth of approaches and treatments in portraying the financial operations of an enterprise. What may be proper or not in an accountant's exercise of judgment is governed by rules and opinions handed down by the Accounting Standards Board, by the profession's governing body, the American Institute of Certified Public Accountants (AICPA), as well as by law, and by various regulatory agencies, such as the Internal Revenue Service and the Securities and Exchange Commission.

The basic motivation behind any sound accounting decision and the supreme standard that governs all practice is the honest and accurate portrayal of what is actually transpiring within the enterprise. While unscrupulous managements and their accountants may occasionally attempt to falsify records or to hide rather than to disclose facts which owners and stockholders should know, normal practice dictates that the fullest possible information be provided by whatever statements are prepared. The need for disclosure, then, dictates much of the style, format, and methods used in accounting; the desire to leave an accurate impression with the reader of a statement will influence many decisions regarding treatment and fiscal policy.

So fundamental is this concept, and so ready are all parties to honor it, that the government even allows a business to keep two sets of books: one to inform management and ownership of goings-on, the other for tax purposes. Then if under the tax law a business chooses to adopt practices which give it certain advantages but which would result in a distorted or inaccurate portrayal of the business's condition, it will not be forced to confuse the issue by having to share with management the reports designed to take advantage of tax loopholes rather than to disclose facts.

One of the basic concepts in accounting, designed to provide an accurate picture of the health and vitality of a business is that, insofar as logical and possible, the income a business enjoys should be related to the expenses incurred in generating that income. In other words, an expense should be shown on a statement covering the time period during which the income toward which it contributed is shown. For many businesses, including most publishing, this means that very often an expense is not shown when the cash was actually spent, or income when it was actually received, but at the time when the relationship between income and cost can be most meaningfully established. The accounting approach that matches income with expense irrespective of the time of cash flow is known as "accrual" accounting; it is distinguished from the method which records transactions at the time money actually flows and which is therefore known as the "cash" method.

Accrual accounting makes sense. If a large advance is paid to an author this year, yet the book being written will not be published until two years from now, it would not provide a realistic picture of the loss or gain on that book if the advance were reported on this year's statement. It would be more revealing to report the royalties covered by the advance as they are earned by sales, two and three years hence. Similarly if the printing of a book were to arrive late in the year it would be more instructive to report the cost of that printing as the books are sold during the coming year rather than burden this year's sales with expenses unrelated to them.

Time, generally, is a very important factor in accounting. A year is the basis on which major assessments and analyses of businesses are normally undertaken, not only by examining the experiences of the year itself but by comparing it with the previous and even earlier years. During the course of the year, monthly or quarterly statements are usually prepared so that the progress of the enterprise can be carefully watched. Even though short periods, influenced as they often are by incidental factors, are less reliable than longer time spans for revealing trends and patterns, intelligent watch over performance indicators, particularly as they relate to budgets and forecasts prepared in advance, and the ability to make enlightened decisions because of the information provided, are essential to sound management. Incidentally, a "year" or "quarter" may not always mean a calendar year or quarter; many businesses, including some publishing houses, operate on "fiscal" years which may end with any month and which are usually chosen because the seasonal character of the enterprise—or the history of its incorporation—provided some advantages for so doing.

Another very important consideration in accounting is consistency. Once a practice is established it should not be departed from or changed without very strong reason since such changes make comparison with previous periods very difficult if not impossible. If a change becomes inevitable, the statement which incorporates it must be adequately footnoted to call attention to the change and to warn the reader to take it into account.

Accounting for a Small Press

As a first step in observing the accounting function in practice, we shall examine the financial experience of an imaginary small press, from its beginning through its first five years of existence. In the process we shall discover how such a press might plan, record, and summarize its finances.

The imaginary press in question is about to be founded by a young woman who has had extensive experience as an editor of professional reference works. She has investigated and established the need for two regional professional directories in her geographical area, which, with the help of one full-time assistant, she proposes to compile and typeset on a desktop publishing system. One directory will initially appear in each of the first two years, to be revised every two years thereafter, so that she will, in effect, be publishing a new edition every year. Her efforts have been endorsed by the regional societies serving the professions she is addressing. Several professionals have indicated to her that, provided she can demonstrate the profitability of her planned venture, they are prepared to invest in her enterprise.

The directories will carry substantial list prices, $75 and $65 respectively. The publisher anticipates that 80 percent of sales will be made directly to individuals who will pay list price, 15 percent to wholesalers who will receive a 15 percent discount, 3 percent to libraries that will be granted a 10 percent discount, and 2 percent to booksellers who will receive a 20 percent discount.

Our entrepreneur has consulted an attorney who is incorporating the business. Next she must discover what her capital requirements will be. Accordingly, she consults an acccountant who questions her in detail about her plans and produces a cash flow projection based on her expectations (Figure 10).

Projecting Cash Flow

The projection provides data for every quarter, as well as annual totals, for the five-year period, and could apply to either a calendar or a fiscal year. The symbol "($000)" below the heading indicates that dollar signs and three zeros have been dropped from the presentation to facilitate viewing and must mentally be added to entries; in other words, the values shown represent thousands of dollars.

The stub legends at the left identify the entries either as receipts or expenditures, detailing them by source. *Book Sales* are the only source of receipts for the planned enterprise, and these are not expected to begin until year two. During year one Directory A is being compiled, typeset, and manufactured, and while some copies will actually be shipped just before year's end, payments for these shipments will not be received until the first quarter of year two at the earliest. This is due to so-called cash lag—the inevitable delay between billing and the receipt of payments— here estimated to average 30 to 45 days for individuals and 90 days for libraries, booksellers, and wholesalers.

Sales of Directory A, anticipated by the publisher to total 3,800 copies, are to occur as follows: 700 prepublication orders will be shipped at the end of year one, 2,600 copies during year two, and 500 copies during year three. A total of 1,700 of the second-year shipments will be made during the first quarter, the rest will be shipped at a rate of 100 copies per month during the balance of year two and the first five months of year three. No further shipments of the first edition of Directory A are anticipated thereafter, since the second edition will be announced in the summer of year three and shipped before the end of that year.

Directory B, to be prepared during the course of year two, is forecast to sell 3,100 copies according to the following pattern: 700 copies at the end of year two, 1,900 in year three (1,000 during the first quarter) and 500 by the fifth month of year four.

On the second edition of Directory A, the price will increase to $85. Expected sales, totaling 4,300 copies, are to occur as follows: 900 in year three, 2,900 in year four (2,000 in the first quarter) and 500 in year five.

The second edition of Directory B will carry a list price of $70. Total sales will be 3,500, of which 900 will be shipped at the end of year four, 2,100 in year five (1,200 in the first quarter) and 500 beyond the time frame of the cash flow projection in year six.

The first detail under expenditures, *Editorial,* concerns only incidental editorial disbursements—such as travel, source materials, data bank user fees, subscriptions, and memberships—since the principal editorial expense, compensation for a large portion of the owner's time, is included under Payroll.

There will not be an expenditure for *Manufacturing* during the first year, since the first payment—for 4,000 units of Directory A at $10.50 per unit for negatives, printing, paper, binding, and prepacking—will not be made until early in the second year, because the manufacturer's billing allows for a 30-day payment lag. Payment for 3,200 units of Directory B at $9.10 per unit is made a year later. In year four, the second edition of Directory A is payable, involving 4,500 copies at $11.40 per unit; and in year five the second edition of Directory B is paid for, covering 3,600 copies at $9.80 per unit. In projecting future costs, the publisher is providing for 5 percent inflation in manufacturer's charges.

Payroll represents the largest disbursement during year one. Base salaries are $35,000 to the publisher, $18,000 to the assistant, to which allowances for payroll taxes, hospitalization, and other benefits are added ($10,000 for the owner, $5,000 for the assistant). In subsequent years, 5 percent increases in base salaries are provided for.

Furniture and Equipment includes the cash outlays associated with the acquisition of a computer, peripherals, and software, which is being fi-

Professional Small Press
Five-Year Cash Flow Projection
($000)

| | Year One | | | | |
	1st Q	2nd Q	3rd Q	4th Q	Yr Total
Receipts					
Book Sales					
Expenditures					
Editorial	3.0	3.0	3.0	3.0	12.0
Manufacturing					
Payroll	17.0	17.0	17.0	17.0	68.0
Furniture &					
Equipment	3.8	0.4	0.4	0.4	5.0
Professional Fees	1.0		0.3		1.3
Marketing			7.1	10.4	17.5
Fulfillment				2.5	2.5
Rent	1.5	1.5	1.5	1.5	6.0
Office Expense	3.0	3.0	3.0	3.0	12.0
Surplus (Deficit)	(29.3)	(24.9)	(32.3)	(37.8)	(124.3)
Cumulative		(54.2)	(86.5)	(124.3)	(124.3)

| | Year Two | | | | |
	1st Q	2nd Q	3rd Q	4th Q	Yr Total
Receipts					
Book Sales	152.1	27.8	31.0	31.0	241.9
Expenditures					
Editorial	3.2	3.1	3.2	3.1	12.6
Manufacturing	42.1				42.1
Payroll	17.9	17.9	17.9	17.9	71.6
Furniture &					
Equipment	0.4	0.4	0.4	0.4	1.6
Professional Fees	0.8		0.3		1.1
Marketing	6.4		7.9	11.1	25.4
Fulfillment	6.4	1.1	1.0	1.0	9.5
Rent	1.6	1.6	1.6	1.6	6.4
Office Expense	3.1	3.1	3.1	3.1	12.4
Surplus (Deficit)	70.2	0.6	(4.4)	(7.2)	59.2
Cumulative	(54.1)	(53.5)	(57.9)	(65.1)	(65.1)

		Year Three			
	1st Q	2nd Q	3rd Q	4th Q	Yr Total
Receipts					
Book Sales	146.9	29.2	24.0	9.2	209.3
Expenditures					
Editorial	3.3	3.3	3.3	3.3	13.2
Manufacturing	28.8				28.8
Payroll	18.8	18.8	18.8	18.8	75.2
Furniture &					
Equipment	0.4	0.4	0.4	0.4	1.6
Professional Fees	0.8		0.4		1.2
Marketing	6.6		7.3	10.4	24.3
Fulfillment	6.2	1.1	1.0	1.0	9.3
Rent	1.7	1.7	1.7	1.7	6.8
Office Expense	3.1	3.1	3.1	3.1	12.4
Surplus (Deficit)	77.2	0.8	(12.0)	(29.5)	36.5
Cumulative	12.1	12.9	0.9	(28.6)	(28.6)

		Year Four			
	1st Q	2nd Q	3rd Q	4th Q	Yr Total
Receipts					
Book Sales	215.3	63.4	41.0	27.1	346.8
Expenditures					
Editorial	3.5	3.5	3.5	3.5	14.0
Manufacturing	51.3				51.3
Payroll	19.7	19.7	19.7	19.7	78.8
Furniture &					
Equipment	0.4	0.4	0.4	0.4	1.6
Professional Fees	0.9		0.4		1.3
Marketing	6.9		7.6	10.9	25.4
Fulfillment	6.4	1.1	1.1	1.1	9.7
Rent	1.8	1.8	1.8	1.8	7.2
Office Expense	3.2	3.2	3.3	3.2	12.9
Surplus (Deficit)	121.2	33.7	3.2	(13.5)	144.6
Cumulative	92.6	126.3	129.5	116.0	116.0

	1st Q	2nd Q	3rd Q	4th Q	Yr Total
			Year Five		
Receipts					
Book Sales	151.8	47.5	26.1	19.8	245.2
Expenditures					
Editorial	3.7	3.6	3.7	3.6	14.6
Manufacturing	35.3				35.3
Payroll	20.7	20.7	20.7	20.7	82.8
Furniture &					
Equipment	0.4	0.4	0.4	0.4	1.6
Professional Fees	1.0		0.5		1.5
Marketing	7.3		7.9	11.3	26.5
Fulfillment	6.6	1.2	1.2	1.2	10.2
Rent	1.9	1.9	1.9	1.9	7.6
Office Expense	3.4	3.4	3.4	3.4	13.6
Surplus (Deficit)	71.5	16.3	(13.6)	(22.7)	51.5
Cumulative	187.5	203.8	190.2	167.5	167.5

Figure 10.

nanced with monthly payments through a bank, as well as purchases of a reconditioned copying machine and used office furniture.

Professional Fees cover the costs of incorporation and other legal and accounting fees. *Marketing* embraces the expenses of promotional mailings before and after publication, ads in regional professional media, the distribution of complimentary copies, exhibits, and other promotional efforts. *Fulfillment* represents payments to the book manufacturer who will bill and ship the directories, as well as postage that will not be recovered from customers. Since the enterprise will be located in the owner's home, *Rent* will be payable to her for the space occupied. Finally, *Office Expense* includes telephone, stationery and supplies, service contracts, automobile expense, and similar items.

The projection has two bottom lines. The upper shows the positive or negative amount of cash flow generated during each quarter or year. (Negative amounts appear in parentheses.) The lower carries a cumulative total value forward from quarter to quarter and year to year. Thus, during the first quarter of year one, a cash deficit of $29,300 is generated. which is augmented by $24,900 during the second quarter for a cumulative total of $54,200. Although the deficit reaches a cumulative level of $124,300 at the end of year one, during the first quarter of year two a surplus of $70,200 is generated, which reduces the cumulative deficit to $54,100. Fluctuating during the remaining quarters, the cumulative deficit reaches $65,100 at the end of year two, is reduced to $28,600 at the end of year three, and is converted to a surplus of $92,600 during the first quarter of year four. Although three of the subsequent quarters in years four and five produce deficits, cumulative cash flow remains positive, growing to $167,500 at the end of the fifth year.

Viewed in its entirety, the projection shows that the planned venture is sound and has excellent prospects for earning solid profits for investors. That the operation will show deficits for three years before becoming profitable is not unusual, nor is the fact that ebbs in cash flow continue even after the corner has been turned. Given the business cycle of the enterprise, in which sales receipts are seasonally concentrated, periods in which disbursements will exceed receipts are to be expected. In fact, the reason why accountants advocate quarterly or monthly cash flow projections is that they allow clients to anticipate periods when ebbs will occur and enable them to make provisions in advance to avoid embarrassment or disaster.

What does the projection reveal regarding the amount of capital required to launch the enterprise? The peak deficit is nearly $125,000, so one might assume that this would be the amount of working capital required. That could turn out to be a risky assumption, however. What if the publication of Directory A were delayed by three months?—not an unimaginable prospect in an untried enterprise. That would add $40,000 to disbursements before any receipts ever materialized, raising the peak cumulative deficit to $165,000. Should not such a contingency be provided for?

The answer advocated under the circumstances by the accountant in our example is that the publisher should approach her investors with the projection in hand, advising them that she required their joint commitment for $125,000. Since the need for this amount would be reached only gradually over a two-year period, their initial payment would be invested in interest-bearing securities, the earnings from which would provide some hedge against a possible shortfall. Should this hedge prove insufficient, the publisher would reapproach the investors for the additional capital required.

Recording Daily Operations

Assume now that the enterprise is launched and functions completely as forecast, which is not likely in reality but convenient for our purpose. How will its experiences be recorded on a day-to-day basis, and how will its progress be documented in its principal financial reports: the operating statement and the balance sheet?

The tool used to account for daily financial transactions is the Double-Entry Accounting (Bookkeeping) System, an ingenious though basically simple invention. Although mastery of the system's advanced applications requires extensive training, a high school–taught bookkeeper can usually cope with its routine demands.

The system is designed around the two basic documents it produces— the operating statement and the balance sheet. The *Operating Statement* (or Income Statement or Profit-and-Loss Statement as it is sometimes known), is fundamentally a financial history of a given time period, such as a month, a quarter, or a year. It summarizes the income and expenses of the period and establishes the extent of profit or loss realized during its course, in accordance with the formula "income minus expense equals profit (or loss)."

The *Balance Sheet,* on the other hand, is a portrait of the financial condition of an enterprise at a given point in time, such as the last day of a month, a quarter, or a year. The statement summarizes the firm's holdings and debts owed to it by others (assets) as well as its debts to others (liabilities) and the value of the owners' investment in the enterprise (capital). Balance sheets follow the formula "assets equal liabilities plus capital."

Operating statements and balance sheets bear a close relationship to one another. Every fiscal period summarized by an operating statement begins and ends with a balance sheet, so it is appropriate to say that "beginning assets, liabilities, and capital plus operating results equal ending assets, liabilities, and capital." In other words, all elements of the total financial experience have a mathematical relationship to the whole and to one another.

The Double-Entry system derives its efficacy from the fact that when one of the elements in a financial universe is augmented or diminished, a countervailing subtraction or addition elsewhere in that universe becomes necessary to maintain total balance. Or, to use the system's own terminology, every debit must be balanced by an offsetting credit.

The various elements in a universe, known as "accounts," are categorized in accordance with the role they play in constructing the two principal financial statements. Thus sales and rights income are called "Income Accounts," and editorial, production, marketing, fulfillment, and administrative expenses are "Expense Accounts." Income and expense accounts may also be referred to as "Operating Accounts." Cash, investments, payments owed by customers (accounts receivable) and inventory are "Asset Accounts"; payments owed to vendors (accounts payable), and debts to lenders are "Liability Accounts"; and the value of owners' investment (equity) in the firm is represented by the "Capital Account." Asset, liability, and capital accounts may also be classified as "Balance Sheet Accounts."

To organize these accounts, every enterprise devises a numbered "Chart of Accounts." A small press might assign five-digit numbers to its accounts, the first digit of which would be devoted to classifying its category, say 10000 for assets, 20000 for income, 30000 for expenses, 40000 for liabilities, and 50000 for capital. In detailing and subdetailing account categories, additional digits are utilized. The method of recording financial data day to day has been greatly simplified by computers and automated bookkeeping programs. In the days when such work had to be performed manually—or where it is still so performed today—it begins with an ongoing log of transactions, known as the "Journal." Journal entries consist of the date of the transaction, the name and number of the account and the amount to be debited, the account and amount to be credited, and a brief explanation of the transaction.

Asset and expense accounts are augmented by debit and reduced by credit. Income, liability, and capital accounts are augmented by credit and reduced by debit. Neophytes often find it difficult to adjust to this rule, because they naturally associate credits with additions and debits with subtractions, based on their experience with bank and charge accounts.

From the vantage point of a bank or store, of course, the terms assume these particular meanings because payments from customers are classified as income, which is one of the categories added to by credit and subtracted from by debit in the Double-Entry system.

In manual bookkeeping, journal entries are then recorded (posted) to the appropriate account categories maintained in "ledgers." To make certain that data have been correctly posted, a test known as a "trial balance" is conducted before accounts are "closed" and statements are prepared for a given period. In a trial balance all accounts are first summarized by adding new debit and credit entries to the prior account balance—the net debit or credit amount, if any, that had resulted from the previous summary—thereby establishing a new balance for each account. If after the new balances are added up, total debits do not equal total credits, it appears that an error had been made which must be searched for and corrected. Not the least-useful feature of Double-Entry is the way it polices itself, making it very difficult to proceed if an error has been made. Difficult, but not impossible. It is conceivable, for example, that an amount correctly debited or credited could be posted to the wrong account and therefore not be detected in a trial balance. However, since many transactions involve cash, errors of this kind usually come to light when a firm reconciles its bank statement.

In computerized bookkeeping the posting to accounts is, of course, automatic as is the instantaneous updating of account balances and the issuance of a warning when an error has occurred. Also automated is the preparation of statements, once all necessary data have been keyed into the computer.

First-Quarter Financial Statements

Assume now that our sample press has faithfully entered all financial transactions which occurred during its first quarter and is issuing its first set of financial statements (Figure 11). To understand these statements and interpret their meaning correctly, we must comprehend the steps the press had to take to complete and record the various transactions.

Let's begin by examining the structure of the two statements. The Operating Statement opens with Net Sales and Cost of Sales—the latter consisting of manufacturing expense only in the present case—which have as yet not been activated. When Cost of Sales is deducted from Net Sales it yields Operating Income, which represents the publisher's "gross margin," one of the efficiency measures by which performance is often judged.

Operating Expenses are listed next. Notice that the arrangement of the

Professional Small Press

OPERATING STATEMENT				BALANCE SHEET	
First Quarter—Year One				**Last Day, First Quarter, Year One**	
Net Sales	—		Assets		
Cost of Sales	=		Current Assets		
Operating Income	—		Cash		15,109
Operating Expenses			Investments		80,000
Editorial	3,000		Accrued interest		1,500
Marketing	—		Accounts Receivable (net		
Fulfillment	—		of allowance for doubtful		
Genl. & Admin.			accounts)		—
Salaries	13,250		Inventories (net of write-		
Benefits	2,687		down provision)		—
Rent	1,500		Total Current Assets		96,609
Office Exp.	4,200		Fixtures & Equip.—at cost		12,400
Other	2,774		Less: depreciation		620
Total Genl. & Admin.	24,411				11,780
Total Operating Expenses	27,411		Prepaid & deferred expenses		4,350
Other Income (Expense)	1,580				112,739
Net Income (Loss) before Taxes	(25,831)		**Liabilities and Capital**		
Income Taxes	—		Current Liabilities		
Net Income (Loss) after Taxes	(25,831)		Accounts Payable		1,200
			Accrued Income Taxes		—
			Other accrued liabilities		774
			Total Current Liabil.		1,974
			Long-term Debt		11,596
			Capital		
			Paid-in Capital		125,000
			Accrued Loss		(25,831)
			Total Capital		99,169
					112,739

Figure 11.

captions in this listing differs somewhat from the one provided in the Cash Flow Projection in Figure 10, in order to make the statement more compatible with the format employed in AAP surveys. Conforming their reporting methods to industry standards is advantageous for all publishers, large or small, because it enables them to compare data with industry surveys and other publishers without stumbling over variations in format, terminology, or definitions.

Also, in accrual accounting a fundamental distinction must be made between "Expenditures" shown in a Cash Flow Projection and "Expenses" listed in an Operating Statement. The former are simply disbursements of cash. The latter designate whole or partial costs being matched as closely as possible with related revenues. While not every expense needs literally to be matched—in the present case, for example, we are not asked to defer all expenses until sales commence—the accrual rules are designed to achieve such matching to the greatest extent reasonable and prudent under the circumstances. As a general policy, we are not required to defer data or make disclosures in instances where the cost of compliance would exceed the value of benefits received.

Generally, in accrual accounting, sales are recorded (recognized) when billed (booked) by the publisher, and costs of sales are matched directly to the recognized sales. Expenses for equipment, furniture, and other property with long-term utility, receive gradual recognition (depreciation) during the course of their useful existence. Expenses for consumable goods and services are recognized on receipt of vendors' invoices, and internal expenses when incurred. All appear in statements accordingly, without regard to when payments were received from customers or disbursed to vendors.

As it happens, the amounts for Editorial Expense and Rent shown in the present Operating Statement are identical to those forecast in the Cash Flow Projection. But here all similarity ends. In the Operating Statement several of the items that appeared separately in the Cash Flow Projection are grouped under the subheading General and Administrative (G & A) Expense. Payroll Expense has been separated into three parts, two of which—Salaries and Benefits—are listed separately because of their significance and the third, Payroll Taxes, is included under "Other" G & A expense. Office Expense not only includes the $3,000 forecast in the Cash Flow Projection, but an additional $1,200 invoiced by vendors, which will not be paid until the second quarter.

After totals for G & A Expense, and for all Operating Expenses, there appears a line for Other Income (Expense), where primarily interest earned or paid is recorded. The $1,580 shown includes $500 already received, as well as $1,500 accrued, from investments, from which $420 in interest paid on the computer loan has been deducted. After a line for Income Taxes, which won't become relevant until the press shows a profit, we encounter the famous "bottom line" which, not surprisingly, shows a first-quarter loss of $25,831.

Now turn to the Balance Sheet. You will notice that it contains two segments, each of which ends with an identical bottom-line figure, $112,739. (Bottom lines are followed by double rules or underlining.) The upper segment lists Assets, the lower Liabilities and Capital, which, in accordance with the statement's name, must balance one another. Under Assets we distinguish between Current Assets—likely to be disposed of or changed substantially during the course of the accounting year—and other property of longer-lasting character. A similar definition applies to Current Liabilities as distinguished from debts of greater duration.

The first Current Asset listed is Cash. Notice that only a modest amount of Cash is kept on hand and in banks—just enough to meet obligations during the next few weeks. Conversely, the following entry, Investments, is more substantial since the firm wants to earn as much interest as possible while some of its initial paid-in capital is still liquid. That this strategy is working is indicated by the listing of Accrued Interest in conjunction with Investments, i.e. interest earned but not yet received. The need to recognize Accrued Interest applies in the present case because the press has invested short term, in certificates of deposit and other instruments earning fixed interest.

Fixtures and Equipment includes the acquisition values of the computer, copier, and office furniture. Under the accrual rules, that value will be depreciated over the period of time the equipment is expected to be useful, in this case five years. There are several methods by which property can be depreciated, the choice depending on whether the value of the equipment is expected to decline at an even pace throughout its useful life, or more rapidly at the beginning and then decelerate, or moderately at the beginning and then accelerate. The method chosen here (straight-line) anticipates an even-paced decline, utilizing equal quarterly amounts to retire the value.

Prepaid and Deferred Expenses is a holding bin for costs incurred currently that cannot be recognized until a later date under the accrual rules. Included in the present entry of $4,350 is the interest balance on the computer loan (interest on the first three monthly payments was charged to Other G & A Expenses), and the accumulation of three days' vacation salaries, benefits, and payroll taxes earned by the publisher and her assistant.

Under Accounts Payable we find current unpaid bills. Good money management requires that while the press should pay its bills when due, it should also take advantage of every day of permissible delay. Accrued Income Taxes has not yet been activated. Other Accrued Liabilities balance the three days' accumulated vacation pay now held in Deferred Expenses. Long-term debt acknowledges the unpaid total balance of the Computer Loan.

Capital represents investors' current equity in the press. Therefore the original investment is shown under Paid-in Capital, and the loss thus far incurred, identified on the bottom line of the Operating Statement, is deducted from Paid-in Capital to arrive at the current equity value.

How were the entries resulting in the two statements formulated on a daily basis? When the initial capital was deposited, Cash was debited with $125,000, and Paid-in Capital was credited with a like amount. When funds were invested, they were debited to Investments and credited to Cash.

When the first interest of $500 was earned, Cash was debited and Other Income credited. The subsequent $1,500, accrued though not yet paid, were debited to Accrued Interest and credited to Other Income. Expense entries involving payments were debited to the appropriate expense accounts and credited to Cash. The three days' vacation pay earned by the staff were debited to Prepaid and Deferred Expenses and credited to Accrued Liabilities. The principal of the computer loan, representing the value of the equipment, was debited to Fixtures and Equipment, and the Interest to Prepaid and Deferred Expenses, while the entire amount was credited to Long-term Debt. The three monthly loan payments were debited to Long-term Debt and credited to Cash. At the same time, Other Income was debited, and Prepaid and Deferred Expenses was credited, with the loan interest on the three payments. Also at that time, Other G & A Expense was debited, and Furniture Depreciation was credited, with the monthly depreciation on the computer and other furniture. Office Expense was debited, and Accounts Receivable credited, when invoices for $1,200 worth of stationery and supplies not payable until the second quarter were received.

Yearly Statements

At the end of Year One (Figure 12) all statement lines, except those pertaining to taxes, have become activated. In the Operating Statement, we have recorded the Net Sales booked just before the end of the year, and because no payments have yet been received, the entire billing has been acknowledged as Accounts Receivable on the Balance Sheet. Notice, however, that an "allowance for doubtful accounts" has been deducted from Receivables. This allowance anticipates that a few purchasers will default on their payments. Without any experience in the matter, we can only guess at the volume of that default and trust that after two or three years of measuring actual write-offs, our estimates will become more accurate.

We have also recognized the receipt of our stock of Directory A by recording its value under Inventories on the Balance Sheet. As we anticipate that some inventory will remain undistributed after the first edition becomes outdated, we have set up a small provision for "write-down" of its value, which will be recognized as a Cost of Sales when the time comes. Currently, the value of copies actually sold has been recorded as Cost of Sales and that of copies distributed free for promotional purposes as part of Marketing Expense. Because we won't be paying the manufacturer's bill until the first quarter or Year Two, we have added the amount due to Accounts Payable. Also added to Payables was the manufacturer's charge

Professional Small Press

OPERATING STATEMENT Year One		BALANCE SHEET Last Day, Year One	
Net Sales	50,164	**Assets**	
Cost of Sales	7,350	Current Assets	
Operating Income	42,814	Cash	5,659
Operating Expenses		Investments	0
Editorial	12,000	Accrued interest	0
Marketing	17,500	Accounts Receivable (net	
Fulfillment	2,520	of allowance for doubtful	
Genl. & Admin.		accounts)	49,411
Salaries	53,000	Inventories (net of write-	
Benefits	10,394	down provision)	33,694
Rent	6,000	Total Current Assets	88,764
Office Exp.	13,200	Fixtures & Equip.—at cost	12,400
Other	8,786	Less: depreciation	2,870
Total Genl. & Admin.	91,380		9,530
Total Operating Expenses	123,400	Prepaid & deferred expenses	5,824
Other Income (Expense)	3,331		104,118
Net Income (Loss) before Taxes	(77,255)	**Liabilities and Capital**	
Income Taxes	—	Current Liabilities	
Net Income (Loss) after Taxes	(77,255)	Accounts Payable	46,220
		Accrued Income Taxes	—
		Other accrued liabilities	1,806
		Total Current Liabil.	48,026
		Long-term Debt	8,347
		Capital	
		Paid-in Capital	125,000
		Accrued Loss	(77,255)
		Total Capital	47,745
			104,118

Figure 12.

for shipping services, which has been recognized as Fulfillment Expense in the Operating Statement.

Investments on the Balance Sheet have all been cashed in to provide needed working capital. Prepaid and Deferred Expenses was credited, and Accrued Liabilities debited, when the staff took five days' vacation, but further accumulation of monthly vacation credits remain on the Balance Sheet. The Prepaid and Deferred Expense account was also utilized to debit the doubtful accounts and write-down provisions credited to Accounts Receivable and Inventories. Investors' equity has been reduced substantially by the loss accrued to date.

Things begin to look up by Year Two (Figure 13). Initial sales of Directory B and continued sales of Directory A bolster revenues so that a profit materializes for the first time. This also leads to a tax liability,

Professional Small Press

OPERATING STATEMENT Year Two		BALANCE SHEET Last Day, Year Two	
Net Sales	229,823	**Assets**	
Cost of Sales	33,670	Current Assets	
Operating Income	196,153	Cash	6,127
Operating Expenses		Investments	45,000
Editorial	12,600	Accrued interest	1,375
Marketing	25,400	Accounts Receivable (net	
Fulfillment	9,500	of allowance for doubtful	
Genl. & Admin.		accounts)	57,722
Salaries	55,650	Inventories (net of write-	
Benefits	10,914	down provision)	28,513
Rent	6,400	Total Current Assets	138,737
Office Exp.	12,400	Fixtures & Equip.—at cost	12,400
Other	8,947	Less: depreciation	5,870
Total Genl. & Admin.	94,311		6,530
Total Operating Expenses	141,811	Prepaid & deferred expenses	5,117
Other Income (Expense)	2,043		150,384
Net Income (Loss) before Taxes	56,385	**Liabilities and Capital**	
Income Taxes	22,554	Current Liabilities	
Net Income (Loss) after Taxes	33,831	Accounts Payable	39,800
		Accrued Income Taxes	22,554
		Other accrued liabilities	2,439
		Total Current Liabil.	64,793
		Long-term Debt	4,015
		Capital	
		Paid-in Capital	125,000
		Accrued Loss	(43,424)
		Total Capital	81,576
			150,384

Figure 13.

activating the tax lines on both the Operating Statement and the Balance Sheet. Nevertheless, the press is able to reinvest some of its cash, and the loss in investors' equity is substantially reduced.

By Year Three (Figure 14), the loss reduction has progressed further and Long-term Debt has been eliminated. Although sales are somewhat lower than in Year Two, (mainly because Directory B, the principal revenue producer this year, is lower priced and less of a seller than Directory A,) the press does not need to dip into investments to maintain its liquidity.

In Year Four (Figure 15) the investment made in the press really begins to pay off. Instead of a capital loss, the firm shows a solid gain, signified by the substantial "Retained Earnings" added to capital holdings. The health of the enterprise is substantiated by the fact that the house has been able to build up its investment balance to $190,000. As a result, a dividend of $60,000 is declared, giving investors a total return on their capital thus far of 48 percent, an average of 12 percent per year for the first four years.

The healthy trend continues into Year Five (Figure 16), even though this is another year in which sales of Directory B predominate. A solid profit of $43,018 on sales of $262,750 (16.4 percent) is realized, boding well for the future. A further dividend of $40,000 is declared, giving investors a return on investment (ROI) of 32 percent for the year, 16 percent of an average for each of the past five years. Thought can be given to winding down the capital investment in the firm altogether since the press appears now able to generate its own working capital.

Professional Small Press

OPERATING STATEMENT Year Three		BALANCE SHEET Last Day, Year Three	
Net Sales	226,932	**Assets**	
Cost of Sales	33,480	Current Assets	
Operating Income	193,452	Cash	4,116
Operating Expenses		Investments	45,000
Editorial	13,200	Accrued interest	2,225
Marketing	24,300	Accounts Receivable (net	
Fulfillment	9,300	of allowance for doubtful	
Genl. & Admin.		accounts)	91,206
Salaries	58,433	Inventories (net of write-	
Benefits	11,460	down provision)	45,584
Rent	6,800	Total Current Assets	188,131
Office Exp.	12,400	Fixtures & Equip.—at cost	12,400
Other	9,939	Less: depreciation	8,870
Total Genl. & Admin.	99,032		3,530
Total Operating Expenses	145,832	Prepaid & deferred expenses	5,027
Other Income (Expense)	2,990		196,688
Net Income (Loss) before Taxes	50,610	**Liabilities and Capital**	
Income Taxes	20,244	Current Liabilities	
Net Income (Loss) after Taxes	30,366	Accounts Payable	61,900
		Accrued Income Taxes	20,244
		Other accrued liabilities	2,602
		Total Current Liabil.	84,746
		Long-term Debt	0
		Capital	
		Paid-in Capital	125,000
		Accrued Loss	(13,058)
		Total Capital	111,942
			196,688

Figure 14.

Professional Small Press

OPERATING STATEMENT Year Four		BALANCE SHEET Last Day, Year Four	
Net Sales	326,781	**Assets**	
Cost of Sales	47,340	Current Assets	
Operating Income	279,441	Cash	5,540
Operating Expenses		Investments	190,000
Editorial	14,000	Accrued interest	3,360
Marketing	25,400	Accounts Receivable (net	
Fulfillment	9,700	of allowance for doubtful	
Genl. & Admin.		accounts)	59,293
Salaries	61,355	Inventories (net of write-	
Benefits	12,033	down provision)	32,957
Rent	7,200	Total Current Assets	291,150
Office Exp.	12,900	Fixtures & Equip.—at cost	12,400
Other	10,546	Less: depreciation	11,870
Total Genl. & Admin.	104,034		530
Total Operating Expenses	153,134	Prepaid & deferred expenses	5,442
Other Income (Expense)	9,600		297,122
Net Income (Loss) before Taxes	135,907	**Liabilities and Capital**	
Income Taxes	61,158	Current Liabilities	
Net Income (Loss) after Taxes	74,749	Accounts Payable	46,500
		Accrued Income Taxes	61,158
		Other accrued liabilities	2,773
		Total Current Liabil.	110,431
		Long-term Debt	0
		Capital	
		Paid-in Capital	125,000
		Retained Earnings	61,691
		Total Capital	186,691
			297,122

Figure 15.

Trade Publishers' Statement Formats

In the foregoing example, we have deliberately disregarded certain complications, such as the need to disclose ownership share and investment details on the Balance Sheet, and to enumerate accounting treatments and policies in notes to the statements. We have also not discussed the preparation of a required statement of cash flow, because, given our assumption that events would conform to our forecast, such a statement would not differ materially from the cash flow projection we have already furnished.

Even had we added these complexities, however, our example would have remained a very simple one. Our enterprise was tiny, engaged in a limited kind of publishing, featuring only two titles produced entirely in-house. When we compare this simple venture with the highly complex operations of a larger trade house, it becomes obvious that the statement formats used to account for the activities of the trade publisher would have to be considerably more sophisticated. Just how much more sophisticated is illustrated in Figure 17, which pictures the Operating Statement and Balance Sheet formats of a hypothetical trade-book operation.

Let's begin again with the Operating Statement. Note that it opens with Gross Sales in deference to the fact that some books shipped will be returned to the publisher by booksellers and wholesalers. Actual returns, as well as credits allowed to dealers to enable them to mark down overstock without returning it, would be entered on the Returns and Allowances line. Returns to mainstream trade publishers have risen steadily over the years; in 1987 AAP Statistics reports indicated that for the

Professional Small Press

OPERATING STATEMENT Year Five		BALANCE SHEET Last Day, Year Five	
Net Sales	262,750	**Assets**	
Cost of Sales	39,765	Current Assets	
Operating Income	222,985	Cash	6,871
Operating Expenses		Investments	135,000
Editorial	14,600	Accrued interest	5,330
Marketing	26,500	Accounts Receivable (net	
Fulfillment	10,200	of allowance for doubtful	
Genl. & Admin.		accounts)	81,115
Salaries	64,423	Inventories (net of write-	
Benefits	12,635	down provision)	48,703
Rent	7,600	Total Current Assets	277,019
Office Exp.	13,600	Fixtures & Equip.—at cost	12,400
Other	8,543	Less: depreciation	12,400
Total Genl. & Admin.	106,801		0
Total Operating Expenses	158,101	Prepaid & deferred expenses	5,363
Other Income (Expense)	13,330		282,382
Net Income (Loss) before Taxes	78,214	**Liabilities and Capital**	
Income Taxes	35,196	Current Liabilities	
Net Income (Loss) after Taxes	43,018	Accounts Payable	74,525
		Accrued Income Taxes	35,196
		Other accrued liabilities	2,952
		Total Current Liabil.	112,673
		Long-term Debt	0
		Capital	
		Paid-in Capital	125,000
		Retained Earnings	44,709
		Total Capital	169,709
			282,382

Figure 16.

Trade Publisher

OPERATING STATEMENT FORMAT	BALANCE SHEET FORMAT
Gross Sales	**Assets**
Less: Returns and Allowances	Current Assets
Net Sales	Cash
Cost of Sales	Marketable Securities
Manufacturing	Accounts Receivable (net of Provisions
Royalties	for Returns and Allowances and
Total Cost of Sales	Doubtful Accounts)
Gross Margin on Sales	Inventories (net of Provisions for Re-
Other Publishing Income	turns and Write-downs)
Total Operating Income	Finished Goods
Operating Expenses	Work-in-Process
Editorial	Paper & Other Raw Materials
Production	Total Current Assets
Marketing	Fixtures and Equipment—at cost
Sales Salaries & Commissions	Less: Accumulated Depreciation and
Advertising & Promotion	Amortization
Free Copies (incl. postage)	Royalty Advances
Departmental Salaries	Less: Reserve for Write-off of Unearned
Travel & Entertainment	Guarantees
Other Marketing Expense	Prepaid and Deferred Expenses
Total Marketing Expense	**Liabilities and Shareholders' Equity**
Fulfillment	Current Liabilities
Order Processing	Accounts Payable
Shipping and Warehousing	Royalties Payable
Total Fulfillment Expense	Notes Payable
General & Administrative	Accrued Income Taxes
Management Salaries	Other Accrued Liabilities
Other Salaries	Total Current Liabilities
Occupancy	Long-term Debt
Employee Benefits	Shareholders' Equity
Other General & Administrative	Capital Stock
Total General & Administrative	Additional Paid-in Capital
Total Operating Expense	Retained Earnings
Other (nonpublishing) Income (or Expense)	Total Shareholders' Equity
Net Income (or Loss) Before Taxes	
Federal, State & Local Income Taxes	
Net Income (or Loss) after Taxes	

Figure 17.

publishers reporting Returns averaged 35 percent of Net Sales on adult hardcover books, 25 percent on adult paperbound books, 12 percent on juvenile hardbound, and 15 percent on juvenile paperbound titles.

Cost of Sales includes Manufacturing costs as well as Royalties to authors of the books sold. The Manufacturing cost is calculated on a unit basis when the books are placed in inventory, and is added to Cost of Sales as copies are sold or, if deemed unsalable, when they are remaindered or pulped. Royalties, computed in accordance with contracted rates, are debited to Royalty expense at the time of shipment.

Other Publishing Income is a vital category for mainstream trade houses. In fact, were it not for revenues from subsidiary rights, many adult hardbound publishers would be losing money. In 1986, for example, Other Publishing Income of the adult hardcover houses reporting to AAP averaged 11.7 percent of Net Sales—Net Sales representing a yardstick by which operating performance is commonly measured—while their Income from Operations (before taxes and fees to parent corporations), amounted to only 7.8 percent. Even when sales from other types of titles were added, Other Publishing Income still represented 8.1 percent, or most of the 10.6 percent Income from Operations which twenty-one publishers with collective Net Sales of $692 million reported to the survey. Understandably, then, the Other Publishing Income entry represents a key component of a trade publishers' Operating report.

The major ingredient of the various Operating Expense entries are departmental salaries (although employee benefits are entered as a sub-category of G & A Expense). Departmental breakdowns also include outside service and free-lance costs, and supplies.

In order to keep traditional financial formats intact, I have included Tax lines in both statements and Equity lines in the Balance Sheet. These would not apply, of course, if the statement were prepared for a corporate subsidiary. An internal corporate Operating Statement would most likely end with "Income from Operations," before taxes and assessments for corporate services, and its corresponding Balance Sheet would simply provide an entry for "Equity" or "Net Worth," representing the parent corporation's investment in the enterprise.

Turning now to the Balance Sheet, we note that Accounts Receivable is reduced by Provisions not only for Doubtful Accounts but also for Returns. The latter is required when a business sells goods on a returnable basis to prevent Receivables from becoming unrealistically overstated. The specific amounts of the provisions, which are computed on the basis of historical experience, should be disclosed in the statement or its notes.

Inventories are detailed to distinguish between bound books, titles in various stages of manufacture, and the publisher's deposits of paper, cloth, and other materials at printing plants and binderies.

There are two species of Royalty Advances: Guarantees, which are not returned to the author even if they are not earned subsequently through sales, and advance payments that authors must repay if not earned. When a book on which an unearned Guarantee is held on the Balance Sheet has run its course, the unearned balance must be written off by debiting Royalty Expense and crediting Royalty Advances.

Furthermore, royalty settlements are commonly made only twice or three times a year, and in the interim sizable fortunes can accumulate in Royalties Payable. Effectively such accumulations represent interest-free loans by authors to publishers, who readily employ such funds for working or investment capital or to aid the cash flow of their parent corporations.

Elhi Publishers' Statement Formats

Figure 18 pictures another variation, the statement formats of an imaginary Elhi publisher. Once again the peculiarities of the publisher's activities are reflected in the accounting measures the house employs to reflect its financial experience. Thus under Manufacturing Costs, two subcategories are identified: Plant Costs and Paper, Printing & Binding. Unlike trade books, whose careers tend to be meteoric, school texts have a longer life expectancy, usually some five years in their current edition. Also unlike trade books, school texts often entail multimillion-dollar investments before publication. Under accrual and tax rules, such development expenses must be deferred and retired gradually parallel with sales. Since typically a school text is reprinted repeatedly over its lifetime, the device employed in trade and professional publishing of writing plant costs into inventory will not suffice here. Instead, Plant and, if applicable, other development costs are "amortized" over the title's anticipated life span. The portions being amortized are debited to Plant Costs (or Development Costs), while the uncapitalized portions appear under Unamortized Plant Costs on the Balance Sheet. Under Marketing Expense we find such characteristically Elhi entries as Compensation to Sales People and Consultants and Depository Expense. On the other hand, because Returns are minor, no provisions need be made for their anticipated arrival. And because large-scale Royalty Guarantees are practically unknown in this sector, there is no requirement to provide for their possible write-off.

Statements of Multidivisional Publishers

We have looked at the statement formats of fictitious houses engaged in different kinds of publishing. The statements of a multidivisional house would require certain modifications in the formats we have discussed. To begin with, the house would probably "consolidate" its statement to stockholders, i.e., it would combine the various divisional data under rather broad headings that would minimize their differences. However, management would still want to be able to assess the performance of each division, and would want the divisional manager to be fully apprised of

Elhi Publisher

OPERATING STATEMENT FORMAT

Gross Sales
  Less: Returns and Allowances
Net Sales
Cost of Sales
  Manufacturing
  Plant Costs
  Paper, Printing, & Binding
  Royalties
    Total Cost of Sales
Gross Margin on Sales
Other Publishing Income
  Total Operating Income
Operating Expenses
  Editorial
  Production
  Marketing
    Compensation to Sales People and Consultants
    Depository Expense
    Free Copies
    Departmental Salaries
    Travel & Entertainment
    Other Marketing Expense
      Total Marketing Expense
  Fulfillment
    Order Processing
    Shipping and Warehousing
      Total Fulfillment Expense
  General & Administrative
    Management Salaries
    Other Salaries
    Occupancy
    Employee Benefits
    Other General & Administrative
      Total General & Administrative
      Total Operating Expense
Other (nonpublishing) Income (or Expense)
Net Income (or Loss) Before Taxes
Federal, State & Local Income Taxes
Net Income (or Loss) after Taxes

BALANCE SHEET FORMAT

Assets
  Current Assets
    Cash
    Marketable Securities
    Accounts Receivable (net of Allowances for Doubtful Accounts)
    Inventories (net of Provisions for Write-downs)
      Finished Goods
      Work-in-Process
      Paper & Other Raw Materials
        Total Current Assets
  Fixtures and Equipment—at cost
    Less: Accumulated Depreciation and Amortization
  Royalty Advances
  Unamortized Plant Costs
  Prepaid and Deferred Expenses
Liabilities and Shareholders' Equity
  Current Liabilities
    Accounts Payable
    Royalties Payable
    Notes Payable
    Accrued Income Taxes
    Other Accrued Liabilities
      Total Current Liabilities
  Long-term Debt
  Shareholders' Equity
    Capital Stock
    Additional Paid-in Capital
    Retained Earnings
      Total Shareholders' Equity

Figure 18.

that performance. Consequently at least simple operating statements would be prepared regularly for each publishing unit.

This would raise certain problems. Most divisions share the services of some departments: production, fulfillment, and accounting, for example; they often occupy the same building, use some of the same equipment, and are directed by the same top management. How is the use of these shared talents and facilities to be accounted for? There are two basic approaches, each with fervent advocates and opponents. The more common method produces a complete statement down to the bottom line of profit. It measures all expenses incurred solely by the division directly: manufacturing, royalty, editorial, and marketing expense, and/or any other over which the division has exclusive control, are simply recorded and detailed. Shared expenses are "allocated," i.e., estimated portions of the expense are assigned to each division on the basis of some formula, such as a relationship to net dollar sales, or number of units sold, or a combination of both, or time consumed by managers in working with divisions, or time-based utilization of EDP and other equipment, etc.

The alternative method reports only the direct expense over which the division has substantial control. The resulting profit margin is regarded as the division's "contribution" to a common pool of revenues from which shared expenses are met and profits derived. Because of its character, this method is said to employ the "contribution concept" of cost accounting.

Advocates of the contribution concept point out that all allocations are essentially arbitrary. Short of undertaking extremely detailed and expensive time-and-motion studies and space utilization surveys, there is no way of doing full justice to a division when charging it with estimated costs. Are dollar net sales to be the basis for allocation? Then high-priced books are likely to receive an excessive share of the expense and cheaper books are likely to escape much of the burden. Are units to be the basis? Then cheaper books will suffer while costly titles will be favored. Even dollar-weighted unit figures cannot achieve just attributions of fulfillment costs where the size of a transaction (i.e., the number of books billed and shipped at one time) has a considerable bearing on actual expense incurred. Nor do most allocation formulas take into account the substantial costs of processing returns incurred by some books and not by others, or the expense created by books that are not selling at all.

Defenders of the allocation approach retort that these problems may be real enough, but contribution-based reporting is not the answer. While it is true that a divisional manager does not have sole control over shared services or facilities, the manager's decisions, the volume of the division's output, and the nature of the product still have a great deal to do with the costs incurred on the division's behalf. Therefore the manager should share some responsibility for those costs. Furthermore, bottom-line profit is profoundly affected by the performance of the divisions and should be related specifically to their performance. Under the contribution method, net profit is not so related, thus failing to disclose the full effect of divisional activities on the earnings of the company.

My own inclination is to favor allocation, to devise the best possible and most equitable formulations for attributing costs, while fully recognizing their limitations. (Constructing allocation formulas is becoming easier after all with the help of computers now utilized by most multidivisional houses.) Not only do I find the argument relating bottom-line profit to divisional performance persuasive, but I think the initiative of a divisional manager will be stimulated more by the more complete disclosure resulting from a full report. Contribution may be a "purer" method in the sense of including a greater proportion of "hard" figures, but purity is not our prime objective here. Producing information designed to facilitate planning and decision making is our objective. If in the process of accomplishing this goal we have to work with estimates that are a little "softer" than actual cost data would be, so be it, so long as the estimates are intelligently and conscientiously prepared.

There is another reason why allocations are essential, in my judgment. The basic decision in publishing is made when an individual title is selected for publication and therefore the most important profit or loss analysis is that which involves the individual book. Such analyses are impossible to construct without making use of some allocations, and in multidivisional companies they cannot be made at all unless divisional allocations have been devised first.

Analyses of Individual Title Performances

To illustrate the importance and value, as well as some possible methods of analyzing the profit performance of specific books, I have devised three fictitious statements which examine alternative approaches to the same title. The title in question we imagine to be a work of history, written by a professor at a prominent university. Some 350 pages in length, illustrated with a few plates and maps, well written and well conceived, it appeals solidly to historians and students as well as to laypersons interested in the subject. It is being published by a trade house (perhaps the one whose statement format we examined earlier).

The publisher has guaranteed the author a $44.00 advance against royalties (10 percent of list price) and subsidiary rights income. The contract grants only domestic rights to the publisher; foreign publication will be negotiated by the author directly. A small book club has selected the title, and the royalty income from the book club sale, representing 10 percent of the club's price to members, is to be shared equally by author and publisher. Reprint rights have also been sold to a trade paperback house which will release its edition, intended principally for use in college courses, 18 months after hardcover publication. The paperback publisher

Profit/Loss Analysis

History Title: Alternative One (List price $35.00—Trade discount)

	Dollars	Percent of Net Sales
Gross sales: 8,100 copies at full price	158,760	111.0
2,450 remaindered at $1.60	3,920	2.7
Total gross sales	162,680	113.7
Less: returns and allowances	19,600	13.7
Net sales	**143,080**	**100.00**
Cost of sales		
Plant costs	16,000	11.2
Paper, printing, and binding	44,620	31.2
Royalties	24,850	17.4
Total cost of sales	85,470	59.7
Gross margin on sales	57,610	40.3
Other publishing income	19,940	13.9
Total operating income	77,550	54.2
Operating expenses		
Editorial	11,800	8.3
Production	3,600	2.5
Marketing		
Advertising	15,000	10.4
Free books	1,380	1.0
Other	16,800	11.7
Total marketing expense	33,180	23.1
Fulfillment	15,400	10.8
General and administrative	13,600	9.5
Total operating expense	77,580	54.2
Net income (or loss)	(30)	(0.0)

Figure 19.

has advanced $20,000, which the contract provides will be shared—60 percent by the author, 40 percent by the original publisher.

The first alternative is illustrated in Figure 19. Here the publisher has decided to price the book at $35.00, extend the customary trade discount (averaging 44 percent) to retailers and wholesalers, and to print initially 10,000 copies; 300 copies are being distributed free, mostly to reviewers, and $15,000 is being appropriated for advertising in general and specialized media. To offer an attractive saving compared with the publisher's list price, the book club plans to sell its edition for $23.90 and is advancing $23,880 on its anticipated distribution of 10,000 copies.

As so often happens in publishing, not everything goes according to plan. During the first eight months of the book's existence, 5,100 copies are sold, but 1,000 are returned at the end of that period. In the succeeding ten months 3,000 more copies are sold, but by that time the sale has slowed to a trickle and the paperback edition is due to be released. The publisher reviews its inventory, remainders 2,450 copies for $1.60 per book, and writes off 150 copies which have disappeared, been stolen or damaged, as a total loss. The publisher then examines the record and discovers that the title has just about broken even.

Let's look at the statement. Gross sales cover the 8,100 copies shipped, at full price, as well as the yield from the remaindered copies; returns represent the 1,000 copies that came back. Cost of sales show plant costs separately, then the paper, printing, and binding of 10,000 copies at $4.60 per copy, less the cost of the 300 copies given away. Royalties represent $3.50 per copy on 7,100 copies sold at full price (remainder sales are, as is customary, exempted contractually from royalties). Other publishing income shows only the publisher's share, of course. It includes $11,940 from the book club and $8,000 from the paperback house.

Operating expense was computed as follows. Editorial, production, and most marketing expenses were established directly by surveying the time involvements of the editors and of the production and marketing staff, determining sales commissions, advertising expenditures, and the value of free books distributed. Fulfillment expense was allocated in accordance with the number and size of the transactions involved in invoicing, shipping, and processing returns of the title, as well as its warehouse occupancy during the period of its life. General and administrative expenses were variously treated. Management and general salaries, occupancy, and other largely indirect expenses were apportioned in accordance with the book's list price and the number of units sold (the formula employed in effect assigns lower proportionate costs to titles with higher list prices). Salary-related costs (such as fringe benefits and payroll taxes) followed directly whatever salaries were directly attributed, but were subject to the list price/unit formula insofar as they were attached to indirectly allocated salary expenses. (Since "other nonpublishing income or expense" or income taxes have no direct bearing on the profitability of a title, our analysis is carried no further than to net operating profit.)

Now let's look at alternative approach number two, illustrated in Figure 20. Here the publisher decides to be more aggressive. After having experienced the sort of disappointment demonstrated in the first alternative with this type of title before, the publisher hopes to overcome it with a slightly harder sell. The decision is made to price the book at only $30, trusting that this will expedite sales and improve earnings. The publisher also decides to give away more copies, 350, and to spend more money on advertising, $17,000. It works—up to a point. The first printing (10,000 copies) sells out in six months (too early to have received any sizable returns), and the publisher rushes into a reprint of 3,000 copies (at a cost

Profit/Loss Analysis

History Title: Alternative Two (List price $30.00—Trade discount)

	Dollars	Percent of Net Sales
Gross sales: 11,650 copies at full price	195,720	113.8
2,450 remaindered at $1.60	3,920	2.3
Total gross sales	199,640	116.1
Less: returns and allowances	27,720	16.1
Net sales	**171,920**	**100.00**
Cost of sales		
Plant costs	16,000	9.3
Paper, printing, and binding	60,170	35.0
Royalties	30,000	17.5
Total cost of sales	106,170	61.8
Gross margin on sales	65,750	38.2
Other publishing income	19,634	11.4
Total operating income	85,384	49.6
Operating expenses		
Editorial	11,800	6.9
Production	4,200	2.4
Marketing		
Advertising	17,000	9.9
Free books	1,610	1.0
Other	21,600	12.5
Total marketing expense	40,210	23.4
Fulfillment	22,200	12.9
General and administrative	15,200	8.8
Total operating expense	93,610	54.4
Net income (or loss)	**(8,226)**	**(4.8)**

Figure 20.

of $5.26 per copy). Of the second printing 1,650 are also sold, but returns cancel out these additional sales, resulting, after 18 months, in a total net sale of 10,000 copies. In other words, the publisher did accelerate and increase the sale of the book through the lower price and greater sales effort, but was left with as large an inventory, 2,450 copies, in the end. The publisher is forced to remainder these books at $1.60 cents each, writing off losses and damages on 200 copies.

Was it worth the extra effort? Apparently not. Our analysis shows that while net sales were higher than in alternative one, the lower price, higher inventory costs, and increased marketing and fulfillment expense combined to create a sizable loss for the publisher. To aggravate the problem, the publisher had to pay more royalties to the author ($3.00 on each of 10,000 copies), and the book club, basing its price on the title's list price, lowered it to $19.90. While this resulted in a somewhat larger book club sale (nearly 12,000 copies), the net effect was to lower the club's royalty payments to $23,270, of which the publisher's share was $11,634.

Now suppose that our publisher were to conclude that traditional hardcover publishing methods were no longer adequate for a book of this sort and that an entirely new approach should be tried. The publisher might then arrive at the scheme illustrated in our third alternative shown in Figure 21. Here the publisher decides to narrow rather than to broaden the focus, to pinpoint efforts at the core market for the book: historians, libraries, and intensively interested laypeople. Since individuals in this market can be reached with greater effectiveness by direct methods rather than through current bookstore channels, the publisher decides to sell the book at a higher price, $40, and at a short discount (averaging 20 percent). The publisher realizes, of course, that the number of units sold will therefore be substantially fewer than under the other alternatives, and decides on a printing of only 5,000 copies (at a cost of $5.10 per copy). The

Profit/Loss Analysis
History Title: Alternative Three (List price $40.00—Short discount)

	Dollars	Percent of Net Sales
Gross sales: 4,800 copies at full price	172,800	105.7
Less: returns and allowances	9,360	5.7
Net sales	163,440	100.00
Cost of sales		
Plant costs	16,000	9.8
Paper, printing, and binding	24,480	15.0
Royalties	19,200	11.7
Total cost of sales	59,680	36.5
Gross margin on sales	103,760	63.5
Other publishing income	20,834	12.7
Total operating income	124,594	76.2
Operating expenses		
Editorial	11,800	7.2
Production	3,600	2.2
Marketing		
Advertising	10,000	6.1
Free books	1,020	0.6
Other	15,800	9.7
Total marketing expense	26,820	16.4
Fulfillment	13,800	8.4
General and administrative	13,200	8.1
Total operating expense	69,220	42.3
Net income (or loss)	55,374	33.9

Figure 21.

publisher also reduces the number of free copies to 200, limiting them to media that are really likely to review the title and do it some good. Space advertising is also curtailed, to $10,000, to be spent predominantly in specialized media. Marketing efforts will be heavily weighted in favor of direct mail.

The results are spectacular. Gross sales are only 4,800 copies, but of these only 260 are returned, as bookstore involvement is limited largely to special orders. (The returns, including damaged copies, are too few to warrant remaindering at this time, so the stock is simply written off.) Substantial savings in inventory expense, royalties, advertising, and fulfillment work together to produce a substantial profit. Even the book club lends a hand, deciding that it will maintain the higher membership price of $23.90 and that, because of the publisher's more restricted marketing approach, its sales will benefit to the tune of nearly 11,000 copies. The club's guarantee therefore becomes $25,870, of which the publisher's share is $12,834.

Fine, you say. But what about the publisher's responsibility to the book and its author? Is the publisher really exercising the "best effort" for the book, as the contract requires, with the third approach? I think so. I think the publisher has come to recognize that crowded distribution channels make it unwise to attempt marketing a specialized title in the traditional fashion, and that resources must sooner or later give out if that path continues to be followed. The publisher is certainly not evading responsibilities; not only is the publisher making the book available in its own edition but has also sold rights to a book club which will reach additional readers through sales of a hardcover edition and to a paperback house which will keep the work in print, for the benefit of students and consumers, probably for years to come. I don't believe that publishers have a responsibility to lose money or to tread water in developing their program.

It is true, of course, that the author will earn less on the third alternative than on the others. (Interestingly enough, the author will receive the largest income—$53,634—from the second alternative, which is the most ruinous one for the publisher. Alternative one will yield the author $48,790; alternative three $44,034.) This is not to suggest that the long-term interests of authors and publishers are not the same, they obviously are. But it does illustrate the fact that their short-term interests sometimes diverge. Authors would obviously like nothing better than to amass as many sales through bookstores, as many reviews in all sorts of media, and as many promptly earned royalties as possible. They may not give a second thought to the publisher's profitability in this connection. But can they really afford not to?

There are other lessons to be learned from the alternative analyses we have made: for example, that conventional ideas about generating profit may not always work. More sales and larger printings are obviously not always the answer, nor are lower prices and more aggressive marketing. More important than such conventional techniques may be the accurate definition of a market and the choice of optimal means to reach it. Prudence, restraint, and good judgment may be more effective business tools than blind enthusiasm, vigor, and high pressure.

Budgeting and Planning

All the gathering and analysis of financial data will be of little use unless the lessons learned are applied in making decisions on future titles and programs. The time to ask basic questions about the income, cost, and profit of a publishing venture is before, not after, a commitment is made. Accordingly the various revenue and expense factors we have identified in our statements should be estimated and projected for a product in advance of the decision to publish and how to publish. Alternative approaches should be weighed whenever options exist so that the most enlightened decisions regarding format, price, size of printing, promotional efforts, and subsidiary rights arrangements can be made.

A number of publishers have devised sophisticated methods for forecasting profit or loss of titles under consideration, many of them making imaginative use of computer capability. These houses believe that editors, production managers, sales managers, and others involved in making publishing decisions should have the opportunity to view the impact of their plans for the production, pricing, and promotion of forthcoming books before they are required to make a final recommendation. Accordingly these managers prepare forms in which they list basic production specifications and marketing plans. The computer digests these, adds allowances for overhead costs, and produces a financial forecast which indicates whether or not the given specifications will result in a profit that meets the company's standard for return on investment. Should a projection fall short of standard, editors and managers have the opportunity to modify specifications until an acceptable plan results.

No projection is better, of course, than the estimates that go into it, and every forecasting program is therefore dependent on the quality of judgment managers bring to it. But while no forecast is foolproof, it is vastly better to undertake such estimates than to rely on the uncorroborated divinations or inspirations on which so many publishers seem to depend when they make serious publishing decisions. Inspiration has its place, of course. It leads a publisher to discover a potentially important book in the first place, or to recognize the quality of a manuscript on initial reading.

But in today's demanding publishing world, given the sizable risks involved, more than strokes of genius are required to justify a final determination. The muse needs hard facts and figures to demonstrate it is really a muse—not just a dreamer.

If projections are needed to publish individual titles effectively, they are equally necessary to operate a whole program for a season or a year. Most sound businesses make forecasts for each line item on their statements and, as the year progresses, compare actual performance with projections, thus alerting themselves to gains or shortfalls and giving themselves the opportunity to deal effectively with either. In preparing their comprehensive forecasts, publishers will, of course, base them on the projections they have made for individual titles.

Plans involve more than figures or finances, of course. They involve people and working space, warehouses and trucks, computers, furniture, and equipment. Personnel plans must be formulated as carefully as financial forecasts in order to deal efficiently and humanely with any expansion or cutbacks that may be contemplated. It takes time to train new people or to help established personnel adjust to new circumstances. The installation of new facilities, machinery, and systems may involve months, even years of preparation. A good manager, furthermore, must always be conscious of the greater world outside, the economy as a whole, the social and physical environment. A good publisher must be responsive to the world of ideas, the cultural climate, the literary atmosphere. No business executive, and certainly no publisher, is an island.

But there is a limit to planning, especially in a cultural industry. To develop the necessary resources, human as well as financial, one must indeed make long-range forecasts covering periods five or even ten years hence. But such projections will have to be very broad, based more on the experience and imagination of the forecaster than on factual details which are at this point simply unavailable. In book publishing the unknown remains a large factor; one never really knows what will happen in the world of knowledge, education, entertainment, and consumer taste even a year or two years from now. A forecast for next year, based on titles already scheduled or planned for publication, can and should be amply detailed. But a long-range forecast can never be more than a sophisticated, wide-sweeping guess.

Many clever and capable people in other businesses, notably the executives of corporations that own publishing subsidiaries, cannot quite understand this fact. They are accustomed to "scientific" long-term planning and product development, undertaken after years of sophisticated research. Their markets are often more predictable, less dependent on taste and whim or on fashion and mood than the markets for books. These executives cannot believe that the bright young economists who so confidently predict the fate and future of their giant corporations should not be able to do so as readily for publishers.

As a result such corporate owners often demand that some unnecessarily complicated and frequently futile forecasting be done by the managers of their publishing subsidiaries. What is even worse, the owners often take such forecasts quite literally despite the honest disclaimers made by the people who prepare them regarding the impossibility of predicting specific sales and performance details five and ten years into the future.

Like the managers of their publishing companies, these owners should realize that publishing is really much like a poker game: a fascinating exercise combining skill and chance. Like the card player, the publisher who does not react capably to what fortune deals will be quickly forced out of the game. But the publisher who is succesful would be presumptuous to attribute prosperity entirely to his or her own skill. For a publisher never really knows what card will be dealt next when placing a bet.

Capital and Its Sources

For publishers planning their future, raising capital has always been one of the principal problems. Book publishing is reputed to be a field which one can enter with very little capital (which supposedly explains why there are so many small publishing houses in the United States). To a considerable extent this is true, of course. To enter publishing one does not need to build a large plant, purchase expensive machinery, or spend huge sums developing patents. But to establish a significant publishing imprint has always taken a good deal of money, and it takes more today than ever. In school publishing, for example, a major new series may require an investment of several million dollars. In professional and college publishing, building an imprint to competitive size and eminence usually takes years and large sums. And in trade publishing intense competition for good authors and big books is making increasingly heavy cash demands.

The need for capital was one of the principal reasons why so many publishers passed into the hands of larger corporate owners during recent decades. Some of these owners, who acquired publishing houses in the belief that they would fulfill the glowing predictions for growth and prosperity that had been made for them, have since been disappointed. Had some owners known at the time what they know now, they would probably not have acquired their publishing subsidiaries, as witness the corporations that have already divested themselves of their publishing holdings, and others that have indicated strong interest in doing so.

The industry's performance records explain why. While there are outstanding publishing ventures, in both corporate and independent hands, that yearly compile superb earnings records and are a source of great satisfaction to their owners much of the industry is not in such an enviable position.

To raise capital when it is needed is therefore a weighty problem for many publishing executives. There are just too many other opportunities available to the investor who is looking for a quick, easy profit, to make many publishing stocks seem a prize. And in times when the stock market is despondent and the vision of investors is jaundiced, even the shares of highly successful publishers with outstanding earnings records have been known to post very low values. Of course other cultural industries, and even other mercantile and manufacturing enterprises, are in the same boat. That is small comfort for the publisher who is looking vainly for operating capital.

Yet there are still investors, corporations as well as individuals, willing to invest in even the less glamorous and the less profitable publishing houses and publishing stocks. Interested in more than money, they are looking for cultural as well as cash dividends. Like patrons in other ages, they are prepared to risk capital in the pursuit of intangible profits.

The problem has always been to find such people. There never seem to be enough to go around. But although the task of the publisher seeking venture money remains an ardous one, we should not be too surprised to discover that even in this respect publishing experience extends beyond the purely monetary or material. For in the last analysis, the very existence of books, and of the enterprises that publish them, is concrete testimony to the fact that we do not live by bread alone.

Epilogue: What Does the Future Hold?

On the whole, the future of book publishing looks bright. There is every reason to believe that books will continue to gain favor with American consumers, whose rising educational level, deepening cultural maturation, and persistent affluence have proved to be powerful incentives for augmenting book consumption in the past. The BISG consumer studies revealed that 94 percent of the population reads at least newspapers and magazines. New converts to book readership have been recruited from that larger universe, and since only some 50 percent of our people are now book buyers, the potential for further growth is enormous.

Even present book buyers show great promise, however. The baby boomers, whose enthusiasm for books has had such a profound impact on the recent past, are currently entering the age bracket when their disposable income will reach its lifetime peak. Their additional expenditures should more than compensate the industry for the reduced numbers of book buyers following in their wake, particularly as the baby bust cohort has otherwise displayed as vigorous an appetite for books as their predecessors. As for the population boomlet following the bust, we had a taste of its inclinations when it drove juvenile sales to unprecedented levels.

Professional book markets are growing by leaps and bounds, driven by the rapidly growing sophistication of the workplace, and the urgent need for advanced training and retraining experienced by millions of the labor force. Similarly, persistant calls for improved textbooks along with renewed recognition of the vital role played by books in the educational process, appear to be building a new national commitment to quality materials for colleges and schools.

We may hope that professional and educational publishers will respond positively to these opportunities. Whether consumer publishers will do likewise is an open question. The past is not very reassuring. Often it has seemed as though progress in the field was made despite of rather than because of publishers on the scene, and that only consumers' hunger for books and authors' heroic persistence in reaching their readers has made the entire miracle possible. Imagine what a glorious state U.S. book consumption might be in today if trade and mass market publishers had been consistently alert to their readers' interests and efficient at marketing and distributing their books!

Will mainstream trade houses reform and abandon the myths of the 1920s? Will they embrace modern technology and contemporary research methods? Will they recruit new talent with an eye toward the long-term future and provide adequately for their employees' professional training?

The future of popular publishing is entirely in mainstream hands. The giants may be able to count on small presses to take up the slack created by their abandoning specialized publishing, but small presses could not possibly muster the resources necessary to launch most popular books. The giants' success or failure will determine not only their own future but that of popular books and reading, and therefore of popular culture, in America.

Personally, I am more optimistic about the future of serious than of popular publishing, because I believe that the small press is a much sounder institution, from a human and economic point of view, than the trade giant. It remains to be seen, however, whether small presses *as a community* can meet the cultural need created by the giants' flight from small-market, low-profit ventures. To do so, that community would have to mature professionally and to develop a greater consciousness of its opportunities and responsibilities than it has thus far demonstrated. Small presses would have to become more confident about courting quality authors, and many would have to raise the editorial and production standards of their lists.

However, if the giants were to become genuinely responsive to their readers, and small presses were to rise to the challenge of fully supplying the nation's specialized book needs, the coming era could witness a book boom that would make any we have thus far seen seem minuscule by comparison. Thus the industry stands to make or break its own fortune: the consumer is merely waiting in the wings, poised and ready to respond.

One missing ingredient vital to the industry's future is a unifying publishing organization. AAP serves only the mainstream and small-press associations, though numerous, are fragmented. There are too many common interests and concerns, too much need for sharing experiences and ideas, too many occasions when a united front would serve the good of all, to afford publishers the continued luxury of splendid isolation. Now mainstream and small-press people largely ignore each other—and pay the price. To the observer it is overwhelmingly apparent that the sooner the two groups join in a common forum, the sooner they will strengthen and reinforce one another in their common endeavor, and in serving their common constituency.

Glossary

AA—author's alteration: text change in proof made by author

AAP—Association of American Publishers

AAUP—Association of American University Presses

ABA—American Booksellers Association

acid-free paper—(also permanent, neutral PH paper) paper milled to last for a century or longer

accountability—demand for demonstrable results, e.g., from educational programs and materials

accounts receivable—monies due from customers

accrual—accounting method that reports expense not necessarily when incurred but in coordination with related income

adoption—choice of educational materials for classroom use

advance—1. monies paid to author prior to publication, to be earned subsequently from royalties on sales. 2. (advance sale) books ordered by customers prior to publication

advance dating—use of future date on invoice delaying requirement for payment

agency plan—marketing arrangement enabling bookseller to earn preferential discount on short-discount titles in return for a commitment to stock a minimal title selection

agent—author's or artist's representative

AIGA—American Institute of Graphic Arts

ALA—American Library Association

allocation—attribution of indirect expense

alternate—secondary book club offering

amortize—to spread out accounting of an expense over a period of time

antique finish—velvety surface texture of paper

auction (of a book or manuscript)—simultaneous submission to several publishers, receiving successive rounds of bids, and awarding contract to highest bidder

audiovisual materials—educational and professional products utilizing pictorial or sound media to communicate: films, cassettes, records, slides

autographing party—author's visit to bookstore to inscribe copies and meet admirers *backbone* (also *spine*)—back of bound book

backlist—titles selling steadily year after year; may sometimes also denote titles published prior to the current season and still available

balance sheet—financial report, balancing the assets of a business against its liabilities and capital

binding—the folding, gathering, gluing or sewing of press sheets and the attaching of covers

binding die—form used to stamp binding case

BISAC—Book Industry Systems Advisory Committee (a committee of BISG)

BISG—Book Industry Study Group

bleed—extending printing image to the very edge of the page

blind stamping—blank stamping, without ink or foil

BMI—Book Manufacturers' Institute

body—base on which type character is mounted

body type—type employed in setting main text, exclusive of headings and footnotes

boldface—heavyweight type (**abc**)

book club—marketing organization that distributes special editions of books to its members on preferential terms in return for their minimal purchasing commitment

book post—parcel post at special book rates

broken price—merchandising technique which prices books slightly below amounts customarily employed (e.g., 99 cents, $2.49, $4.95)

building-in machine—device intended to set (stablilize) finished bound books by pressure and heat in a few seconds.

bulk—thickness of book paper or book

burning a plate—etching of an offset printing plate

burst binding—(also notch binding) a form of perfect binding in which glue is forced between the pages through notches applied while folding the signatures

calendered paper—paper processed between cylinders for smooth finish

Cameron Belt Press—printing press in which plates for individual pages are hung on a movable belt and which prints, cuts, folds, trims, and perfect-binds books in one continuous operation

cap—capital letter

capitalize—1. to invest capital in. 2. (also *amortize*) to spread out accounting of an expense over a period of time

carload price—cost of book paper in rail freight car lots

case binding—hardcover binding

cash discount—discount given for prompt payment of bills

casting off—1. breaking type into pages. 2. estimating number of pages or columns of type a manuscript or other copy will occupy

character—single type letter or symbol

character count—determining exact length of manuscript prior to design

coated paper—paper surfaced with clay, enamel, or plastic, particularly suited for printing illustrations

codex—a manuscript book, leaves bound at one edge as opposed to a scroll

cold type—direct-impression composition, e.g., process, by typewriter or computer, which dispenses with the hot metal castings of traditional techniques

collating (also *gathering*)—assembling folded press sheets in sequence

college store—retailer, institutionally or privately owned, catering predominantly to college faculty and students

colophon—common though disputed term for publisher's device or trademark; logo; trademark; in traditional usage, a printer's or publisher's statement at the end of a book

color separation—method of preparing several separate images photographically or electronically, from which color printing plates are made

commission man (woman)—free-lance salesperson representing several publishers

comp—complimentary copy; also, abbreviation for *compositor*

comparative price—quotation of original and reduced prices in promoting markdowns or remainders

composition—typesetting

compositor—typesetter

computer composition—methods of typesetting utilizing computers instead of traditional systems

computer program—instructions to computer for performing a routine

condensed type—type compressed in width

consignment—merchandise shipped to customer which does not become payable until sold

consultant—in educational publishing, usually a teacher retained by elhi publisher to demonstrate products

consumable book—educational book designed to be marked up, cut up, or otherwise used up, during its employment

continuity program—mail order marketing arrangement in which the customer agrees to accept periodic shipments of books in series, with option to cancel at any time

cooperative advertising—ad run by bookseller, the cost of which is shared by publisher *copy*—single book unit

copyediting—meticulous working over of manuscript prior to typesetting

copyright—legal protection enjoyed by literary property

Copyright Clearance Center—organization established by publishers to collect fees from photocopying

copyright page—verso of title page listing copyright notice

CPDA—Council for Periodical Distributors Associations: trade association for wholesalers of magazines and mass market paperbacks

crash—sturdy gauze glued to backs of pages and to boards under endpapers, in case-bound books

creative editor—editor who conceives of a book project and subsequently finds an author to execute it

credit—in accounting, the convention by which values are added to income, liabilities and capital, and deducted from assets and expenses.

credit control—screening out unfavorable credit risks from customer list and denying further credit to past due accounts

crop—to trim an illustration or indicate which part of an image is to be reproduced

customer service—handling of order inquiries and complaints

cut—a letterpress engraving

debit—in accounting, the convention by which values are added to assets and expenses, and deducted from income, liabilities and capital

deep-etched plate—offset printing plate that can be used repeatedly

defer—to delay the accounting of an expense, usually in order to achieve better coordination with related income

depository—state-designated warehouse where adopted titles must be stored

depth—vertical measurement of type on page

desk copy—copy furnished free to college teacher upon adoption of a text

desktop publishing—generic name applied to personal computer-based typesetting and page makeup systems

development expense—cost incurred in developing a new product

display type—type used for headings of title pages, usually larger or bolder than text type

dummy—mock-up of pages or book; layout for guidance of stripper or printer

dump bin—combination shipping carton and display unit favored by mass market paperback publishers

dustcover—jacket or plain wrapper placed over binding

ECPA—Evangelical Christian Publishers Association

editing—1. selecting, creating, or soliciting materials for publication. 2. close working over of manuscript to prepare it for typesetting

edition—specific version of a book which may differ from other versions because of content, format, or market (e.g., revised edition, paperbound edition, text edition)

elhi—embraces elementary (grades K-8) and high school (grades 9–12)

em—lateral measure, same as the body size of a given font to type; basic measurement for length and cost of typesetting; see also *pica*

endpapers—heavy, sometimes decorated pages at beginning and end of case-bound books

engraving—halftone or line printing plate

even forms—full utilization of press sheets; no blank pages at end of book

examination copy—complimentary or on-approval copy furnished to college teacher for possible adoption

exhibit—book display at professional, scholarly, or book-trade meetings

extended type—a version of a typeface featuring wider characters than the basic design

fair use—limited quotation of copyrighted matter which does not constitute violation of copyright

F & G's—folded and gathered sheets

first reading—initial review of manuscript to determine whether it should be considered further or rejected

first serialization—see *serialization*

flat sheets—unfolded, printed sheets

flatbed press—letterpress printing machine in which type form lies flat and moves beneath rotating cylinders that carry the paper

folio—page number

font—the characters which are available for a given typeface in a specific size, slant, or weight

foreign rights—right to translate and/or publish a work abroad

form—section of pages printed on one side of press sheet

Frankfurt Book Fair—major international publishing meeting; held each October in Frankfurt am Main, West Germany

free sheet—book paper free of low-grade pulp, therefore of somewhat longer lasting quality, but still containing self-destructive acids.

front matter—material preceding the main body of a book: title, copyright, and dedication pages, preface or foreword, acknowledgments, and table of contents

fulfillment—activities embracing order processing, invoicing, handling of accounts receivable, payments and collections, credit control, shipping and warehousing, and the maintenance of sales and inventory records

G & A—general and administrative costs; incurred on a companywide, as opposed to a departmental, basis

galleys—proofs to typeset material, taken prior to arrangement in layouts or pages; also trays for holding metal type

gathering (also *collating*)—assembling folded press sheets in sequence

grain—direction in which paper fibers flow

gravure (also *intaglio*)—printing process in which impression is made from plates into which image has been depressed to hold ink after surface is wiped

guarantee—minimum royalty agreed upon, usually paid in advance of publication

gutter—margin adjoining inside unbound edge of page

half title—the recto, preceding the title page or a section of a book, on which the title or the name of the section is shown, normally in display type

halftone—the reproduction of a shaded image such as a photograph or painting

hardware—see *software*

head- and footbands—woven, often brightly colored ribands decorating the back edges of the sheets in case-bound books

home field—market of homes and offices covered directly by field representatives of subscription reference book publishers

ID—independent distribution: dissemination of mass market paperbacks through independent wholesalers

IIA—Information Industry Association

imposition—arrangement of pages on the press sheet which results in correct sequence after folding

imprint—name of publisher or series, identified on title pages and bindings

imprint editor—prominent editor whose name becomes part of the imprint and who enjoys some ownership interest in the books edited

income statement—see *operating statement*

independent wholesaler—local wholesaler of magazines and mass market paperbound books

initial galleys—copies of new titles shipped automatically to wholesalers by mass market paperback publisher

instant book—work of great current interest written, produced, and marketed on a crash schedule

integrated book manufacturer—enterprise capable of manufacturing complete books, from composition to bound and jacketed copy

IPA—International Publishers Association

ISBN—International Standard Book Numbering System; assigns identifying numbers to books and publishers (see also *SAN*)

italics—slanted version of type *(abc)*

jacket—decorative, printed paper cover placed over binding for protection and promotional purposes *jobber*—wholesaler to bookstores or libraries

justify—to set type in lines of equal width, resulting in even right-hand margin

juvenile—children's book

lamination—plastic coating applied to covers

leading—spacing between lines of type

letterpress—printing process in which impression on paper is made by raised surfaces

library reprint (also *scholarly reprint*)—short-run, hardcover reprint of out-of-print title

lightface—type of regular weight; sometimes, however, a still lighter version, when "regular" is denoted "medium"

line illustration—illustration without tones or shadings, e.g., a geometric diagram or a pen-and-ink drawing

Linotype—a metal typesetting process, casting text by the line

list—publisher's entire output of titles, in-print and forthcoming

list cleaner—service provided by post office informing mailing list owner of address changes

literary agent—author's representative

lithography—see *offset printing*

live returns—new books in unopened cartons returned by wholesaler to mass market paperback publisher

LMP—*Literary Market Place:* annual directory of book publishing industry

logo—trade device or mark

lowercase—small letter

mail order publication—title produced primarily for distribution by mail directly to the general consumer

makeready—setting up of press in preparation of print run

manipulative materials—educational materials that are touched and handled rather than read or viewed: rocks, sea shells, toys, games, craft kits, etc.

manufacturing—process of making the physical book, principally typesetting, printing, and binding

manuscript editing—see *copyediting*

mass market—book market that extends beyond traditional trade outlets (such as book, department, and stationery stores) to include newsstands, drugstores, chain stores, convenience stores, and supermarkets

mass market paperback—see *paperback*

measure—width over which a line of type is set

module—unit or section of multiunit educational product

monograph—narrowly specialized, scholarly study

Monotype—registered name of metal typesetting process by which each character is cast individually

ms.—manuscript

multimedia product—educational materials package containing components in two or more media: books and cassettes, filmstrips and records, booklets, cards, slides, and tapes, etc.

multiple contract—agreement binding author and publisher for the publication of two or more books

multiple insertion—use of several enclosures in direct mail

NACS—National Association of College Stores

NCES—National Center for Education Statistics

negative—photographic transparency used in preparing offset printing plates

negative option—book club marketing technique whereby members receive selection automatically unless they notify club to the contrary

neutral PH paper—acid-free paper

NO—not our publication

notch binding—see *burst binding*

NYP—not yet published

objective test—testing materials sold in conjunction with textbooks or materials to measure student's learning progress

offset printing (also *photo-offset, lithography*)—process in which impression on paper is made by rubber blanket on which print image has been "offset" from photographically etched cylindrical plate

on-approval copy—book furnished to college teacher for possible adoption, which must be returned or paid for if not adopted

on-demand publishing—method of publication which manufactures books only in response to specific purchase orders

OP—out of print: stock exhausted; no longer available

opacity—density of paper which prevents image on reverse page from showing through

operating statement—financial report establishing the profit or loss of a business by showing its income and expenses

option—opportunity of first refusal granted by an author to a publisher on a future manuscript, or by one publisher to another in negotiating for reprint or foreign publication rights

order editing—review and annotation of customers' orders to ensure their accurate processing

OS—out of stock; temporarily unavailable

over the transom—unsolicited manuscript

packager—entrepreneur who provides editorial and production services in developing a book subsequently marketed and distributed by a publisher

page proof—final proof in typesetting process

pallet—see *skid*

paper merchant—wholesaler stocking book papers from several mills

paperback—softbound book. Trade paperbacks are distributed largely through book and college stores; mass market paperbacks are distributed, in addition, through chain stores, drugstores, supermarkets, convenience stores and newsstands

PE—printer's error: error made by typesetter

perfect binding—process in which the backs of folded press sheets are abrased and the cover is attached with a strong adhesive; adhesive binding

perfector press—prints both sides of sheet simultaneously

permanent paper—acid-free paper with long-lasting characteristics

permission—granting of the right to use a book excerpt

photo-offset—see *offset printing*

pica—type measurement, a little less than ⅟₁₆ inch (12 points); a pica em is the basic measure in printing; see also *em*

plant costs—nonrecurring manufacturing costs (such as typesetting, negatives, and reusable plates) plus artwork (outside artwork only in the case of educational books). Some publishers may include certain editorial and other development expenses as well

plate—metal or other surface from which printing image is impressed or transferred by offset onto paper

PMA—Publishers' Marketing Association

point—type measurement, a shade less than ⅟₇₂ of an inch

printing—1. process of transferring images to paper 2. (also *impression*) a particular lot of copies printed at one time

process color—method of full-color reproduction, requiring separation of colors by a special photographic or electronic process

production—task of planning and supervising manufacturing process

professional books—books created predominantly as tools of work for the professions and the trades

profit-or-loss statement—see *operating statement*

promotion—marketing activity other than direct personal selling, such as space advertising, direct mail, exhibits, and publicity

proportional spacing—making allowances for the varying widths of letters in equalizing the spacing between them

proprietary textbook—college textbook published exclusively for an instructor's use in his or her own course *publicity*—achieving news and review exposure for books and authors

publishers' overstock—see *remainders*

pulping—destruction of unsalable books

PW—*Publishers Weekly,* the industry journal

rack allowance—contribution made by mass market paperback publisher to the cost of customer's display racks

ream—500 sheets of paper

recto—right-hand page

religious books—Bibles, testaments, hymnals, prayer books, and other works of specifically religious content

remainders (also *publishers' overstock*)—unsold books disposed of by publisher, usually below cost, to wholesalers, retailers, and consumers

reprint—1. new printing in original format. 2. reissue in new format (e.g., paperback)

reproduction proof—proof of exceptional quality used as the source for negatives or plates

resource center—facility, similar to a library, serving one or several schools

returns—1. unsold books shipped back to publisher. 2. responses to direct mailing

review copy—free book furnished to newspaper or other medium for review purposes

rivers—unsightly blank streaks running through pages of inexpertly set type

rotary press—press that prints from curved plates fastened to a cylinder; may be sheet-fed or web-fed

rough front and foot—pages of a book that are untrimmed at the front and bottom edges

royalties—shares of sales income, paid to authors and others, usually based on the number and price of copies sold

running heads—captions at tops of pages identifying book, parts, or chapters

saddle-wire stitch—wire-stapling booklets through the backs

SAN—standard account number assigned to mercantile and institutional book purchaser

sans serif—typeface that lacks serifs (cross strokes at line endings)

scholarly books—books in highly specialized areas of knowledge and advanced research

school books (also *elhi books*)—textbooks for grades K-12

score—indentations on sheets and covers facilitating folding

screen—transparency, marked with crisscross lines or other pattern, used in preparing images for halftone reproduction

second serialization—see *serialization*

selection—title chosen by book club as its prime offering

self-mailer—brochure mailable without envelope

serialization—publication of a book in installments by a periodical, either before (first serialization) or after (second serialization) publication

sheet-fed press—press that prints from sheets of paper rather than rolls; see also *web-fed press*

sheets—unbound printed pages

short discount—lower than the standard trade discount of 40 percent

short run—small printing

side-sewing—stitching signatures through the sides rather than through the backs

signature—folded press sheets, usually making 32 or 16 pages but possibly 8 or 64

sizing—1. coating paper preparatory to offset printing. 2. specifying the reduction, enlargement, or cropping of illustrations

skid (also *pallet*)—wooden platform used to store books, sheets, or paper

smyth-sewing—threading signatures together prior to attaching covers

software—1. computer software: programs as distinguished from computer hardware: machinery and equipment. 2. audiovisual software: films, filmstrips, tapes, etc., as distinguished from audiovisual hardware: cameras, projectors, players, etc.

space advertising—advertisement in periodical or newspaper

special library—library limited to business, industrial, professional, music, art, historical, or other special collections

special order—order for title not carried in bookseller's regular stock

special sales—sales outside normal distribution channels

spine—back of bound book

split test—simultaneous sampling of several direct mail approaches

spoilage—sheets and raw materials damaged beyond repair during printing or binding

square-backed—bindings with backs which have not been rounded

SSP—Society for Scholarly Publishing

stamping—imprinting or embossing of titles and other matter on binding case

standardized test—test measuring intelligence, ability, aptitude, achievement, and other personality traits

state adoption—approval of elhi materials by state selection board, permitting purchase by local school districts

STOP—Single Title Order Plan: ABA-sponsored plan in which booksellers earn preferential discounts on prepaid orders for single books

stripping—preparation and assemblage of offset negatives or transparencies prior to platemaking

subscription reference books—multivolume encyclopedias marketed predominantly to the consumer on a door-to-door or direct-mail basis

subsidiary rights—rights to use of a book in ways other than original publication: reprint, book club distribution, serialization, translation, film adaptation, etc.

substance weight—ream weight of paper in standard sheet size (25 inches × 38 inches for book papers)

superior number—small raised number (^{1}) used in references to footnotes

test—1. standardized test: measures intelligence, ability, or personality traits, not related to specific books or materials. 2. objective test: accompanies specific textbooks and materials to measure student's learning progress. 3. direct-mail test: measures appeal of title or promotional approach by means of small sample mailing

textbook—book created predominantly for use in formal educational settings and equipped with educational apparatus, such as summaries and test questions

title—1. name of a book. 2. a specific book on publisher's list

title page—page at book's beginning, usually of special design, listing title, author, and publisher

TOP—temporarily out of print: plans for reprinting title are indefinite

top-stain—color applied to top edges of pages

trade books—titles created predominantly for the general consumer and marketed through bookstores and to libraries

trade customs—industry-approved policy standards for printers and binders

trade discount—40 percent or better

trade list—publisher's complete catalog of books in print

trim—the machine trimming of the top, front, and bottom (foot) edges of the bound (not yet covered or cased) pages of a book; full trim—smooth trimming of all three edges; top trim only—smooth trim at top only (see *rough front and foot*); top and front trim only—smooth top and front edges

trim size—page size, exclusive of binding

typeface—specific design in which various sizes and weights of type are available

typography—art of designing typefaces and arranging type

university press—publishing arm of a university, museum, or research institution

unjustified margin—ragged right-hand margin, resulting from type set in lines of unequal width *unsolicited manuscript*— (also manuscript received *over the transom*)— manuscript submitted to publisher directly by author (not through an agent) and which publisher has not specifically requested for consideration

uppercase—capital letter

validation—field-testing and verifying the effectiveness of educational materials

vanity publishing—publication entirely or substantially paid for by the author

varnish—light protective coating applied to some jackets and covers

venture capital—cash sought for funding a new enterprise

verso—left-hand page

web—roll of paper

web-fed press—press that prints on rolls of paper; see also *sheet-fed press*

welding—binding process which heat-seals paper coated with plastic resin

widow—dangling word or short line at top of page or end of paragraph, preferably eliminated during typesetting

word processing—computer-supported system of copy preparation in which the encoding and editing of text are performed electronically

working capital—cash tied up in enterprise; amount is determined by deducting current liabilities from current assets

write-down—to reduce the value of inventory or other asset in financial reports

write-off—to show an expense in full, or to fully eliminate the value of an asset, such as inventory, in financial reports

Bibliographic Note

The literature on publishing, sparse and inadequate when the first edition of this volume appeared in 1974, has grown along with the industry's population. Where once one could count the available titles on the fingers of one hand, now the neophyte is confronted by such a plethora of publications, particularly by self-taught small-press people, that the problem is no longer to discover what is available but rather to choose what is reliable.

Three source lists are worth consulting in this context. *Literary Market Place* (R. R. Bowker, 245 W. Seventeenth Street, New York, New York 10011) contains an excellent bibliography compiled by Bowker librarian Jean Peters. John Kremer's *The Independent Publisher's Book Shelf* (Ad-Lib Publications, 51 N. Fifth Street, Fairfield, Iowa 52556) provides sound evaluations of books addressed to the small-press audience. And Judith Appelbaum's *How to Get Happily Published* (Harper & Row, New American Library) contains a superb resource section, including capsule assessments of books and periodicals.

Index

Note: Page numbers for table and figure entries are italic.